SERIES "C" BLACK LIGHTNING MODEL

SERIES "C" BLACK SHADOW MODEL

VINCENT WORKSHOP MANUAL

INCLUDES MAINTENANCE AND REPAIR DATA FOR ALL MODELS

1935 - 1955

1,000cc: Rapide, Shadow, Lightning, Knight and Prince

500cc: Meteor, Comet and Flash

ISBN: 1-58850-072-1

ORIGINALLY PUBLISHED BY FLOYD CLYMER IN 1955
THIS EDITION REPUBLISHED BY VELOCEPRESS IN 2007

COPYRIGHT 2007 VELOCE ENTERPRISES INC.,
SAN ANTONIO, TX 78230, USA.

ALL RIGHTS RESERVED. THIS WORK MAY NOT BE REPRODUCED OR TRANSMITTED IN ANY FORM WITHOUT THE EXPRESS WRITTEN CONSENT OF THE PUBLISHER

INTRODUCTION

Welcome to the world of digital publishing ~ Using state of the art digital technology and equipment, **VelocePress** is able to bring titles back in print allowing you to access the information that you need, when you need it. Never has information been so accessible and it is our hope that this book serves your informational needs for years to come. While this edition is presented unchanged from the original 1955 edition, it has been reproduced using the latest print-on-demand technology.

If this is your first exposure to digital publishing, we hope that you are pleased with the results. Many more titles of interest to the classic automobile and motorcycle enthusiast are available via our website at **www.VelocePress.com**. We hope that you find this title as interesting as we do.

TRADEMARKS

We recognize that some words, model names and designations, for example, mentioned herein are the property of the trademark holder. We use them for identification purposes only. This is not an official publication.

INFORMATION ON THE USE OF THIS PUBLICATION

The information presented is unchanged from the original edition and has not been updated to reflect changes in common practice, new technology, availability of improved materials and increased awareness of chemical toxicity. As such, it is advised that the user consult with an experienced professional prior to undertaking any procedure described herein. While every care has been taken to ensure correctness of information, it is obviously not possible to guarantee complete freedom from errors or omissions or to accept liability arising from such errors or omissions. Therefore, any individual that uses the information contained within, or elects to perform or participate in do-it-yourself repairs or modifications acknowledges that there is a risk factor involved and that the publisher or its associates cannot be held responsible for personal injury or property damage resulting from the use of the information or the outcome of such procedures.

VINCENT MOTOR CYCLES

A PRACTICAL GUIDE COVERING ALL VINCENT AND VINCENT H.R.D. MODELS FROM 1935

This book is a practical guide for repairing and servicing all Vincent and Vincent H.R.D. models from 1935. We have arranged for the U.S. publication rights from C. Arthur Pearson, Ltd. Paul Richardson, the author, is technical information manager of Vincent Engineers, Ltd., and is an authority on the care and operation of Vincent motorcycles.

We believe that every Vincent owner and enthusiast will find this book most interesting and informative.

Published by

FLOYD CLYMER

World"s Largest Publisher of Books Relating to Automobiles, Motorcycles, Motor Racing, and Americana

1268 SOUTH ALVARADO STREET, LOS ANGELES 6, CALIFORNIA

Copyright 1955 by Floyd Clymer

PREFACE

THIS book has been compiled from experience gained on Vincent motor cycles in service, competitions and private ownership over a number of years. Its aim is to assist those riders who derive additional satisfaction from carrying out their own maintenance, as well as mechanics requiring the maximum of information for guidance or reference.

It was not intended to provide a step-by-step workshop manual, but in the design of this range of interesting machines some departures from conventional motor-cycle engineering practice are incorporated, and the book endeavours to give the answer to many questions.

While completely covering the comprehensive subject from a practical angle, the contents are in many respects complementary to the very informative publications issued by the manufacturers, and it has been assumed that readers are already familiar with certain principles of general maintenance.

The author wishes to express his gratitude for the assistance received from Messrs. Vincent Engineers (Stevenage), Ltd., Amal, Ltd., Joseph Lucas, Ltd., H. Burman & Sons, Ltd., Renold Chains, Ltd., The Avon India Rubber Co., Ltd., Blacknell Sidecars, Ltd., K.L.G. Sparking Plugs, Ltd., *Motor Cycling*, *The Motor Cycle*, J. E. Hampshire, and R. S. Allan, A.R.P.S.

Valuable comments on the manuscript were passed by

J. M. Sugg, Esq., Service Manager to Messrs. Vincent Engineers, and the publishers are indebted to the manufacturers for their permission to use the Vincent trademark in the design of the cover.

PAUL RICHARDSON

CONTENTS

CHAP.		PAGE
I.	THE FRONT END	11

Introduction—Upper Frame Member—Head-races—Head Brackets—Brampton Pattern Forks—"Girdraulic" Forks—Hydraulic Dampers—Steering Complaints—Rims and Wheel Balance—Hubs—Brakes—Handlebar and Controls—Speedometer—Front Stand—500-c.c. Models.

II.	THE REAR END	33

Removal—Rear Suspension—Frame Springs—Rear Fork—Crash Damage—Friction Dampers—Rear-wheel Fitting—Rear Brakes—500-c.c. Models.

III.	CYLINDER HEAD, BARREL AND PISTON	42

Tappet Adjustment—Decarbonising—Rockers and Bearings—Valve Guides—Valve Springs—Seat Rings—Cylinder Barrel—Pistons—Piston-rings—Running-in.

IV.	THE LOWER ENGINE HALF	54

Crankcase—Splitting Crankcase—Crankcase Fittings—Flywheels and Mainshafts—Main Bearings—Big End—500-c.c. Models.

V.	PRIMARY DRIVE AND CLUTCH	64

Lubrication—Adjustment of Tensioner—Primary Chain—Noisy Drive—Shock Absorber—Clutch—Clutch Slip—Shoes and Linings—500-c.c. Models.

VI.	GEARBOX AND SECONDARY DRIVE	75

Lubrication—Gear-change Adjustment—Alternative Specifications—Oil Retention—Dismantling—Assembling—Ratchet Shaft and Bevel—Diagnosing Trouble—Chain and Sprockets—500-c.c. Gearboxes — Service Notes — Inspecting and Re-assembling.

CHAP.		PAGE
VII.	THE LUBRICATION SYSTEM	93

Description—Oil Recommendations—Maintenance and Adjustments—Oil Change—Oil Tank—Oil Pump—Lubrication Troubles—Breathing—General Lubrication—500-c.c. Models.

VIII.	FUEL SYSTEM, TIMING GEAR AND EXHAUST SYSTEM	106

Petrol Tank—The Tie-bolt and Distance Piece—Carburetters—Carburation Troubles—Push-rods and Cam-followers—Camshafts—Idler Gear—Half-time Pinion—Valve Timing—Mark III Cams—Exhaust Lifter—Exhaust System—500-c.c. Models.

IX.	IGNITION AND ELECTRICAL EQUIPMENT	122

Sparking-plugs—Interference Suppressors—Magneto—Timing the Magneto—Ignition Trouble—Headlamp—Electric Horn—Battery—Wiring—Dynamo—Voltage Regulator—500-c.c. Models.

X.	RACING	140

General Observations—Standard Specifications—Weight Reduction—Engine Tuning—Primary Drive and Gearbox—Carburation and Fuels—Ignition and Revolution Counter—Exhaust Systems—Cycle Parts—Sprockets and Gearing—500-c.c. Models—Gearbox—Speedway Engine.

XI.	SIDECARS, ACCESSORIES AND EXTRA EQUIPMENT	161

Sidecars—Sidecar Alignment—Sidecar Conversion—Touring Models—Tyres and Pressures—The Dualseat—The Tool-kit—Panniers and Crashbars—Air Cleaners—Petrol-tank Cover—Handlebar Screens—U.S.A. Specification—Service Exchange—Vincent Owners Club.

XII.	THE SERIES "A" MODELS	172

Introduction—Frame and Forks—Wheels and Brakes—Cylinder Head and Barrel—Valve Gear—Crankcase and Flywheel Assembly—Primary Drive and Clutch—Gearbox and Secondary Drive—Lubrication System—Oil Pump—Oil Filters—Fuel

CONTENTS

System—Ignition and Electrical Equipment—Comet Special—T.T. Replica—Rapide, Series A—Sidecars.

APPENDIX. TABULATED INFORMATION ON ALL MODELS 1935 ONWARDS 198

General Data—Lubrication Chart—Sparking-plugs—Tyre Pressures—Sprocket Sizes and Ratios—Carburetter Settings—Piston-rings—Power Unit Ball and Roller Bearings—Rear Frame Springs—Service Exchange—Detail Modifications.

INDEX 212

R. Madsen-Mygdal Competing in the Clubmans T.T. 1000 c.c. (1953).

[Photograph by R. S. Allan, A.R.P.S.

CHAPTER I

THE FRONT END

UNDERSTANDING of the technical details is bound to give keen riders the best results from their mounts, and many are sufficiently experienced to carry out their own maintenance and straightforward renovations to a high standard of workmanship. It is appropriate, however, to issue a word of warning to those attempting overhauls without the necessary mechanical aptitude or working facilities. In certain paragraphs of this book reference is made to jobs which are generally considered outside the scope of the owner-rider, and in case of doubt it is wise to obtain expert advice. Frequently, an opinion on a problem can be formulated only after examination of the job; seeking local qualified assistance is therefore in some instances preferable to writing to the manufacturers, especially on matters which are not peculiar to the Vincent machine.

Great accessibility for maintenance and overhauls has always been amongst the outstanding features of the motor cycles described in the following pages. Separate chapters devoted to the front and rear ends of the Series B and C models emphasise the fact that it takes but little time to remove these main assemblies from the power unit. This enables more than one person to work on the same machine without interference, apart from ease of storing or transporting in confined spaces. The pre-1940 range described in Chapter XII has a conventional front frame, but the rear end detaches in a similar manner.

Upper Frame Member

On a high-performance motor cycle fine steering qualities are of utmost importance, and Vincent machines have always set a very high standard in this respect. In the post-war series so much attention has been paid to rigidity of the power unit that it is possible to dispense with a frame in the normally accepted sense, and the head-lug is supported by a triangulated upper frame member which also acts as oil tank.

The head-lug is fitted to the oil tank by means of five special bolts, the countersunk nuts of which are riveted over after tightening. For all practical purposes, however, the upper frame member assembly is to be regarded as one unit which *must not be separated*. In case of crash damage to the machine the upper frame member may well maintain its alignment due to its immense strength, but it is advisable to carry out a check.

This is done by passing a $\frac{1}{2}$-in. (12·70-mm.) bar through the steering-head engine-bracket lug or lugs in order that the part may be set up in V-blocks on a surface plate. By supporting the rear of the oil tank a mandril can be inserted through the head-races for checking with a square and two distance pieces. In normal use the alignment will never be affected, but assemblies which have sustained accidental damage must be returned to the manufacturers or to Vincent repair specialists for possible rectification.

Of the three cross-tubes at the rear of the upper frame-member, the top one carries the dualseat pivot tube in self-oiling bushes, the middle tube takes the frame-spring bolt sleeve (divided on Series C models) and the bottom tube can be used for a $\frac{5}{8}$-in. (15·87-mm.) sidecar-mounting bolt.

During 1951, production was simplified by the introduction of a modified head-lug used in conjunction with a

THE FRONT END

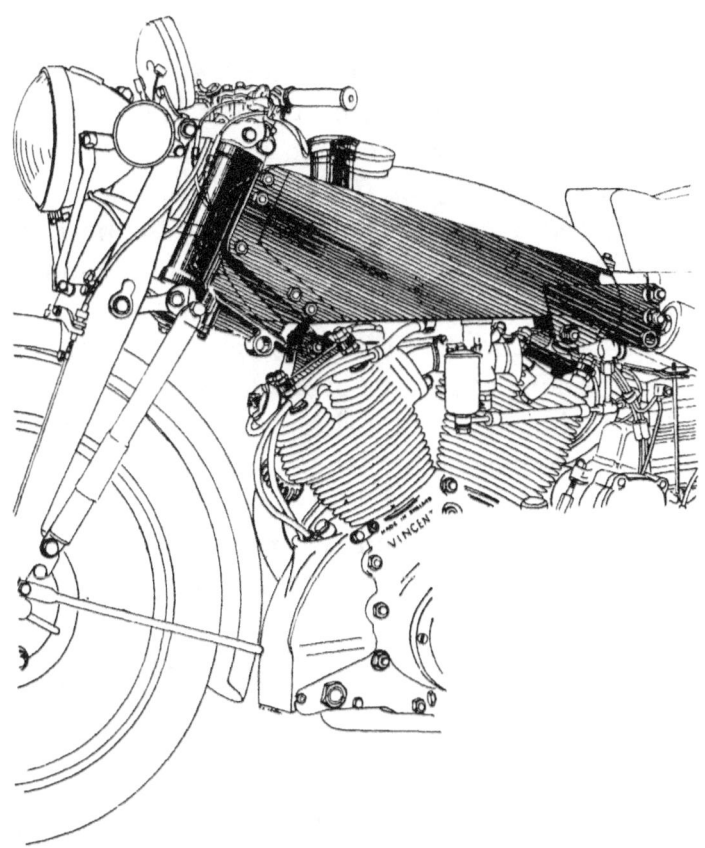

Fig. 1.—The Upper Frame Member.

different front-cylinder head-bracket, engine-mounting bolt and spigot nuts. Upper frame members featuring the earlier head-lug are not normally supplied as a spare, but the complete group of later components is interchangeable with the earlier pattern. Head-races should be left in position in any upper-frame-member assemblies returned to the manufacturers for checking or repair, but oil-pipe unions, filler cap, chain-oiler needle valve and steering-head grease nipple should be removed.

Head-races

Cups and cones are used on post-war machines, the former being pressed into the head-lug, the latter on the forks. Although each bearing will take twenty-one, *not more than twenty*, ¼-in. (6·35-mm.) dia. steel balls may be used in each race. During assembly, the bearings are packed with high-melting-point grease, and the lower race which takes the thrust, is provided with a grease nipple. Occasional application of the grease-gun is recommended, but over-greasing should be avoided, especially on earlier models, on which excess lubricant may find its way on to the engine through the head-lug.

When correctly adjusted, there should be no perceptible play in the steering-column, yet the forks should fall to full lock by their own weight with the machine on the front stand and the front wheel removed. There is a clamping bolt in the head-clip just below the steering-damper knob, and unscrewing the nut a few turns will release the grip of the pad bushes on the fork stem. The head-clip nut can then be tightened until the aforementioned adjustment is obtained, and re-tightening the clamping-bolt nut completes the operation. Loose head-races will wear rapidly, and over-tightening will result in pitting, particularly of the cups; faults of this nature are bound to affect the steering, and damaged components must be renewed without delay.

Bearing cups can be driven out of the head-lug with the aid of a mild-steel drift of sufficient length and diameter. The top fork cone sits in a shroud in which, if not already provided, two holes must be drilled; a thin drift can be used to drive out this part. New cups are best drawn into position by means of a large-diameter bolt with large washers of the appropriate thickness bearing on the outer edges of the races. Each bearing recess must be perfectly

THE FRONT END

FIG. 2.—FRONT AND REAR ENGINE-MOUNTING BOLTS.

Nut (*A*) should be first tightened fully, then slackened one-sixth turn and outer nut locked up. This procedure will permit joint to creep under the influence of engine expansion on 1000-c.c. models.

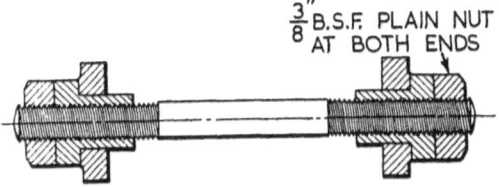

FRONT, ALL NUTS FULLY TIGHTENED

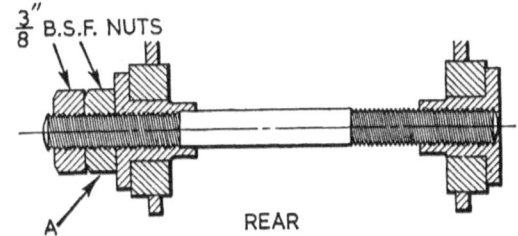

REAR

clean and free from foreign matter, as tilt in a cup of the order of 0·003 in. (0·07 mm.) is enough to be noticeable in handling. Cones are carefully tapped on to their seatings, taking care that they are also fitted squarely.

Head Brackets

On 1000-c.c. models the raised portion of the cylinder-head bracket lies to the right on the front cylinder and to the left on the rear. This also applies to the 1951-pattern front bracket, which is not interchangeable with the rear component as on earlier models. It should be noted that the upper-frame-member stresses are not carried by the engine-mounting bolts but by spigot nuts and bushes, and one of the latter is welded to its bolt for fitting to the right-hand side of the upper frame member. The rear lugs are slotted and, in order to enable the light-alloy engine to expand under influences of temperature, the nut of the rear mounting bolt is fully tightened and then slackened off 60 degrees before the lock-nut is drawn up. On all models the nuts and lock-nuts of the front mounting bolt should be dead tight.

Forks

Brampton Pattern Forks

Series B machines are fitted with Brampton-type girder forks similar to the pre-war pattern but—on account of difference in head-stem—not interchangeable, the post-war head-lug being longer. The Series B forks feature self-oiling bushes, indicated by the absence of lubrication nipples; should these have been fitted at a later date, oil must be used for additional lubrication, not grease. The self-oiling properties of porous bronze bushes may vary to some extent; the occasional application of oil to various fork joints is therefore good practice.

Top and bottom spindles are machined from heat-treated bar, and differ in length as well as diameter; they are square-ended for adjustment. The left-hand lock-nuts, links and spindle ends have left-hand threads, the top spindles $\frac{7}{16}$ in. $\times$ 26 C.E.I. and the bottom spindles $\frac{1}{2}$ in. $\times$ 26 C.E.I. Left-hand-threaded nuts are stamped " L ". The solo top links measure $3\frac{3}{8}$ in. (85·72 mm.) between centres, and are stamped " 41L " and " 41R " on the inside. Sidecar links are 3 in. between centres, and are stamped " 6L " and " 6R ". The hand-operated friction damper is fitted to the right-hand lower link, and its efficiency is mainly dependent upon the friction discs remaining free from oil or grease.

LINK ADJUSTMENT.—The need for link adjustment is often indicated by a knocking noise when the handlebars are moved from lock to lock. Turning the spindles clockwise after slackening off the lock-nuts takes up play, and the adjustment is correct if one of the knurled washers of each spindle can be turned with the fingers. Before adjusting the lower links the friction damper must, of course, be slackened off completely.

REMOVING THE FORKS.—In the case of slight accidental damage a girder can be trued up and checked, but badly dented tubes must be replaced. When removing the forks complete it is probably easier to detach the wiring loom from the machine rather than disconnect various leads from the headlamp. A $\tfrac{3}{16}$-in. grooved pin in the right-hand fork end locks the wheel-spindle nut. The steering-damper pressure plate is riveted to a sleeve

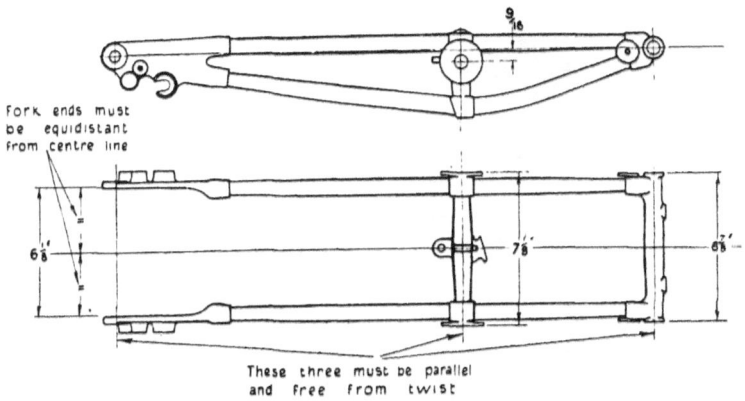

FIG. 3.—FORK GIRDER TRUEING DETAILS.

retained by the rear bottom-fork spindle, which must be removed for taking the steering-damper apart. The operating rod is prevented from slackening off by a rubber washer fitted inside the head-clip bore.

REBUSHING THE FORKS.—When rebushing the forks the old bushes can be removed with a sharp chisel or narrow hacksaw blade. Another method is to tap the old bush to take a bolt; this bolt is then driven out from the other side together with the bush. Each pair of spindles must be unscrewed simultaneously to avoid jamming in the link. The new bushes are pressed-in or drawn into position with a long bolt and washers. It is important to note that these self-oiling bushes *must not be reamed*, and any tight spots should be removed with a scraper.

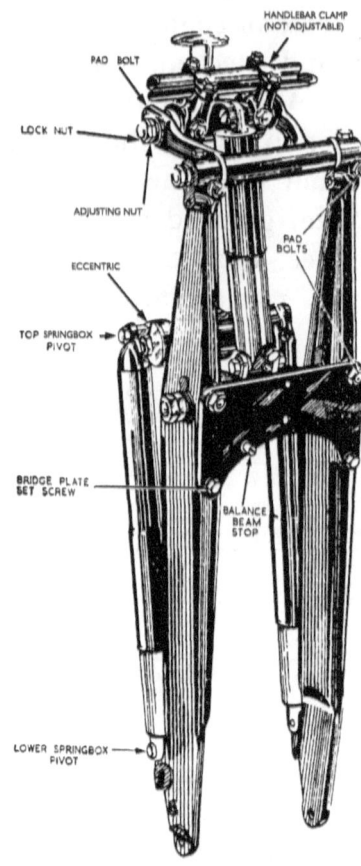

FIG. 4.—VINCENT "GIRDRAULIC" FORKS.

"Girdraulic" * Forks

As these forks are also fitted with self-oiling bushes, lubrication is confined to the application of a few drops of engine oil to the moving parts every 3000 miles (5000 km.). A few machines were fitted with lubrication nipples to the lower link at a time when self-oiling bushes were not available. Worn bushes can easily be renewed, but must be scraped, *not reamed*, if too tight on the spindles.

For sidecar use the trail and spring strength are altered at the same time by simultaneously rotating the lower link eccentrics until the stop plates come up against the opposite pegs in the crown lug, after the spindle nut has been slackened off. It is not essential to detach the spring-boxes for this operation, provided the front wheel is clear of the ground; leaving them in position simplifies the job considerably, and avoids the possibility of damage to pivot threads, spring-boxes, etc. Re-tightening the spindle nut after variation of trail should not be forgotten.

ADJUSTMENT OF SPINDLES.—Adjustment is correct when it is possible to rotate one dust-washer of each spindle by hand, and whilst there must be no perceptible play, the

* British Registered Trade Mark No. 675,834.

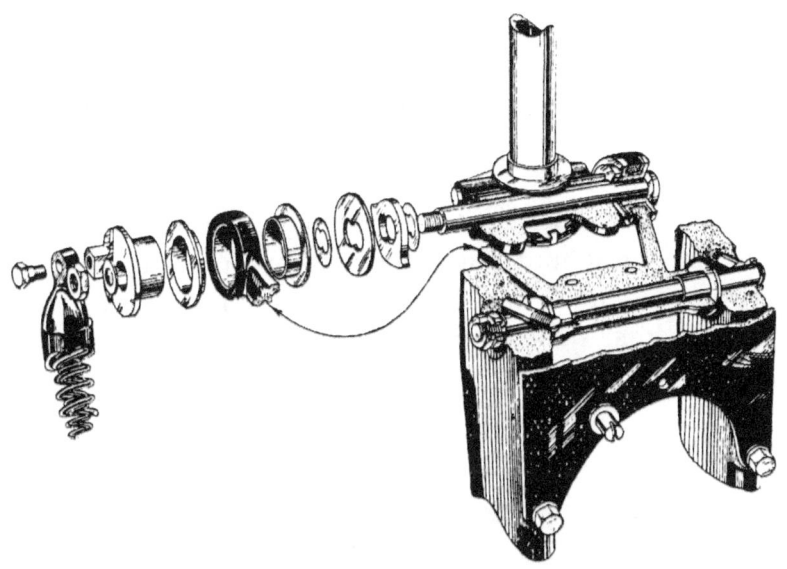

Fig. 5.—" Girdraulic " Fork Bottom Link and Spindle Retention.

blades must move freely relative to the links. Milled pad-bolts retain three of the four spindles, and the nuts of these bolts must be slackened off so that the grip on the spindles will be released before adjustment. There is no need to slacken off both pad-bolts of each spindle; the ones nearest to the spindle nuts suffice, and turning these nuts in a clockwise direction takes up play. The pad-bolts are provided with screwdriver slots, but it is, of course, not possible to turn or withdraw them with the spindles in position. For adjustment of the lower front spindle the bridge plate set-screws must be slackened, and fork adjustments are best performed with the wheel removed. After adjustment all set-screws and lock-nuts should be re-tightened.

The Fitting of Shims.—It is a popular misconception that shims are added when play develops in the rear bottom-link bearings; that this is not so will be clear once it is realised that the width of each pair of bushes in a link eye is greater than the width of the eccentric. Consequently, the difference must be made up by shims between eccentric and thrust-washer to obtain the necessary working clearance of 0·003 in. (0·07 mm.). As the flanges of the bushes wear in service, the overall width of each pair decreases, and the eccentric will have to follow suit, the reduction being effected by removal of shims between eccentric and thrust-washer. It will be noted, however, that this removal of shims tends to distort the

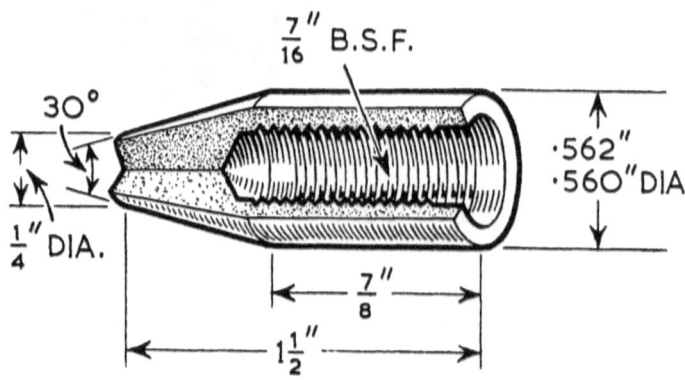

Fig. 6.—Bottom-link Assembly Bullet for "Girdraulic" Forks.

lower link by pulling-up the eyes towards each other when the spindle nut is tightened.

For this reason shims may have to be re-fitted between the stop plates and the crown-column lug. The positioning of the correct shims may call for some experimenting by trial and error; whilst the link must be clear of the fork blades it is not necessary to dismantle these, as they can be swung upwards complete with wheel, etc., after the front lower spindle has been withdrawn from the circlip and collar end. The lining-up of rear bottom-link components and shims is greatly facilitated by the use of a bullet-shape assembly tool which screws on to the threaded portion of the spindle, thereby reducing the possibility of damage to the threads during spindle removal.

REMOVING AND RE-FITTING SPRING-BOXES.—For removal of the spring-boxes the forks must extend to the extremity of downward travel with the hydraulic damper detached. It is advisable to remove the lower pivot first, as the load on this component can be eased with a narrow screwdriver inserted between the bottom of the spring-box and the lug on the fork. Conversely, it is better to re-fit a spring-box at the top pivot first, as the same screwdriver is again used to lever the inner spring-box upwards, using the fork-lug as a fulcrum; the lower pivot can then be inserted without difficulty.

THE STEERING DAMPER.—This is meant to be *used*, and experienced riders always have the damper " just biting " on the open road. The layout differs from the Series A and B models, although Series C machines also had a single friction disc until 1953. The dished spring plate is dismantled by removing the $\frac{1}{4}$-in. B.S.F. nut and the special damper lock-nut at the bottom end of the operating rod. This exposes the anchor plate, retained by the head-stem being peened over.

If it is necessary to renew the anchor plate or friction disc the stem must be carefully dressed back to release the plate. After the new parts have been fitted the stem is again peened over with a ball-end hammer, taking care that the anchor plate remains free to rotate. The top damper disc has a tongue which locates in the head-stem, and this tongue also prevents the damper nut from falling down when the knob is slackened off. The anchor pin must be a slack fit in the head-lug to assist self-centralising.

If a damper tends to slacken itself, the ball and spring in the detent housing may have rusted, and if so the application of some penetrating oil or the fitting of a new spring is called for. Models from late 1953 onwards are

[*By courtesy of "The Motor Cycle", London.*
Fig. 7.—Steering Damper with Two Friction Discs.

fitted with double friction discs, and the construction of the steel plates is such that self-slackening is virtually impossible; this renders this damper eminently suitable for sidecar work. Earlier dampers can easily be converted; on the later pattern the head-stem is not peened over.

" Girdraulic " forks which have been involved in a crash should be returned to the Works or Vincent specialists for check and replacement of any damaged component with genuine Vincent spares. The blades and top link are made from light alloy, which is heat-treated in furnaces of special design; local rectification is not permissible.

Hydraulic Dampers

As not all riders are equally sensitive to deterioration in road holding due to insufficient damping, it is recommended that the dampers are removed for topping up every 2000 miles (3000 km.), although most units give perfectly satisfactory service for longer periods without attention. The lower mounting, however, must be greased periodically, and as angle nipples are not practical from a production point of view, the lower headlamp brackets must be released from the retaining eye bolt. For access to the rear-damper grease nipple the dualseat can be raised.

When filling the damper utmost cleanliness of oil and utensils is essential. The component is inverted with the filling orifice facing upwards; the hexagon plug removed and the damper fully extended in a position approximately 15 degrees from vertical. Oil is injected until full, and air is allowed to escape for approximately two hours; then the damper is slowly compressed to nearly the extent of its travel with the plug seal loose. Finally, the damper is fully compressed and the plug tightened. S.A.E. 20 engine oil is recommended, and less prone to leakage than the shock-absorber fluids used until 1952, but these fluids are still suitable for use in extremely cold climates. A new or recently overhauled unit may lose some oil during the time the new seals bed down, but if the leakage persists, dismantling is necessary. The top eye end is screwed on and retained by a grooved pin, which must be driven out after the enamelled shroud has been removed. The eye end can be unscrewed with an adjustable spanner, and the flats of the top plug are gripped in a vice so that the body can be unscrewed with a tommy bar inserted through the eye. Driving the piston through the cylinder will dislodge the bottom cut-off. The top cut-off need be removed only if its bore has worn oval, and if so it must be renewed to prevent damage to the cylinder. This part will also suffer if the bearing surface of the piston is scored. A scored piston-rod will cause leakage, even if the seals are renewed, and a badly worn or scored cylinder should be replaced.

The fibre washer and the two smaller O-rings should be renewed whenever a damper is serviced, and all component parts are supplied as spares. When mounted, the damper must not be pulled out of line, and if necessary a

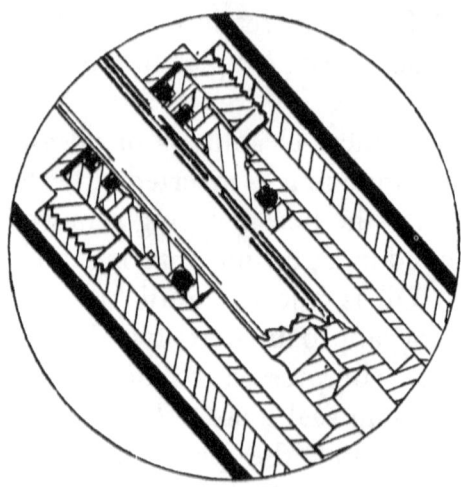

Fig. 8.—Hydraulic Damper "O" Rings.

thin washer can be inserted under one of the retaining eye bolts to ensure that the unit enters the top lug without strain. The top mounting pivot, although provided with a screwdriver slot, is not threaded in the lug, and can be driven out after the lock-nut has been removed. A rear damper can be fitted to Series B models if the middle cross-tube of the upper frame member is slotted with a narrow hacksaw blade and the distance sleeve divided. It is not advisable to ride Series C models with the front damper removed, but the rear damper can be temporarily fitted to the front, provided the rear friction dampers are adequately tightened.

Steering Complaints

If correction of the wheel alignment does not cure a steering defect, such as pulling to one side, the machine requires expert attention, and in the majority of cases an alignment check on the forks, upper frame member or rear frame will be necessary. It is seldom possible to diagnose the cause of the trouble by road test only.

Rims and Wheel Balance

Standard fitting is a 20 in. WM1 rim front and 19 in. WM2 rear; Touring models have a 19 in. WM2 rim front and an 18 in. WM3 rim rear. For good steering the

THE FRONT END

Fig. 9.—Position of Security Bolts and Balance Weights on Wheel Rims (Series B "Black Shadow").
B. Balance weight. S. Security bolt. T. Tyre valve.

wheels must be true, and rims which are badly buckled or show flats should be replaced. A rim defect (or tyre running out of true) becomes noticeable by front-wheel judder at approximately 30 m.p.h. (50 k.p.h.), although the steering may appear satisfactory at higher speeds. For special conditions high-tensile rims can be used, although these are not normally available from the Works; light-alloy racing rims are not recommended for everyday use. Each wheel has forty spokes, usually plain in the front and plain or butted rear. If available, a butted spoke is preferable, on account of less weight for identical strength. Normally, a new spoke can be hooked into the slotted flange without difficulty, but sometimes the hub bolts must be slackened off to provide the necessary clearance between spoke flange and drum. Steel spoke nipples are essential.

Only 1000-c.c. models are fitted with a security bolt, and rule of fitting is that in forward rotation the security bolt leads the tyre valve. During tyre fitting care is necessary to ensure that the inner tube is not nipped. On these machines the wheels are also balanced by weights bolted to the rim. Perfect balance is not essential for road work, but tyre life and handling are improved even with partly balanced wheels. The job is done with the hub felts and brake plates removed, and washers are temporarily fitted between the bearings and the thin nuts.

FIG. 10.—FITTING SECURITY BOLT.

Some experimenting with the weights may be necessary until the wheel does not tend to stop in any one position. On Avon tyres a yellow spot denotes the lightest part, which should be fitted adjacent to the security bolt. Wheels are balanced with the tyre inflated to the recommended pressure.

Hubs

The light-alloy hub is fitted with taper roller bearings, but some 1952 machines featured alternative layouts. Every 10,000 miles (16,000 km.) each bearing should be fully packed with high-melting-point grease, but the space inside the hub body between the bearings may not be more than one-third to half full.

When cold there should be 0·005 in. (0·13 mm.) end

float on the hollow axle relative to the hub body, noticeable by approximately $\frac{1}{32}$ in. (0·79 mm.) shake at the rim. Adjustment is by shims placed between the collars of the hollow axle and the bearings; similar shims are used to obtain brake-plate clearance as required.

With taper roller bearings the cups are dropped into the hub heated up to 200° C. (390° F.). If a cup is no longer a tight fit it may be possible to plate-up the outer diameter to the required oversize, taking care that no plating solution finds its way on to the bearing track.

The foregoing also applies to machines fitted with Metric taper roller bearings, but models with a frame number suffix " D " or " E " are equipped with a ball journal in conjunction with a roller bearing. " D " indicates retention by circlip and " E " retention by screwed and split-pinned lock-ring. These hubs are not adjustable, but the method of shimming out the brake-plates does not differ.

Brakes

The cam spindles should be lubricated periodically through the grease-nipples provided on each cam-plate boss, but overgreasing will cause lubricant to find its way on to the brake linings. It may be necessary to slacken-off a nipple for removal of a cam-spindle. Control cables should be oiled regularly.

Adjustment difficulties on the compensated front brakes are usually caused by friction in the mechanism or uneven tension of the shoe-return springs. Sometimes the stronger spring can be slightly stretched, but the adjustment is much easier on later models fitted with a brake-arm return spring and balance-beam stop. It is important to get the cam arms of the two brakes parallel, and each serration alters the position by 12 degrees. Finer adjustment can be obtained, however, by with-

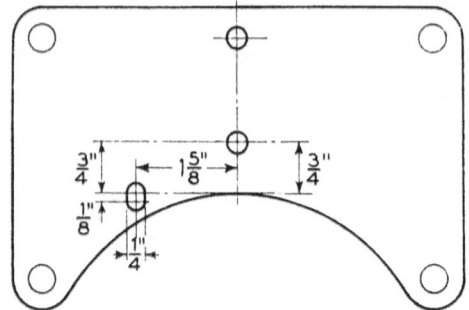

PARTS REQUIRED.
Return spring (FF74/1).
Balance-beam stop
 (FF75/1).
¼-in. B.S.F. nut.
¼-in. B.S.F. flat washer.
Single-coil spring washer.

FIG. 11.—DIMENSIONS FOR DRILLING FORK BRIDGE PLATE FOR BALANCE-BEAM STOP.

The return spring (FF74/1) is mounted to the right-hand cam arm, and modifying earlier machines may necessitate fitting the extended front-brake cable assembly (long), HB9, which is now fitted to the left-hand side of the balance beam, viewed from the rider astride.

drawing the serrated washer from its square and re-fitting after turning through 90 degrees. The cam spindles have cycle threads. Earlier Series C models can be fitted with the balance-beam stop and return spring, provided the extended front-brake cable fitted to the left-hand side of the balance beam is used.

Ferodo MR41 as well as Duron P28 moulded linings have been used; the latter do not bed themselves down in the same way as woven material, and after re-lining the removal of high spots with sand-paper may be necessary. As the shoes are not jig-drilled, replacement linings are supplied undrilled, but owners are advised to take advantage of the Service Exchange scheme, although relining the shoes follows normal motor-cycle practice. Linings must be well chamfered, particularly the leading edges, and the linings must not bulge, as this causes sponginess and squeal. With ribbed brake drums squeal may occur in spite of correctly fitted linings, and as long as there are no rivets standing proud, the noise is not detrimental. Each shoe is retained by a split-pin, and it will be found

THE FRONT END 29

that it is much easier to remove both shoes simultaneously, together with the cam-spindle; the same applies to refitting.

Handlebar and Controls

All post-war handlebars are $\tfrac{7}{8}$ in. (22·22 mm.) O.D., and the standard straight pattern is $25\tfrac{1}{2}$ in. (64·8 cm.)

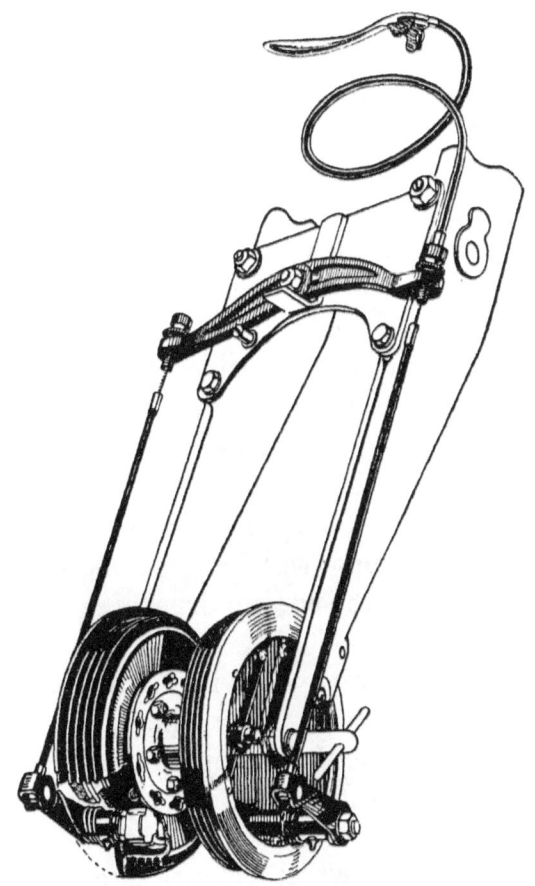

Fig. 12.—Fitting of Front-brake Return Spring.

long. The straight bar is also available 3 in. (7·6 cm.) wider for sidecar work, or alternatively a " cow-horn " handlebar can be fitted by those touring or sidecar enthusiasts who prefer a more upright riding position. Sidecar and touring bars necessitate a longer throttle cable assembly, which is available as a spare.

Control cables should be oiled regularly, and replacements are supplied as complete assemblies ready for fitting. On 1000-c.c. models the clutch and exhaust-lifter cables are interchangeable. A loose dummy grip must be refitted with " Bostik " or similar adhesive without delay.

Speedometer

The speedo gearbox requires greasing regularly through the nipple provided, but overgreasing will cause the lubricant to reach the brake linings or the speedometer head. The gearbox gives a reduction of $1\frac{1}{2}$ to 1, and is adjustable for cable angle. The pinion should project $\frac{7}{32}$ in. (5·55 mm.) from the inside of the brake-plate for correct mesh with the gear ring. This component has forty-one teeth, and on a machine fitted with an Avon tyre the speedo is accurate within 1·8 per cent for the standard wheel. With a 27-in. front wheel (e.g., 3·00 × 21-in. tyre) the reading will be even more accurate, so that no alterations to the speedo drive are necessary if this size is used.

The gear ring is removed with a three-arm sprocket puller, and is only a press fit on the hub body. A discarded piston can be used for tapping the ring home when re-fitting, after which four fresh indentations are made in the hub spigot for retention.

Speedometer heads which require attention should be returned to the manufacturers or their nearest service depot, but Service Exchange also applies in this case. Recurring cable fracture may result from a defect in the head, and in this case the same course should be adopted.

Front Stand

Either the left- or right-hand prop-stand can be used for parking the machine, but it is advisable to always turn the front wheel towards the stand in use. Both stands together form a front stand, but for this purpose the magneto cowl must be slackened on its mountings and the $\frac{5}{16}$-in. B.S.F. set-screw removed from the left-hand engine plate. With the machine placed on the rear stand the front wheel is lifted off the ground to swing the spring-loaded front stand forwards into position. Check occasionally that the prop-stand pivot bolts have not worked loose. The stands on Series C models are longer than on Series B machines, and if the latter are fitted with " Girdraulic " forks the longer-pattern stands should be fitted at the same time.

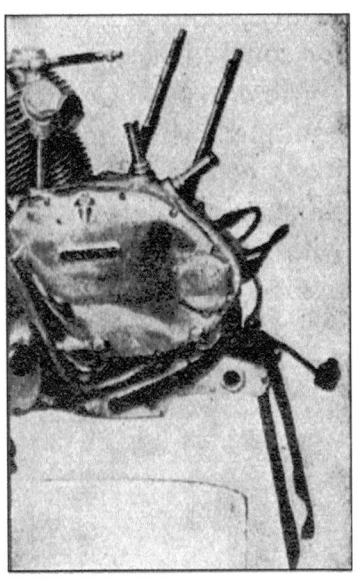

Fig. 13.—Prop-stands Used as Front Stand.

500-c.c. Models

There is no need to slacken-off the rear upper-frame-member retaining bolt 60 degrees before tightening the lock-nut; no engine expansion as on 1000-c.c. machines will occur, and therefore the frame tie bolt should be fully tightened.

Single-cylinder models are fitted with outer front-fork springs only, but inner springs can be added if a heavy sidecar is fitted.

The wheels are not fitted with balance weights; tyre

security bolts are not necessary unless the machine is used for competitions.

Meteor and Grey Flash machines are not normally equipped with prop-stands and magneto cowl, but these items can be added if required. It is possible to mount the engine plates with prop-stand pivot and nuts but without the actual stands or bracket, if it is merely intended to attach a sidecar at the minimum of cost or weight.

CHAPTER II

THE REAR END

It may be convenient or necessary to remove the rear end as a complete unit, and the only parts to be detached are the chain, brake cable, lighting and horn wiring, front dualseat mounting bolt and front spring-box pivot bolt. The *right-hand* nut is then removed from the pivot-bearing bolt, and this part driven out to the left, after which the rear end can be pulled clear of the plates. With the rear stand down, the whole assembly is easily parked upright on the tyre. When refitting make sure that the nuts on the pivot-bearing hollow axle are a good fit between the plates; shim up if necessary.

Rear Suspension

An exclusive feature is the rear mounting of the dualseat (British Patent No. 424,644), which gives a comfortable ride without sensitivity to varying loads. This makes it unnecessary to change the frame springs to accommodate normal variations in the weight of rider and/or passenger. The triangulated rear fork is free from twist without unduly increasing the unsprung weight relative to the total weight of the machine. Damping is provided by adjustable friction dampers incorporated in the seat stays. On Series C models a hydraulic damper is an additional refinement.

To obtain maximum comfort, some owners mount the dualseat fully sprung by supporting the rear end of the seat on extended stays bolted to the pillion footrest plates. Heavier frame springs are likely to be necessary, and whilst a modification of this nature may well be successful,

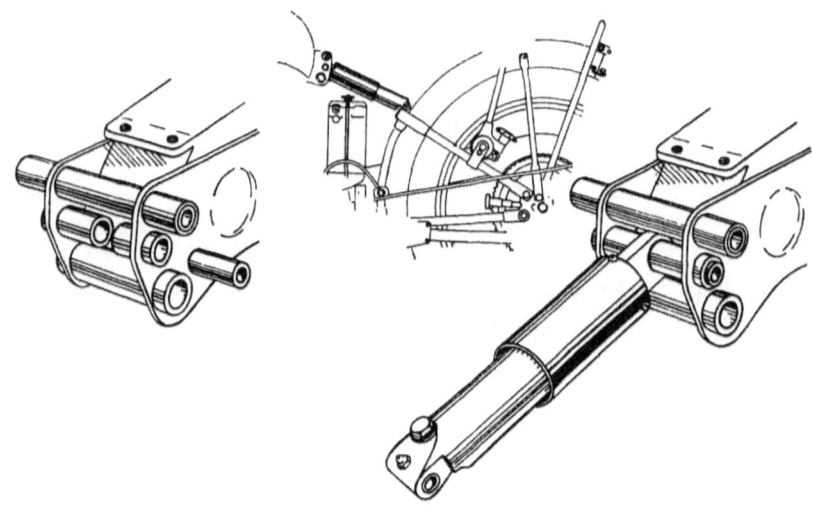

Fig. 14.—Fitting of Rear Damper.

the manufacturers accept no responsibility, and the guarantee, where applicable, will be invalidated.

Frame Springs

The fully enclosed coil springs are packed in high-melting-point grease during assembly, and do not require additional lubrication. The same applies to the spring-box pivot bolts, which bear in self-oiling bushes, but here the occasional application of some oil will do no harm.

The uninitiated mechanic is apt to regard the frame springs with awe when it comes to removal, but this is a simple operation, entirely without danger. The job is greatly facilitated if the weight is taken off the springs by placing a jack or box of suitable height under the power unit. Just remove the spindle nuts adjacent to the eye bolts of each spring-box and withdraw the assembly.

After slackening-off the lock-nut, the eye bolt can be unscrewed; this releases the spring-box and exposes the spring for examination. The rate and wire diameter of the springs is given in Table IX of the Appendix.

THE REAR END

The free length is 6¾ in. With the rider seated, 1¼ in. (32 mm.) of inner spring-case should project, and springs which have settled down appreciably should be renewed, as otherwise the steering will be affected. Springs are " unscrewed " from their claws by tapping the end of the coil with hammer and drift, but they are re-fitted with both hands. When fitting sidecar springs, the claws may require easing with a round file. When mounting the spring-box assembly to the machine, it is advisable to tighten-up the lock-nuts of the eye bolts last, to avoid spring torsion during the job.

Rear Fork

The fork is supported by taper roller bearings identical to those used on the hubs, but each race is provided with a grease-nipple which also feeds the rear-brake cross shaft. Adjustment of the pivot bearing is correct if the hollow axle can be rotated with the fingers, and, if necessary, shims are inserted between the collars of the hollow axle

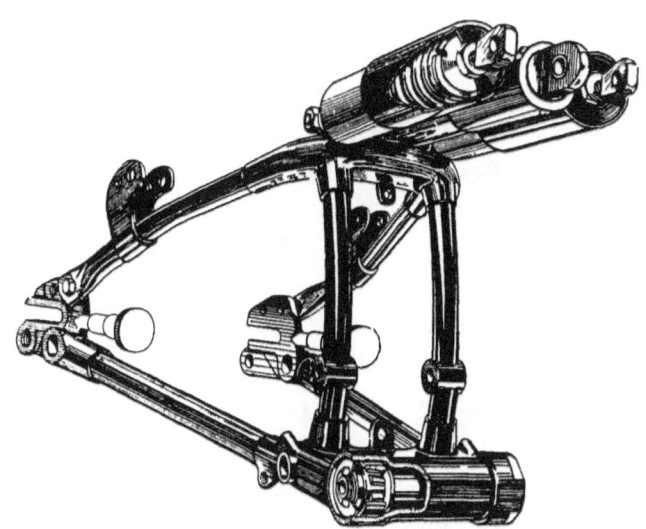

FIG. 15.—LATE PATTERN REAR-FORK ASSEMBLY.

and each bearing, no end float being required. The rear fork pivots at a point $4\frac{1}{2}$ in. (11·43 cm.) to the rear of the gearbox final-drive sprocket, and variation in rear-chain sprocket centres never exceeds $\frac{1}{16}$ in. (1·5 mm.) between mid position and full travel.

On early Series B models the fork measured $17\frac{1}{2}$ in. (44·45 cm.) from the pivot centre to the rear-axle centre in its foremost position, but on later machines this dimension was increased to 18 in. (45·72 cm.) to enable the use of a 27-in.-diameter rear wheel for racing or competitions. With the introduction of the 500-c.c. models a different brake-cable stop and curved seat-stay lugs became standard to render the component interchangeable for the whole range.

Crash Damage

Slight lateral bending can sometimes be corrected by heating the tubes adjacent to the lugs and re-setting each fork end individually. Mandrils inserted through the pivot bearing and the rear-axle slots should be parallel, and the maximum permissible twist is $\frac{3}{32}$ in. (2·38 mm.) per foot of mandril. The inner fork-end faces should be parallel, $8\frac{3}{8}$ in. (21·27 cm.) apart; the right-hand face is $\frac{9}{16}$ in. (14·28 mm.) outside the face of the pivot-bearing lug, and on the left-hand side the dimension is $1\frac{1}{4}$ in. (31·75 mm.) relative to the left-hand face of the pivot-bearing lug. The apex lug is central to the fork ends, and the ears of the seat-stay lugs should also be parallel. Wherever possible, advantage will be taken of the " Service Exchange Scheme ", as the component parts of the fork are not normally supplied as spares, and brazing must be done in a definite sequence in order to avoid distortion.

For repairs or service exchange, the bearing cups must

be driven out; the dust-washers fitted to the inside of each cup are sufficiently sturdy to withstand the impact of a drift. When re-fitting the pivot bearing, each race must be re-assembled in its original cup. The self-oiling spring-bolt bushes should be removed as well; when it is found on re-fitting that they are loose in the apex lug they can be carefully squeezed endways in a vice to increase the diameter. As with many other parts of the machine, the standard finish is high-grade stove enamel, which is very durable and unlikely to chip or flake.

Friction Dampers

The application of some thin oil will cure a squeaking noise emanated by the dampers when the drums foul the light-alloy clamps, alternatively, it is possible to ease slightly the recess of the offending clamp. For normal fast touring the friction dampers should be "just biting", but more tightening is required on machines which are not fitted with a hydraulic damper.

It has happened on some earlier Series B models that the right-hand damper knob fouls the chain guard. Not only does this dent the guard, but the damper may lock momentarily, causing the clamp to fracture or the shank to bend. An easy cure is to lower slightly the rear mounting of the chain guard by means of a tab.

On earlier machines the damper drums were located by 2 B.A. screws, but as these may not be strong enough for sidecar work or regular pillion riding, it is advisable to fit $\frac{1}{4}$-in. B.S.F. screws with nuts, as are standard on later models. Closing up of the damper-clamp slot indicates that the friction linings are due for renewal, and the fresh material is stuck to the clamp with "Bostik" or similar adhesive. The length of each lining is $5\frac{5}{8}$ in. (14·28 cm.). Note that the seat-stay ends are adjustable for height.

Fig. 16.—Rear-brake Torque Arms and Cross Shaft.

Rear-wheel Fitting

The brake torque arms are fitted to the outer face of the lug on the pivot-bearing housing and retained by a $\frac{3}{8}$ in. × 26 C.E.I. screw with a lock-nut on the inside. Occasional lubrication of the spring-loaded clips will facilitate wheel removal.

In order not to interfere with the silencer, the tommy bar of the rear axle should be on the left-hand side of the machine. As the component is designed for tightening by hand, it is *never* permissible to increase the leverage by using a ring spanner or similar tool on the tommy bar. The axle nut is lipped; damage to the rear fork end has occurred due to garage attendants trying to unscrew this stainless-steel part with the aid of a spanner, not being aware of the lip. This must always lie to the *rear*; for if fitted the wrong way round, the lip is bound to foul the chain adjuster which may bend when the axle is tightened;

THE REAR END

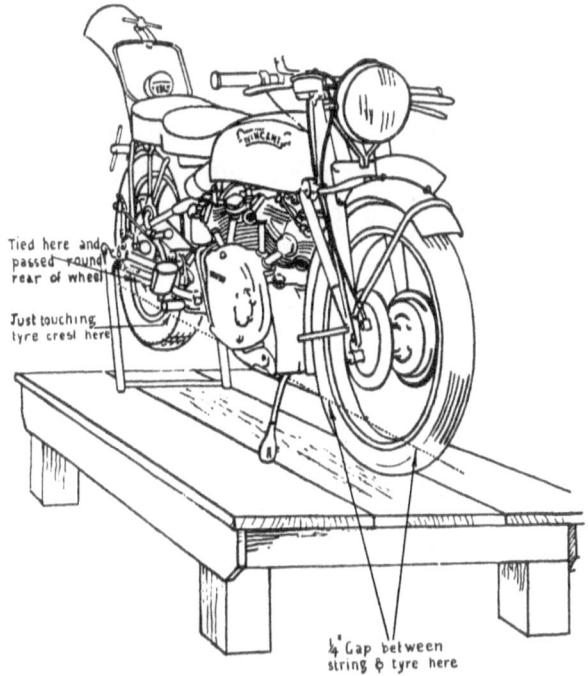

FIG. 17.—CHECKING WHEEL ALIGNMENT.

fracture of the fork end is just as likely to occur in this case.

The time spent on correct wheel alignment with the aid of a length of string or straight edge is well worth while; allowance must be made for the difference in front and rear tyre sizes.

Rear Brakes

These are not compensated and individually adjusted. The procedure is to screw up each wing-nut until the brake binds, and then to count the number of half-turns required to free the brake when unscrewing. Adjust the opposite brake to bind in the same manner, and then slacken off that wing-nut an equal number of half-turns to obtain simultaneous operation. As on the front brakes, the cam arms can be re-set on their serrated washers when the adjustment on the threaded stainless-steel rods has been used up.

The rear-brake linings should be well chamfered on the leading as well as on the trailing edges, and re-chamfering may be necessary if a considerable mileage has been

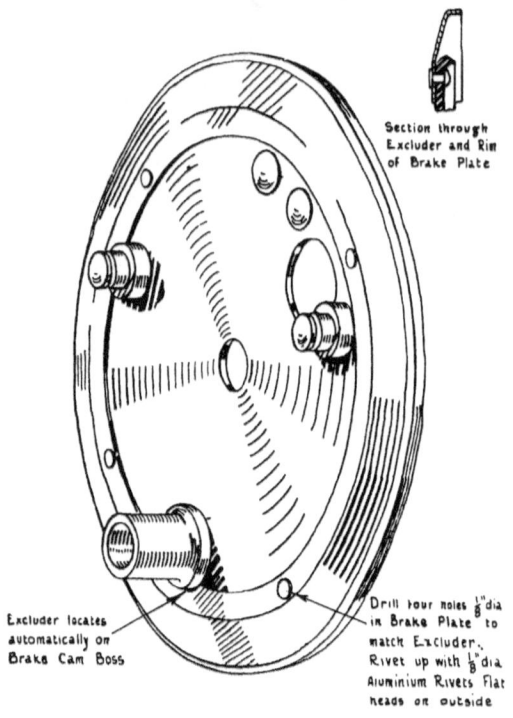

FIG. 18.—BRAKE WATER EXCLUDER.

covered on the same linings. In particular, the trailing edges are apt to get overlooked and when it becomes necessary suddenly to stop a machine rolling backwards by means of the foot-brake, bending of the torque stays or even drum fracture may occur if the brake locks due to insufficient chamfer. The rear-brake leverage has been purposely reduced to prevent lock and it is not permissible to lengthen the cam arms.

Nipples are provided on each cam-spindle boss, *but do not overgrease*! During 1952, a water excluder on one rear brake became standard, but this part cannot be used if the machine is fitted with twin sprockets. It will be found, however, that the sprocket tends to keep water away from the drum, so that the need will not arise. Fitting a water excluder to a brake-plate which was not originally so equipped is straightforward, as the excluder is self-locating, and the holes are used for marking the plate before drilling. There are no objections to the removal of one rear brake complete for special purposes.

500-c.c. Models

The same lifting handle as on the Twins is used, but mounted reversed for the lug to support the chain guard on the left-hand side of the machine. Earlier post-war single-cylinder models were equipped with 0·276 in. (7 mm.) wire diameter frame springs, but this gauge was discontinued as somewhat soft for average conditions. It is pointed out here that there is no need for both springs of a pair to be of equal rating, and the suspension can be varied to suit individual tastes by the fitting of any of the spring combinations listed in the Appendix, Table IX.

Whilst the rear fork is interchangeable with the 1000-c.c. models, there are slight dimensional variations in the mounting, evident by the fact that there is usually less clearance between the tool-tray and spring-boxes. From a practical point of view, the only matter of importance is that a pannier set especially designed to fit a Twin may require slight modification when mounted to a Single.

CHAPTER III

CYLINDER HEAD, BARREL AND PISTON

FOR access to each tappet adjuster the corresponding inspection cap must be removed with the kit spanner. A rocker on lift prevents the removal, and it may be necessary to turn the engine until the corresponding valve is fully closed. Later engines are fitted with "Klingerit" inspection cap washers, which are superior to the copper-asbestos pattern.

Tappet Adjustment

The tappets are adjusted to zero clearance with the engine *cold*; when running-in a new or overhauled unit a check at 500-mile (800-km.) intervals is recommended. Subsequently, attention at infrequent intervals only is required, but the cause of any suddenly developing tappet noise at cruising speeds should be investigated immediately. Frequent need for re-setting one particular tappet should also be watched, as this may be indicative of premature wear in any of the component parts of the valve-operating mechanism. A temporary deficiency in lubrication after prolonged disuse may have been the cause; parts which may be affected in this manner are rocker bearings, followers and cams. These parts will also suffer if an assembly error impedes the full lift of the valve, e.g., coil-bound valve springs or a valve-stem collar fouling the lower guide. In this case rockers, rocker pins or push-rods may wear as well.

A rare phenomenon is a valve which fails to return on its seating due to extreme influences of temperature in the engine, resulting in the collar moving up the valve

CYLINDER HEAD, BARREL AND PISTON

stem and staying in the higher position. Slackening-off the corresponding tappet will restore the engine to its previous efficiency, and when subsequently the valve is removed for inspection the evidence is, of course, destroyed by withdrawal of the collar. The trouble will be avoided if the interference fit is correct, i.e., size-to-size minimum to 0·001 in. (0·02 mm.) maximum.

Tappet clearances tend to increase slightly when the engine gets hot, and complete silence of operation is difficult to obtain as light-alloy cylinder jackets and heads amplify sound. The ⅛ in. B.S.P. tappet-adjuster lock-nut is identical to the one used on the normal clutch adjuster. The latter locknut can be used as a temporary replacement in an emergency.

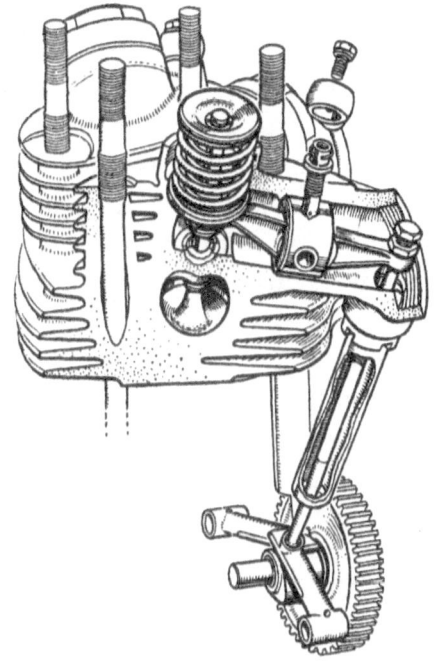

[*By courtesy of "The Motor Cycle", London.*]

FIG. 19.—VALVE-OPERATING MECHANISM.

Decarbonising

The rate of carbon formation is partly dependent on operating conditions, but Vincent engines are known to have covered very large mileages without removal of the cylinder head. Decarbonising at approximately 10,000-mile (16,000-km.) intervals is recommended, mainly for inspection of the valves. These are also remarkably trouble free, and when checking the compression on the kick-starter the throttle must be fully opened.

REMOVAL OF CYLINDER HEAD.—Before the head can be removed the push-rod tubes must be released from the rocker boxes and worked downwards; they are made from stainless steel, and pliers may be used with care. The push-rods will foul the rocker boxes unless the cam-followers are resting on the cam-base circle, but as no gasket is fitted, the head is unlikely to stick on to the barrel. The valves are retained by circlips and split collets, and a standard "C"-type Terry valve-spring compressor can be used for removal. Tapping the valve-stem end with a copper hammer will release the collar; the light-alloy top guide is easily pushed out of its recess with the partly withdrawn valve. Note the 30-degree angle of the valve seat.

The removal of carbon and the grinding of the valves follows normal motor-cycle practice, but valves with badly scored stems should be renewed to prevent the ingress of oil into the combustion chamber; the inlet valve is the larger of the two.

A ground cylinder-head joint is used, and if the liner flange shows signs of gas leakage the joint must be reground using fine emery paste on the liner flange and coarse paste on the wide face, where contact over three-quarters of the width is sufficient. The use of new gaskets and washers is strongly recommended, and pre-packed decarbonising sets are available.

Engines up to No. 1310 are fitted with hollow holding-down bolts, inside of which are separate solid bolts which relieve the barrels and heads of frame stresses. The nuts of these hollow bolts should be tightened to 30 lb.-ft. (4·15 kg.-m.): if a torque-registering wrench is not available, a ring spanner 1 ft. (30 cm.) long can be used in conjunction with a spring balance. Alternatively, a normal-size ring

CYLINDER HEAD, BARREL AND PISTON 45

spanner held mid-way between the ends will do the job. Later machines are fitted with solid bolts, which are just as effective, and on these the nuts can be fully tightened.

Rockers and Bearings

For removal, it is necessary to unscrew only the inspection cap, tappet adjuster and rocker-feed bolt. The

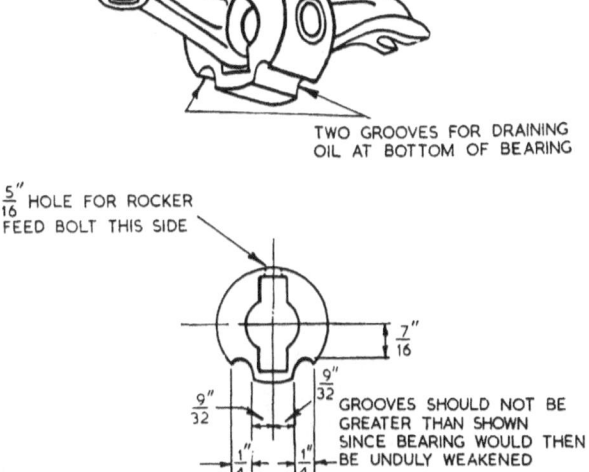

FIG. 20.—DRAINING GROOVES IN ROCKER BEARING.

rocker assembly can then be withdrawn without touching any other part of the engine. The rocker fork should bear evenly on the valve-stem collar, and if necessary the higher prong can be carefully stoned until even bearing is obtained. A rocker with more than 0·010 in. (0·25 mm.) side play may cause noise due to the inside of the fork fouling the valve stem, and should be shimmed up.

The rocker pin is a force fit in the rocker and a running fit in the duralumin bearing which carries the oscillating load. Worn bearings are unlikely to fail suddenly, but should be renewed on account of noise. After prolonged service the pins will eventually wear as well. On engines after No. 2340 all four rocker bearings are grooved for improved oil drainage.

When new, the clearance of the rocker bearing in its tunnel may amount to 0·002 in. (0·05 mm.), but, as the bearing is surrounded by oil, greater clearance developed in service is not necessarily detrimental. If a bearing is considered unduly slack, the fitting of a new component will usually restore the clearance to normal; by way of a temporary measure the original bearing can be carefully squeezed in a vice to take up vertical play. Oversize bearings have at times been available, but may require skimming of the tunnel. The feed bolts have a $\frac{1}{32}$-in. (0·8-mm.) oil jet: the two holes in the base of the bolt need not line up with those in the bearing, as the latter is provided with a chamfer for catchment of the lubricant.

Valve Guides

The lower valve guides, in particular, must be in good condition to avoid oil leakage past the valve stem into the combustion chamber. This fault may show up by smoking from the exhaust shortly after the engine has been started up. A clearance of 0·002–0·003 in. (0·05–0·07 mm.) inlet, and 0·003–0·004 in. (0·07–0·10 mm.) exhaust is recommended, and as a general rule renewal is recommended if wear exceeds 0·003 in. (0·07 mm.), depending upon conditions of operation. The lower guides are dropped into position after the head has been heated to 200° C. (390° F.), preferably in an oven; but, for additional security, they are also retained by screwed rings which are punchlocked after tightening. Experience has shown that private owners may encounter difficulties in the removal of these lock-rings due to not having the simple special tools required. For this reason

CYLINDER HEAD, BARREL AND PISTON 47

the job can better be entrusted to Vincent specialists, who are also equipped for line-reaming the guides, if necessary. Variations in the castings of earlier heads may cause oil to build up over the valve-guide lock-ring, and if so the surplus material can be carefully ground away. Later heads have a $\frac{3}{8}$-in. clearance cut at the bottom of the rocker boxes made to within $\frac{1}{2}$ in. (12·70 mm.) distance from the valve-guide centre line.

Valve Springs

Owing to the air space between the exhaust-port roof and top valve guide supporting the spring, the latter component remains relatively cool, resulting in long life. The Vincent engine is also remarkably free from valve bounce; triple springs are no longer recommended.

The free length of the outer spring is $2\frac{1}{4}$ in. (57·15 mm.), and the inner spring measures $2\frac{7}{32}$ in. (56·35 mm.); both springs must be a good fit in each other, and renewal is necessary if they have shortened to $2\frac{1}{16}$ in. (52·38 mm.).

Seat Rings

These are drawn in position after the head has been heated up to 200° C. (390° F.); then finished with standard Black and Decker equipment, which is also used for re-cutting. Renewing the rings is seldom necessary, but it should be noted that the old rings cannot be removed by application of heat; turning out or carefully breaking up the old components by drilling is the recommended procedure. This job is also safer in the hands of the manufacturers or specialists with machining facilities. Some machines were fitted with oversize seat rings when new, indicated by the figure 10 stamped inside the head; oversizes are also available as spares.

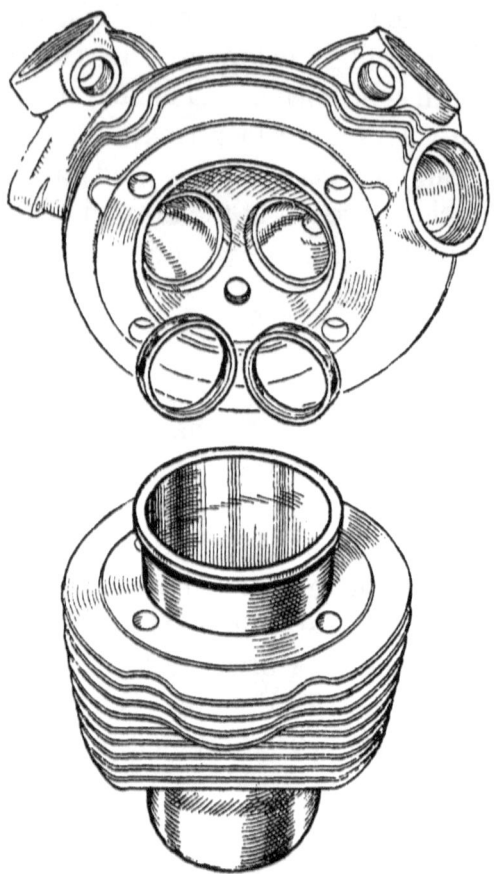

[By courtesy of "The Motor Cycle", London.
FIG. 21.—DETACHABLE VALVE-SEAT RINGS AND CYLINDER LINER.

Cylinder Barrel

The flanged cylinder liner is an interference fit in the light-alloy jacket, which is heated up to 200° C. (390° F.) before fitting. In this instance heat can be applied to the jacket for removal of the old liner, but, as replacement liners only are supplied with *unfinished bores*, owners will take advantage of the "Service Exchange System" whenever possible to avoid having to hone the liner after fitting into the jacket. Cylinder-bore wear is, moreover, remarkably low. Porosity of a liner is most unlikely, but oil weep from a jacket may be experienced if oil under pressure from the cylinder-feed gallery finds its way up past the threads of the cylinder-holding-down bolts. If this happens, re-fitting the offending bolt with some jointing compound will usually be effective, but note the groove provided in these threads to allow the oil to pass.

The liner can be bored up to 0·030 in. (0·76 mm.)

CYLINDER HEAD, BARREL AND PISTON

oversize, and whilst no hard-and-fast rules are laid down as to when re-linering or re-boring is necessary, it is frequently accepted that wear in the top of the liner exceeding 0·008 in. (0·20 mm.) calls for attention. A badly scored barrel should be bored or re-linered irrespective of wear or ovality. Note that liners only, obtained for fitting locally, have no oil-feed hole; this must be drilled after the liner has been fitted. The size is $\frac{3}{32}$ in. (2·38 mm.).

After 1951 the oil hole was positioned lower in the barrel with a view to feeding the oil on to the piston below the scraper ring. On these barrels there is a groove in the outside of the liner which connects the hole with the gallery in the crankcase mouth; the earlier pattern is no longer supplied.

All Rapide and Meteor models left the Works fitted with $\frac{1}{32}$-in. (0·79-mm.) compression plates, and the $\frac{1}{16}$-in. (1·58-mm.) variety, although available, has never been fitted as standard. For use of Premier grade fuels, compression plates can be removed, but as there is bound to be a slight ridge in the top end of the liner after any use, this ridge will have to be removed by honing; it is better therefore to leave the conversion until such time as the engine reaches the overhaul stage. Compression plates are fitted with a paper washer on each side, but no jointing compound is used.

Pistons

Die-cast " Specialloid " pistons are used in all models as well as for racing, and the available compression ratios are 6·8, 7·3, 8, 9, 11 and 12·5; the oversizes normally stocked are 0·005, 0·010, 0·020 and 0·030 in. (0·13, 0·25, 0·50 and 0·76 mm.). When any of these pistons of " Specialloid " manufacture are fitted, no rebalancing of the engine is necessary. The type and size are usually stamped on the crown, but pistons for compression ratios of 6·8 and 7·3 can also be identified by the casting number inside skirt, i.e., H95 for the former and H92 for the latter. The smaller cut-away is usually stamped " Ex " and faces the exhaust valve. When fitting pistons make sure they are installed the correct way round !

PISTON CLEARANCES.—These should be checked as per diagram to avoid misleading conclusions, but on earlier machines clearances were greater, in particular the Black

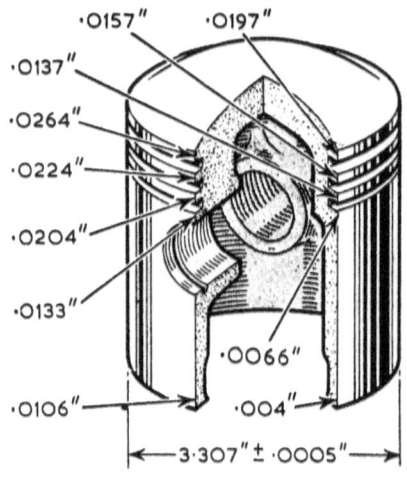

FIG. 22.—PISTON CLEARANCES ON TYPES E7/6 AND E7/7.

Shadow, which was fitted with 0·006–0·0065 in. (0·15–0·16 mm.) at the bottom of the skirt. Engines after No. 3716 are fitted with low-clearance pistons, which are usually stamped " N " on top of the crown. The letters " A ", " U " and " S " stamped on pistons and cylinder-jacket flange indicate fine-grading for initial assembly : " A " pistons are normally fitted into " A " barrels, etc. The installation of new pistons into used barrels, however serviceable these may be, is not recommended on account of noise. Never use emery cloth on pistons, but remove any high spots with a fine file dipped in methylated spirit.

It is important that the gudgeon pin is an easy push fit

when cold, as a tight-fitting pin may lead to distortion of the piston around the gudgeon bosses, and the consequential scuffing may well lead to a seizure at a later date. If necessary, ease these bosses with a $\frac{7}{8}$-in. (22·225-mm.) reamer. The circlips must be a good fit in their grooves, and they are of the wire type. It is as well to renew them once they have been removed. Clearance of the gudgeon pin in the bronze small-end bush is 0·005–0·001 in. (0·01–0·02 mm.), and the latter is provided with two $\frac{3}{16}$-in. (4·8-mm.) oil-holes which must line up with those in the eye of the rod. Service exchange con-rods are normally supplied with a new small-end bush fitted, and although wear on the component is usually very slight, a new bush can be ordered separately. As a new bush contracts after fitting, here again, reaming with a $\frac{7}{8}$-in. reamer is required.

After December 1951 Comet and Rapide models were shipped to the United States with a compression ratio of 7·3, whereas Black Shadows for this market featured a ratio of 8 : 1. With the return of Premier grade fuels in Great Britain a few machines with these higher compression ratios were supplied to the home market.

Piston-rings

"Wellworthy" rings with polished sides are standard fitting, except on some very early models, and it should be noted that the rings of pistons giving ratios of 6·8, 7·3 and 8 : 1 are of narrower radial thickness than those fitted to the racing pistons. The thicker rings must not be used in the touring pistons, which require rings with a radial thickness of 0·118 in. (3 mm.). See Appendix Table VII for clearances, gaps and dimensions on all pistons. A larger ring gap is unlikely to affect the performance in any way, but a smaller gap is not permissible.

There is no point in renewing rings just because the closed gap exceeds the figure of new condition, but it is

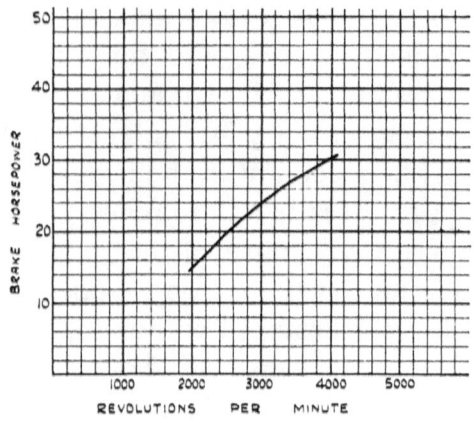

Fig. 23.—Power Curve Showing "Rapide" Performance Range.

Not to be exceeded if maximum engine longevity is required.

difficult to ascertain whether a ring has lost its strength, and in case of doubt renewal is the best plan.

In isolated cases it may be advisable to increase the oil drainage of the piston to cure over-lubrication, and this is done by drilling three additional $\frac{1}{16}$-in. (1·58-mm.) holes in each side of the component, just below the scraper ring, and these holes should be evenly positioned relative to the existing drainage holes of the scraper groove. Chromium-plated top compression rings have never been a standard fitting on Vincent engines. There are no objections to their use.

Running-in

Although the running-in of a new or reconditioned engine follows normal automotive practice, experience has shown that a number of riders are by no means certain of the correct procedure. In view of the great importance of this matter, the following salient points should be noted :

No Vincent touring engine is fully run in before 2000 miles (3200 km.) have been covered, and it is advisable to change the oil at 500, 1000 and 2000 miles (800, 1600 and 3200 km.). Some people seem very concerned about the exact running-in speed, but this is by no means as important as the fact that the engine must bed down *under a light load*, and speeds should be increased progressively after the first 750 miles (1200 km.), full throttle to be avoided until the end of the breaking-in period. Initially 40 m.p.h. (64 k.p.h.) is a suitable solo gait for the single-cylinder models, but for the Twins, 50 m.p.h. (80 k.p.h.) is not too fast. Subsequently, short bursts of higher speeds can be indulged in, still avoiding heavy loads on the engine. Conditions may vary due to the fitting of a sidecar or the nature of the country traversed, but common sense will always be a good guide. An all-alloy engine should be tightened-up all round towards the end of the running-in period.

CHAPTER IV

THE LOWER ENGINE HALF

THE crankcase halves are matched, as a number of machining operations are carried out to the pair assembled; consequently it is by no means always possible to replace a damaged half-case only. Sometimes the damaged half can be repaired by welding, but care is necessary to avoid distortion. The material is a low-silicon alloy.

Rectifying Crankcase Damage

There are standard salvage schemes by means of which a defect in a crankcase half can be rectified, and one instance is stripped threads for the main oil-feed-pipe banjo bolt. The hole can be tapped $\frac{9}{16}$ in. × 20 T.P.I., taking care not to damage the oil-pump sleeve, in order that an adaptor with banjo nut may be screwed into the case to replace the original banjo bolt.

Damage to the drive-side case due to fracture of a worn primary chain is likely to be irreparable. This half also features the camplate spindle boss, which may fracture if the gearbox is abused. Later engines have a separate dynamo cradle which will not take the earlier $3\frac{1}{2}$-in. (88·90-mm.) instrument.

Spindles and Pins

The spindles and pins of the timing-side case are inserted after the case has been heated up to 200° C. (390° F.), and an interference of 0·001 in. (0·02 mm.) is sufficient. Pins or spindles which have worked loose can be re-fitted after their outside diameter has been plated

THE LOWER ENGINE HALF

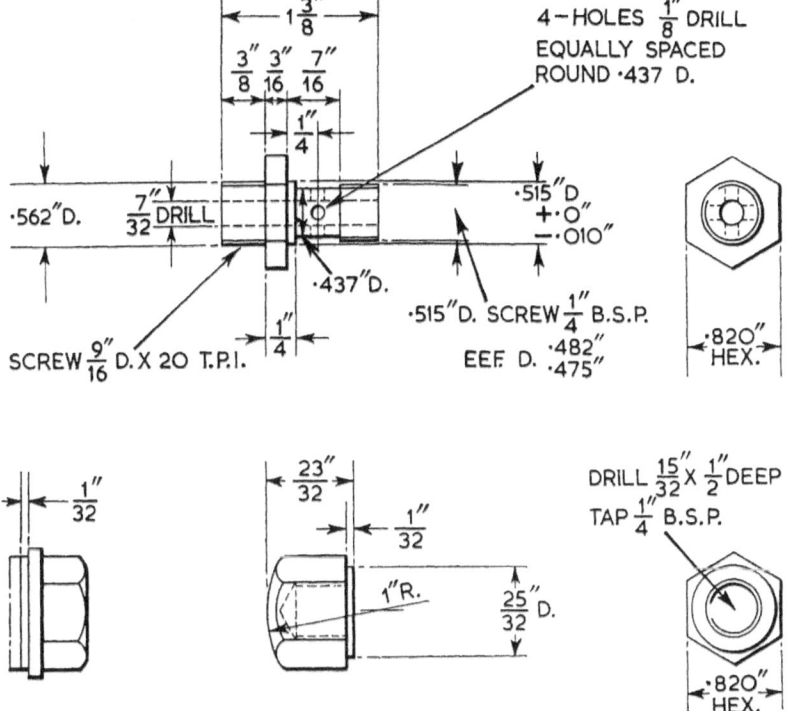

Fig. 24.—Adaptor and Alternative Nuts for Use when Threads for Main Feed Pipe Banjo Bolt Are Stripped in Crankcase (Not Necessary to Remove Engine).

The alternative left-hand nut is a standard carburetter nut (PR5J) shortened as shown.

up to the required oversize, provided the holes have not worn out of round. If these holes require boring, oversize stepped pins or spindles may have to be made up.

Splitting Crankcase

When splitting the case there is no need to remove the magneto, timing gear, oil pump and filter; but primary drive, gearbox and half-time pinion will have to be dismantled. Sixteen bolts and studs are used for retention, and after removal of the nuts the two halves can be

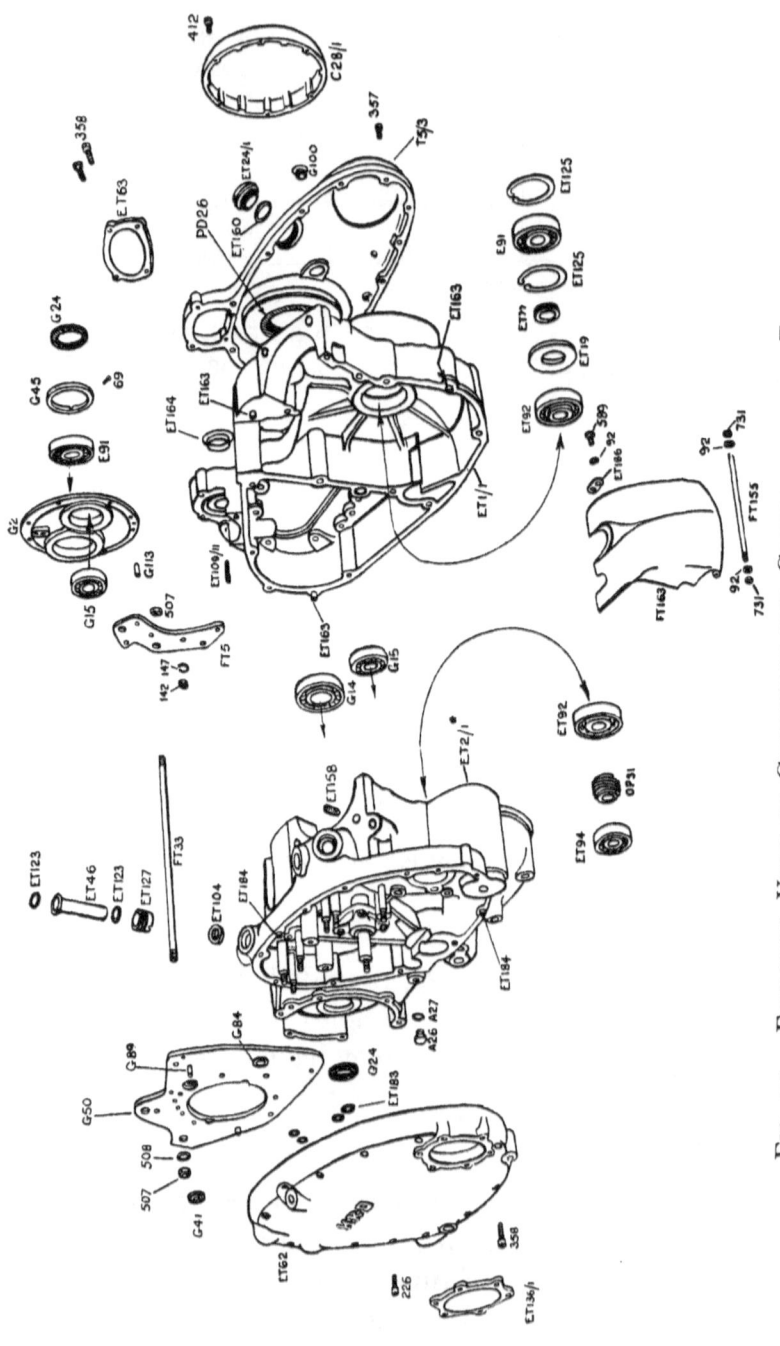

Fig. 25.—Exploded View of Crankcase and Covers, 1000-c.c. Engine.

THE LOWER ENGINE HALF

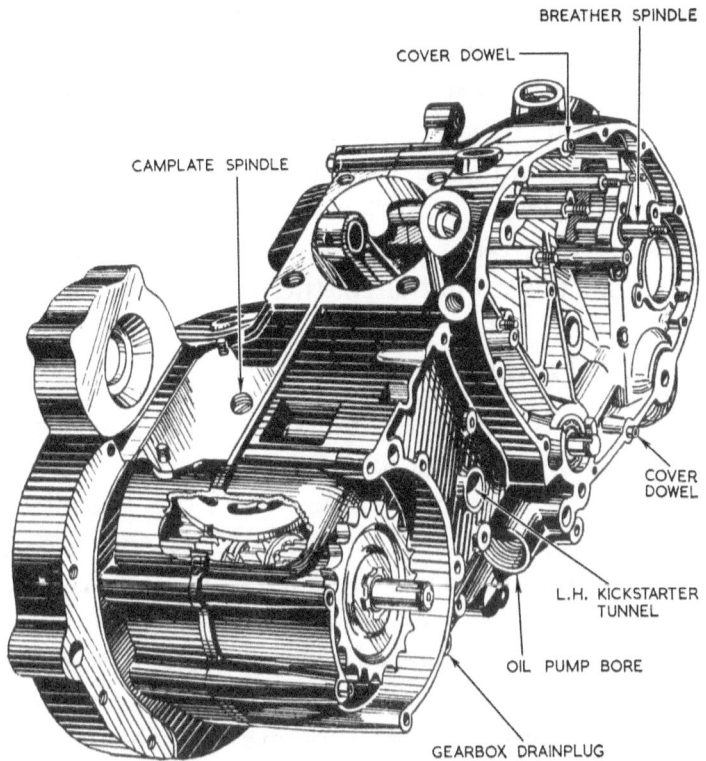

Fig. 26.—The Lower Engine Half.

separated with a rawhide mallet. Note the three hollow dowels provided to maintain alignment of the half-cases.

Bearing races are fitted after the case has been heated-up to 200° C. (390° F.), and the inner rings are furthermore retained by indentations in the crankcase material in four places. The required interference fit is of the order of 0·002 in. (0·05 mm.); if less, a race may work inwards and foul the crank-pin nuts. If this happens, the race can also be plated up to the required oversize and re-fitted after the case has been warmed-up. Keep plating solution away from the bearing track. Excessive interference fit will cause contraction of the race, and affects the bearing running clearance.

Jointing compound but no paper washer is used for reassembling the crankcase halves, and the bearings should be carefully entered into their mating races. If correctly assembled, the flywheel assembly will spin freely, and being located from the drive side, it should continue to do so after the shock absorber has been assembled and tightened. Contrary to common belief, the shock-absorber springs do not affect the flywheel location.

Crankcase Fittings

Oil leaks past crankcase bolts can easily be cured by the application of some jointing compound; watch the lower bolts, as these may cause mysterious loss of lubricant from the primary chaincase. Most nuts are $\frac{5}{16}$ in. B.S.F., and some studs are threaded $\frac{5}{16}$ in. B.S.W. Avoid over-tightening.

The use of new gaskets is sound practice when overhauling any engine, and pre-packed complete gasket sets covering the entire power unit are available. Jointing compound should be used only on the gaskets for the dynamo pinion cover, timing cover, magneto-drive cover, carburetter adaptors and magneto flange.

Flywheels and Mainshafts

Being machined all over, the flywheels have a high finish, but they are polished on Lightnings only. When taken out of the crankcase, the roller bearings usually stay on the mainshafts, and leaving them in position ensures that they are re-assembled into their mated races.

The crank-pin is a parallel fit in the flywheel bores, and whilst the flywheels can be separated after the crank-pin nuts have been removed with a $\frac{3}{4}$ in. B.S.W. solid steel box spanner, it is much better for the private owner to entrust the job to the Works or Vincent specialists. The

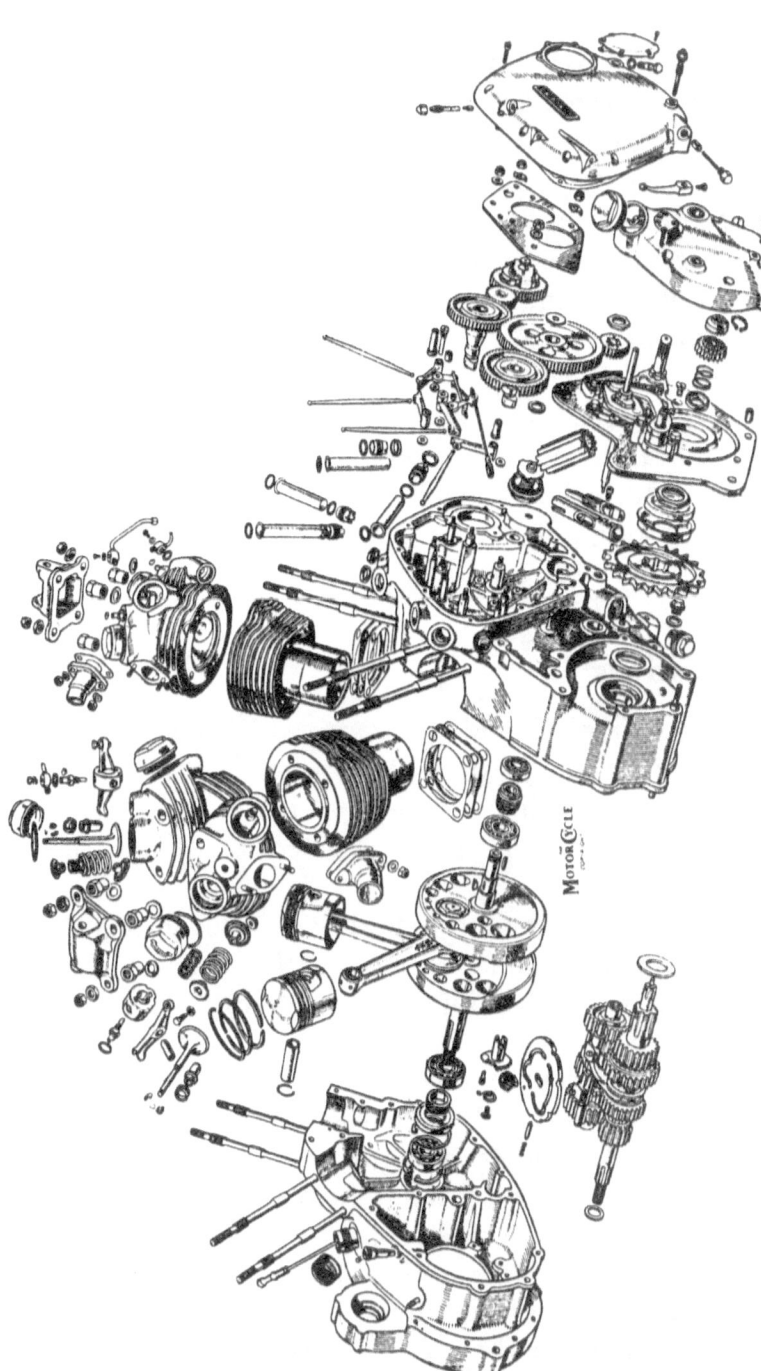

Fig. 27.—Exploded View of "Rapide" Power Unit. [By courtesy of "The Motor Cycle", London.

mainshafts are an interference fit in the flywheels, 0·0039 in. (0·09 mm.) maximum, 0·0031 in. (0·07 mm.) minimum, and further located by a $\frac{3}{16}$-in. (4·76-mm.) grooved pin which is inserted from the inside. Mainshafts are available separately, but the fitting is again to be regarded as a specialist's job. The balance factor for the Twin is 46 per cent of the reciprocating weight.

Shims of 0·010 in. (0·25 mm.) thickness are sometimes used on the drive side of Black Shadow flywheel assemblies to obtain perfect centrality of the small-end bushes in the cylinder registers. If a flywheel boss wears down due to the inner bearing race being loose on a mainshaft, the worn boss can be turned off and substituted by a hardened shim of the appropriate thickness, but a new mainshaft and/or bearing will be necessary.

Main Bearings

Main bearings should be renewed if play exceeds 0·0015 in. (0·03 mm.): mere roughness of a main bearing may render an engine surprisingly noisy, although the running of the unit will not be affected to any noticeable extent.

Some lubricant is bound to find its way out through the mains, and this accounts for the fact that primary chaincases usually require draining-off periodically rather than topping up. If a chaincase fills up at an excessive rate, it need not necessarily be the main bearings which are at fault; other factors, such as excessive crankcase pressure due to incorrect breather timing, may well contribute, but a drive-side seal can be fitted. In the normal course of events main-bearing wear is very low indeed.

The drive-side spacer will come loose if the roller-bearing outer race moves inwards; the noise emanated by this spacer under these conditions will be more pro-

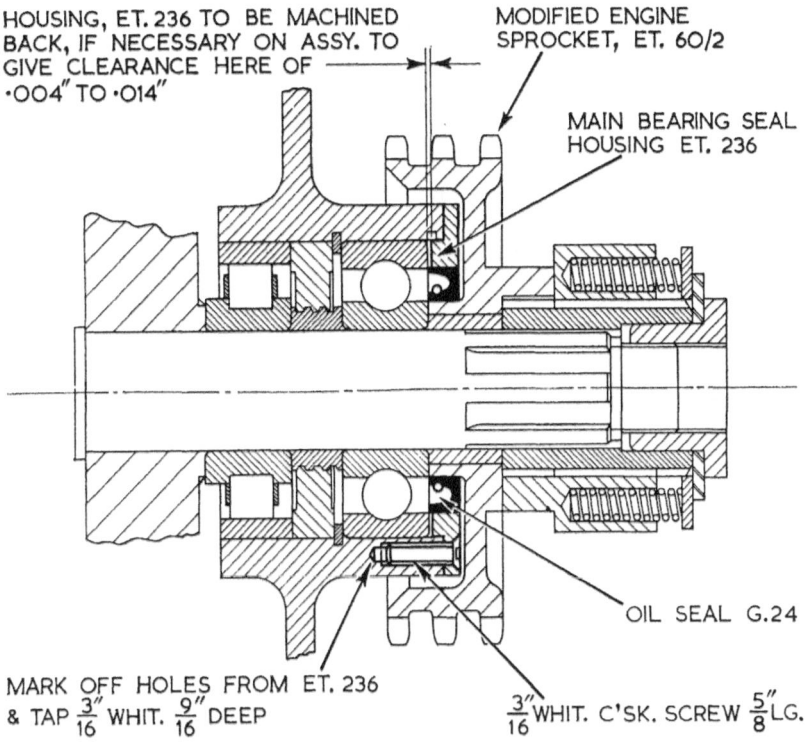

Fig. 28.—Fitting Mainshaft Oil Seal to 1000-c.c. Models.

nounced if the engine is ticking over with the chaincase inspection cap removed.

Each drive-side main is retained by its own circlip, and after removing the outer circlip the ball-race is pressed out from the inside. Then remove the inner circlip, the alloy spacer and press out the roller-race from the outside. Renewal of the small timing-side roller-race necessitates withdrawing the oil-pump sleeve, and an angular drift is used for driving out the large roller-race. The case is heated up as indicated previously, and when fitting new races reverse the procedure of dismantling.

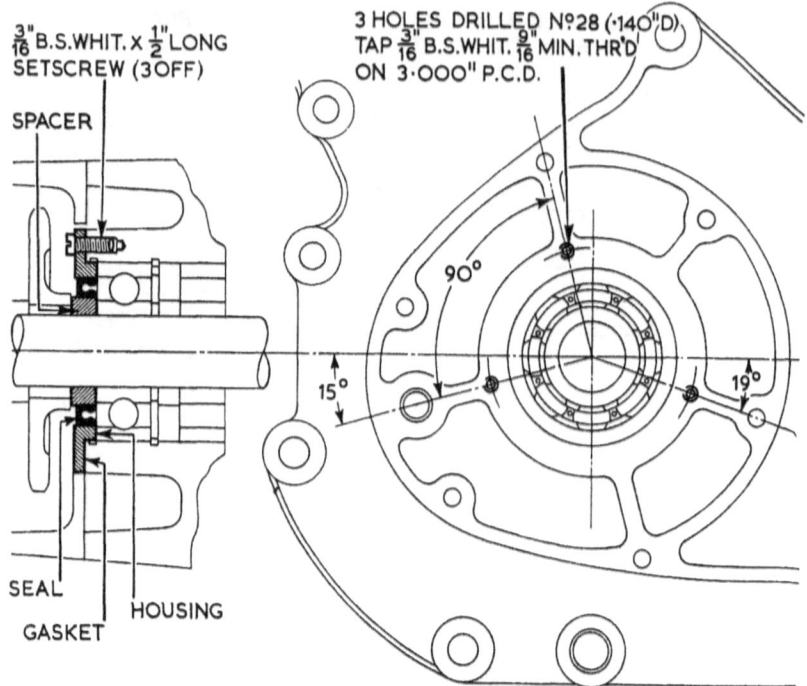

FIG. 29.—FITTING MAINSHAFT OIL SEAL TO 500-C.C. MODELS.

Big End

In each big end the three rows of uncaged 3 × 5-mm. rollers are endwise located by separators; 1000-c.c. models feature a spacer between the con-rods. Due to the smaller load on each roller, this design ensures extreme longevity, provided the revolutions per minute do not normally exceed 5800: on the Black Shadow with 7·2 bottom gear this gives safe speeds in the intermediate ratios of 60, 78 and 104 m.p.h. (96, 122 and 168 k.p.h.); there is certainly no need to give the engine excess revolutions to obtain a high performance.

A big end should be renewed if play exceeds 0·003 in. (0·07 mm.); but side clearance on a con-rod is not detrimental, and $\frac{1}{64}$ in. (0·39 mm.) measured at the small-end bush is normal. Oversize rollers are not available;

in any case, the component parts of the big end are not supplied separately to private owners. The job should therefore be entrusted to the manufacturers or Vincent specialists, who supply completely assembled big ends fitted to service con-rods ready for mounting into the flywheels. Trueing up the flywheels to close limits is also a specialist's job. Coloured paint dabs on component parts indicate grading to fine limits. Black Shadows are fitted with polished high-tensile con-rods, whereas Lightnings and Flashes have polished Vibrac rods.

500-C.C. MODELS

As the primary chaincase is not integral with the crankcase, a separate inner and outer case are used. Note the three countersunk screws behind the engine sprocket: as a general rule it is advisable to remove the engine from the chaincase if overhaul of the lower half is contemplated.

The balance factor of the 500-c.c. models is 66 per cent; here again there is no need to rebalance the engine if one of the alternative pistons is fitted.

As on the Twins, the drive-side main-bearing distance piece is formed to act as an oil spinner, and for this reason no mainshaft oil seal is fitted as standard. It is possible, however, to fit a seal to cure excessive loss of oil from the engine into the primary chain-case through the drive-side main bearings; some single-cylinder models have been so equipped at a later date. The seal fits in a housing which is mounted as illustrated, and the engine-sprocket spacer is replaced by a component with a ground outer face for the lip of the seal.

CHAPTER V

PRIMARY DRIVE AND CLUTCH

IN this chapter it is proposed, first, to deal generally with the lubrication of the components in the above heading, and then individually, with the servicing of the components themselves.

Lubrication

Engine oil is the lubricant for the primary chain on all models, and with the machine *on the rear stand* the level is checked or oil drained off by removal of the ¼-in. B.S.F. set-screw in the cover. If the level is too high oil is likely

[*Photograph by R. S. Allan, A.R.P.S.*

FIG. 30.—SECTIONED POWER UNIT, SHOWING PRIMARY DRIVE.

Fig. 31.—Filling, Drain and Level Plugs.

to leak at the dynamo end face on Twins and on to the rear chain on Singles.

In order to prevent loss or accidental damage, no drain-plug is provided on 1000-c.c. models, but there is sufficient end float in the clutch to partly withdraw the cover after all the retaining screws have been slackened-off a few turns. If desired, the boss on this cover can be drilled and tapped to take a plug, provided this will not lead to loss of lubricant in service.

If a large light-alloy engine is frequently used for runs of very short duration condensation inside the chaincase may emulsify the oil, eventually causing rust and deterioration of the lubricant to a condition sometimes referred to as " coffee-grounds ". It should not immediately be assumed that this trouble is due to a serious mechanical defect in the engine, although a developed fault—such as blow-by past the rings—may affect the matter. In order to avoid premature wear of primary chain, tensioner blade and dynamo bearing, the entire drive should be dismantled and thoroughly cleaned. The chaincase can then be re-filled with one of the modern lubricants containing an anti-corrosive inhibitor, or oil with a proprietary brand of special motor-cycle chaincase additive. A breather on the inspection cap may also help.

Adjustment of Tensioner

The tensioner is not self-adjusting, but operates also when the direction of the drive is reversed, and the external adjuster is very accessible at the underside of the chaincase of 1000-c.c. models. On these the tension is checked occasionally *with the engine hot*. Correct slack in the top run is $\frac{1}{4}$–$\frac{1}{2}$ in. (6–12 mm.) at the tightest point, but mind your fingers when finding this! The adjuster has a lock-nut, and screwing inwards tightens the chain.

Amongst the advantages of this design of tensioner is the fact that it combines efficiency with very low weight of the component parts. After some service the blade will show grooves, but this is normal: the part need not be renewed before these grooves are worn half-way through the blade. A crack will cause collapse of the tensioner. If this happens, the noise emanated by the drive will serve as an indication that immediate renewal is required.

Primary Chain

The " Renold " triplex primary chain is endless, and no component parts are supplied as spares; renewal is necessary when all available adjustment has been taken up or if the dismantled chain shows more than $\frac{1}{4}$ in. per foot (6·35 mm. per 30 cm.) = 2 per cent elongation. Breakage of rollers also calls for immediate replacement.

Whilst fracture of the chain is rare, it should be remembered that serious damage to the crankcase may result if the chain wraps itself around the engine sprocket.

Alternative triplex chains may well fit, but these are unlikely to feature the straight links necessary for running in conjunction with a tensioner, and their temporary use is justified only in an emergency.

For access to the primary drive on Twins the clutch must be dismantled and the drum removed from the sprocket by unscrewing the six slotted screws; note the shake-proof washers under their heads. Sprocket wear is normally very low and misalignment rare.

Noisy Drive

A high-pitched whine noticeable when the engine is pulling at low speeds in the intermediate gears is a developed fault which few riders seem able to trace to its actual source, and some are apt to suspect the clutch as the noise may be more pronounced when the drive is taken up from a standstill. The trouble is, however, merely due to the dynamo sprocket being too deep in mesh, which can easily be verified by temporarily detaching the sprocket. The remedy is to deepen out each tooth-space with a round file, or alternatively, a piece of shimming material can be inserted between the dynamo and its cradle. This cure will not be of much avail if the drive-side dynamo bearing is badly worn, and the noise may also be indicative of a badly stretched primary chain, which should, of course, be renewed without delay.

Shock Absorber

It is important that the retaining nut is dead tight at all times, and this ¾-in. B.S.W. component, which has a right-hand thread, is best tightened with a hammer on a solid steel box spanner. No locking device is provided, but if desired the nut and spring plate can be drilled and wired. A loose shock-absorber nut affects the location of the flywheel assembly, and may cause wear on the flywheel boss as well as spring fracture. There are eighteen concentric springs, and excessive wear on the shock absorber cam is a potential cause of spring fracture; the complete set rather than individual springs should be re-

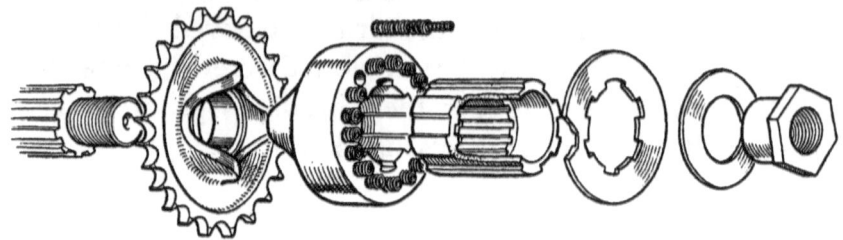

[*By courtesy of "The Motor Cycle", London.*

FIG. 32.—EXPLODED VIEW OF SHOCK ABSORBER.

placed. Owners are apt to struggle with the fitting of the spring plate against the compression of the spring cluster, but the job is so easy if it is remembered that the splined cam sleeve can be partly withdrawn so that there is no need at all to compress the springs by hand! At one end the cam sleeve has splines which should be fitted innermost. The hardened sleeve inside the sprocket can normally be left on the mainshaft unless the crankcase is being split.

Clutch

The main components of the patented Servo clutch on 1000-c.c. models consist of a pair of lined shoes which are expanded through a toggle linkage against the inside of a ribbed cast-iron drum by a single-plate pilot clutch of conventional pattern. The clutch itself requires no lubrication, wear on the shoe linings and floating-plate inserts is very slight, and the design is capable of trans-

PRIMARY DRIVE AND CLUTCH

mitting great power. Only the adjusters of the lifting mechanism require re-setting; this is carried out first on the control cable and then on the kick-starter cover. The former is correctly set if the operating lever just touches the cable abutment, visible through the kick-starter-cover inspection orifice, when the handlebar lever is pulled hard up against the dummy grip; the main adjuster is set to give $\frac{3}{16}$ in (4·76 mm.) cable slack when the clutch is fully

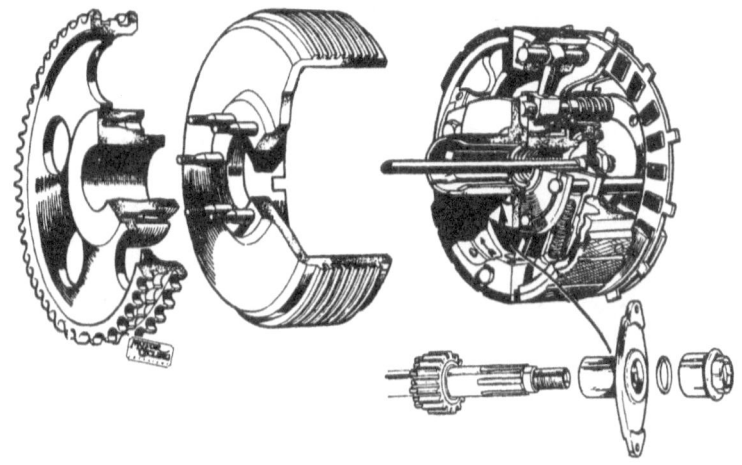

["*Motor Cycling*" Copyright.
FIG. 33.—CLUTCH ASSEMBLY WITH 1954 PATTERN CARRIER SEAL.

engaged. An auxiliary adjuster is fitted to the outer plate of the pilot clutch and used when all the adjustment on the kick-starter cover has been taken up; for access the clutch dome is removed. Note that the auxiliary adjuster features a $\frac{1}{4}$-in. (6·35-mm.) steel ball on earlier machines only.

Fierceness in operation is usually caused by insufficient chamfer on the leading edges of the shoe linings. Most models are fitted with circlips on the shoe pivots, and each shoe can easily be withdrawn for re-chamfering with the aid of a file. Clutch judder produces a noise rather

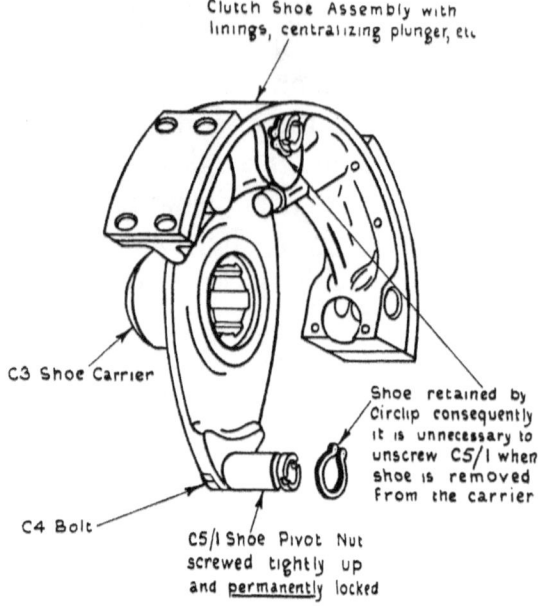

Fig. 34.—Circlip Retention of Clutch Shoes.

reminiscent of a chain jumping its sprocket, and is only noticeable in bottom gear when the drive is taken up. The cause is usually wear of the shoe in the pivot hole, and unless re-bushing is possible renew. Frequent need for clutch adjustment indicates that all is not well with the lifting mechanism, and the parts to examine in this case are the push-rod and the operating lever. The push-rod is $12\frac{5}{16}$ in. (31·27 cm.) long, and if worn appreciably it is better to fit the later-type divided rod, which is fitted with a $\frac{1}{4}$-in. steel ball in the middle. A worn operating lever can possibly be reclaimed by "Stelliting" or a similar process, but the fitting of a new part saves time and ensures a first-class job. At traffic checks of any duration it is always good practice to select neutral rather than keeping the clutch disengaged for long periods.

Clutch Slip

If the clutch slips the cause should be investigated, and it is likely that one of the three seals has failed, causing oil to find its way on to the linings. On a solo machine the pilot clutch alone will transmit power up to speeds of approximately 60 m.p.h. (96 k.p.h.), but the plates will eventually suffer from overheating, evident by blueing in three places. Assuming that the slip is not occasioned by insufficient slack in the lifting mechanism, the assembly will have to be dismantled : if there are signs of oil on Ferodo MR41 linings these must be renewed, as degreasing does not work. The seal in the carrier retained by the clutch nut consists of a steel ring with rubber bonded to it. It is advisable to renew this component whenever the clutch is taken down. Non-setting jointing compound is used on the clutch-shaft splines. The seal between the two bushes of the clutch sprocket is made of synthetic rubber and has a spring-loaded lip which must be undamaged. A similar component, but of large diameter, fits in the chaincase cover and prevents the ingress of oil from the primary case into the clutch housing. When renewing seals of this type, remember that the spring-loaded lip should face the side where the oil comes from, i.e., inwards.

Shoes and Linings

In 1952 Duron P28B moulded shoe linings, which are impervious to oil, were introduced; they should be grooved, and six $\frac{1}{16}$-in. (1·58-mm.) dia. drainage holes in the drum are necessary. If the grooves become clogged with powder after long service, these linings may be washed in clean petrol, roughed up and re-used. Service shoes fitted with these Duron linings are available under the Exchange Scheme. For 1954 a rubber " O "-ring

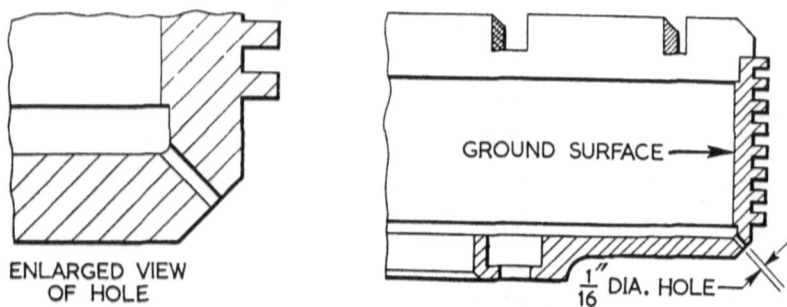

FIG. 35.—DRILLING CLUTCH DRUM FOR MOULDED LININGS.

was introduced to take the place of the bonded carrier seal, but this ring requires a different pattern clutch shaft, carrier and retaining nut; fitting to earlier machines is, therefore, not an economical proposition.

If a replacement-bonded carrier seal is not available a plain hard copper washer 0·062 in. (1·57 mm.) thick, 1·250 in. (31·75 mm.) outside diameter and 0·766 in. (19·45 mm.) inside diameter provides a satisfactory substitute.

The small porous bronze bush in the left-hand end of the clutch shaft was discontinued in 1952. It is advisable

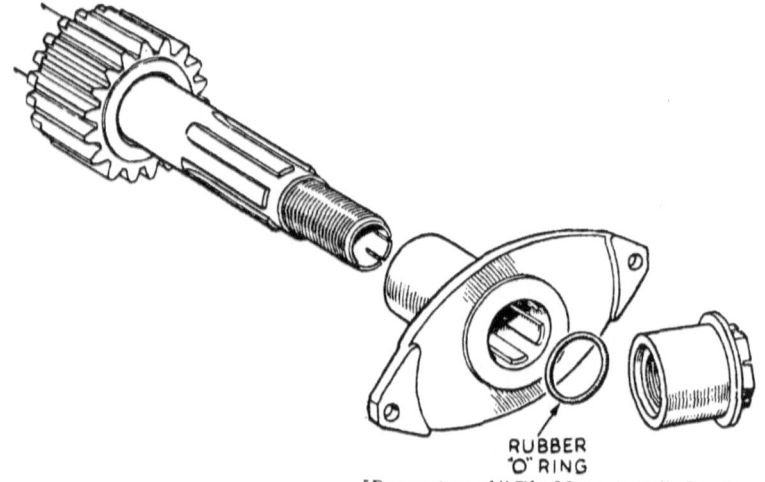

[By courtesy of "The Motor Cycle", London.
FIG. 36.—1954 PATTERN CLUTCH CARRIER SEAL.

to remove this bush on earlier models if trouble with the lifting mechanism is experienced. Symptoms similar to clutch slip may be evident if the constant-mesh pinion in the gearbox is loose on the clutch shaft. This occurrence is most rare, as the pinion is an interference fit as well as keyed; but, if the key shears, the pinion may grip when cold and slip on the shaft when hot.

500-c.c. Models

These models feature a drain-plug as well as a level screw on the primary chaincase. The primary chain is of the single-row pattern and fitted with a spring link. Adjustment is made by moving the gearbox after the mountings have been slackened off, and two adjusting bolts with lock-nuts will be found in the slotted mounting lug at the underside of the shell. The job can be done with the engine cold, and correct up-and-down play at the tightest point is $\frac{1}{4}-\frac{1}{2}$ in. (6·35–12·70 mm.).

The engine-shaft shock absorber is identical to the one used on the Twins, but there is a spacer behind the sprocket.

Clutch Control Cable

Correct adjustment of the clutch-control cable gives approximately $\frac{3}{16}$ in. (4·76 mm.) slack at the handlebar end, and the cable is provided with an adjuster, although stretch is usually compensated by wear on the inserts, which has the effect of increasing the length of the push-rod. The operating lever visible through the slotted inspection cap on the kick-starter cover requires $\frac{3}{32}$ in. (2·38 mm.) play at the top end, and when it becomes necessary to adjust the push-rod length this is done by means of the sleeve nut, which is located by a cap on the cover. Access is gained by removing the two slotted screws which retain the cap, and unscrewing the sleeve nut takes up play. If the push-rod length requires shortening, due to the plates having settled down, the sleeve nut must be turned clockwise.

Clutches

The post-war clutch has five plates, and when new inserts are fitted they should protrude equally on each side of the plate. If difficulty is encountered in re-fitting the re-lined plates these must be rubbed down on a sheet of sand-paper. Glazed inserts can sometimes be rendered serviceable by roughing up; clutch springs are renewed if they have settled down $\frac{1}{4}$ in. (6·36 mm.). The nuts retaining these springs should be equally adjusted to allow the withdrawal plate to lift squarely. Tightening fully and unscrewing four turns is usually correct.

The clutch of the Albion gearbox fitted to Grey Flash models has four plates, but this clutch can be converted to take five and the drum reinforced. The sprocket, when free, runs on ball bearings, and these require lubrication occasionally by de-clutching fully and injecting a few drops of oil down the side of the sprocket.

CHAPTER VI

GEARBOX AND SECONDARY DRIVE

As in the previous chapter, it is proposed first to deal with lubrication generally and then to cover the servicing of the components.

Lubrication

On Twins the gearbox is lubricated by engine oil injected through the filling orifice on the drive-side crankcase, and contrary to earlier recommendations the required quantity is 2 pints (1 litre), which gives a reading to the underside of the dipstick flat. The level is checked with the machine on the rear stand. Occasionally some oil can be squirted over the selector mechanism after the inspection cap on the kick-starter cover has been removed, but this cover is not intended to be oiltight, and any surplus will leak down on to the floor. The drain-plug is rather hidden from sight, but still readily accessible, in the right-hand crankcase wall behind the dural pivot-bearing plate; change the oil at infrequent intervals.

The gearbox breathes through the filling orifice; the dipstick has two or three flats and the filler cap two holes for this purpose. The box also breathes, however, through the ball bearing of the ratchet shaft on the right-hand side of the machine, and oil lost in this manner may not build up a level inside the kick-starter cover, but must leak out without finding its way into the clutch along the push-rod.

Series C models are equipped with a positive rear-chain oiler mounted in the filler neck of the oil tank. This chain oiler cannot be fitted to tanks which were not

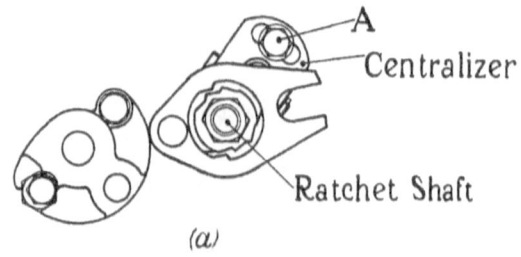

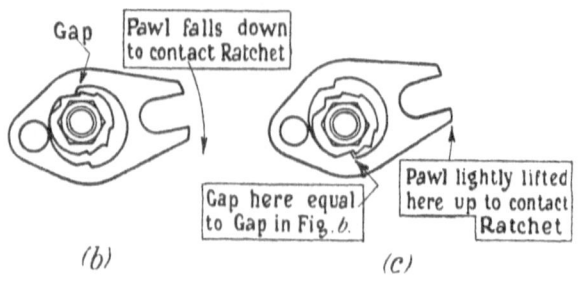

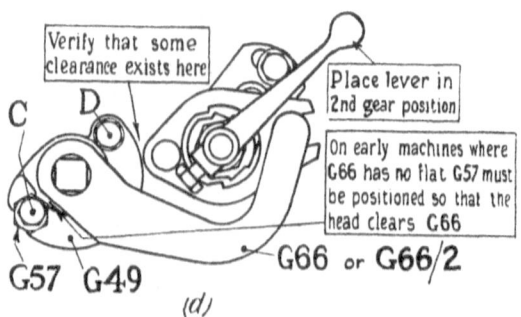

Fig. 37.—Sequence of Adjusting Gear-change Mechanism, 1000-c.c. Models.

Stage 1: Engage ratchet shaft in 2nd gear (*a*).

Stage 2: Adjust centraliser so that pawl engages ratchet equally in up and down positions (*b*) and (*c*) and tighten screw A when this condition is obtained.

Stage 3: Adjust position of lever stop G49 by loosening D and C and then turning eccentric adjuster G57 so that when actuating arm is moved by its squared boss upwards to full extent bottom gear is correctly engaged and when downwards, 3rd gear. Tighten screws C and D.

Stage 4: Check for gear-change. In all ratios ratchet shaft must be firmly notched in position after actuating arm has been slowly moved to its full extent. The indicator lever is used to check this condition. It may be necessary to re-position G49 slightly to obtain correct engagement in all gears.

originally so equipped, and on earlier Series B models the chain received mainly oil mist, also through the oil tank vent pipe. The needle valve is a carburetter pilot screw, and turning clockwise reduces the amount of lubricant by-passed to the chain. Over-tightening should be avoided, as this will damage the taper. The best setting is rather a matter of experiment, opening the needle valve, say half a turn at a time, from fully closed and observing the condition of the chain until the required amount of lubrication is obtained.

Gear-change Adjustment

The Vincent gearbox is unusual as there are two adjustments on the selector mechanism, and any re-setting must be done in the sequence shown in the illustration. Earlier machines were rather sensitive to spot-on adjustment, but detail improvements have rendered the gear-change foolproof, and most of the modified parts can be fitted to earlier models without difficulty or great cost.

The gearbox is unusually robust, and if it jumps out of gear it should not be immediately assumed that it must be dismantled to renew worn parts. The first step is to carefully readjust the gear-change mechanism, and if the actuating arm just falls short of the required amount of travel in one direction, the lobe of the light-alloy lever stop, which restricts the movement, may be very carefully scraped. The earlier pedal linkage was apt to develop play if not well maintained, and the more recent one-piece lever materially improves the operation. For 1953 the pawl-carrier centraliser was re-designed with two stops which restrict the movement of the pawl assembly, thereby preventing over-selection. If the actuating arm shears on its boss the foot-change will be inoperative, but gears can still be selected by hand on the indicator

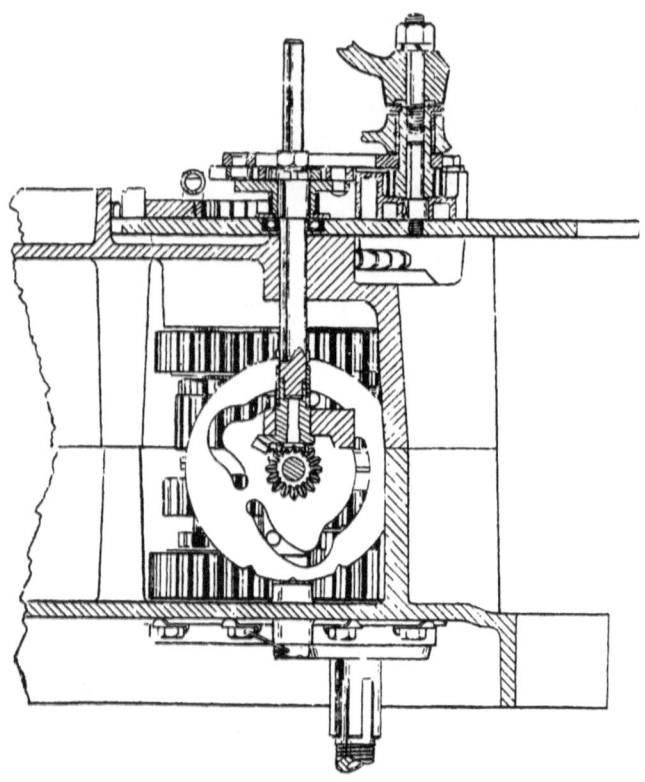

Fig. 38.—Section Through Vincent Gearbox Showing Cam-plate and Bevels.

lever; 1952 and later machines are fitted with a one-piece arm.

Renewing Selector Pawl Spring

Attention to the foregoing details necessitates removal of the kick-starter cover only, and cures gear-change difficulties in the majority of cases. Should gears still slip out of engagement renewal of the selector pawl spring may be required. This spring is retained by the wired plug in the gearbox cover-plate on the left-hand side of the machine, and for access the clutch and primary drive must be dismantled. As a temporary measure a weak spring can be slightly stretched.

The current type cam-plate is an improvement on the two patterns fitted up to Engine No. 1/1400, and changing this component necessitates dismantling the gearbox. Backlash between the operating bevels may also cause gear-change trouble, and if necessary the cam-plate bevel can be shimmed up. Excessive end float on the layshaft can also be taken up with shims, and pinions on which the dogs are badly rounded should be renewed.

Alternative Specifications

Up to June 1951, Black Shadows were fitted with a 7·2 bottom gear ratio against 9·1 on the Rapide, and although many sporting riders like a high bottom gear, it was found that so many Shadows were used with sidecars that the 9·1 ratio became standard for both models. Either ratio can be installed in Shadow or Rapide merely by changing the layshaft first gear and the double gear, but the 7·2 ratio is definitely rather high for sidecar work. In standard form the gearbox is not a racing component, and for serious racing the double-backlash set-up of the Black Lightning is preferable. Here again a standard box can be converted, but the racing specification is not recommended for road work.

A special crank, foot-piece and shaft are available for mounting the kick-starter to the left-hand side of the machine. The shape of the crank reduces the ground clearance on left-hand bends, and this equipment is primarily suited for sidecar work. The shaft is passed through the tunnel which interconnects the chaincase with the kick-starter cover, and the plug of the former is used to blank off the hole in the latter. Similarly, the shaft bush of the kick-starter cover is pressed into the chaincase. The tunnel is sometimes plugged if not in use.

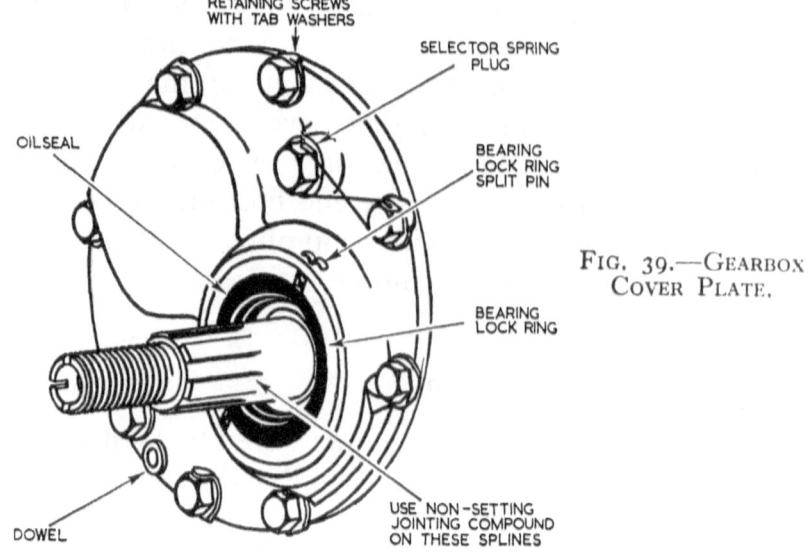

Fig. 39.—Gearbox Cover Plate.

Oil Retention

An oil-seal of the synthetic-rubber spring-loaded pattern is used on the input as well as on the output side of the box, and both seals are identical. Their function is to keep oil inside the gearbox; they are fitted with the lip inwards, and for renewal it is not necessary to strip out the gears.

Failure of the seal in the cover-plate of the gearbox on the left-hand side of the machine causes a drop in oil level in the box, with an equivalent increase of lubricant in the chain-case. A defect in the opposite seal, fitted between the final-drive shaft ball bearing and the sprocket, gives loss of oil on to the rear chain, and from there on to the rear tyre and inside of the number-plate.

Careless fitting of the cover-plate also results in loss of oil into the primary chaincase, but in this event the oil will subside to a lower level in the box than with seal failure. Jointing compound is used on the faces of cover-plate and gearbox wall, as well as on the screws; real

GEARBOX AND SECONDARY DRIVE

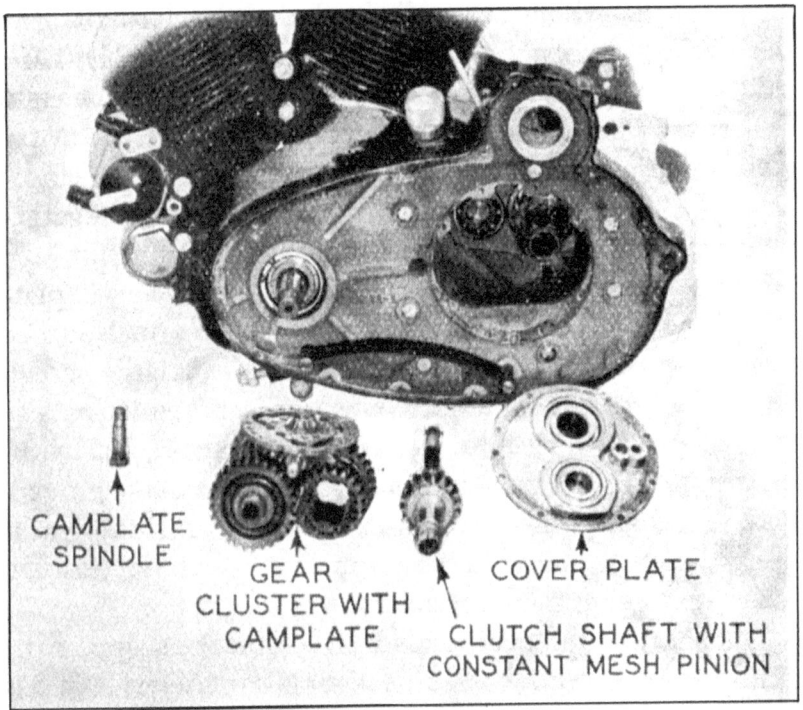

Fig. 40.—Tensioner Blade and Gearbox.

trouble will follow if the dowel is incorrectly fitted or left out altogether. It has already been mentioned that some loss of oil into the kick-starter cover is normal, but if this occurs at an excessive rate the dural pivot-bearing plate can be counterbored behind the ball bearing and a rubber ring fitted on the ratchet shaft; one of the hydraulic damper " O "-rings is very suitable for this purpose. Checks on leakages of the crankcase joint are best performed with petrol.

Dismantling

Preliminary operations involve the removal of the clutch, primary drive, dynamo and kick-starter cover. This exposes on the right-hand side the kick-starter ratchet components, which are pulled off the clutch shaft after the Seeger circlip has been removed. On the left-hand side of the machine the selector pawl (wired) and the eight set-screws (locked by tab washers) are unscrewed. A tap with a copper mallet on the right-hand end of the clutch shaft will free the cover-plate; this is withdrawn, together with the shaft complete with constant mesh pinion, and exposes the other gears still retained by the cam-plate spindle. The latter component is usually punch-locked in the top of the drive-side crankcase and a large screwdriver is required for unscrewing the part, which is also drilled and tapped $\frac{1}{4}$ in. B.S.W. to facilitate final withdrawal. The gearbox internals can now be unshipped, with exception of the final-drive shaft and third-gear pinion, but normally these parts can be left in position when examining their condition.

Dismantling the gearbox is well within the scope of the private owner who has some fitting experience; it has already been stressed, however, that it is rarely necessary to disturb the internals merely to cure gear-change trouble.

Assembling

When assembling gears the first question often concerns the exact location of any thrust-washers, but with the gearbox dismantled as indicated above this matter is easy. There is only one 0·031 in. (0·78 mm.) thick shim fitted between the constant-mesh pinion on the clutch shaft and the bearing in the gearbox cover-plate.

Re-assembling the box requires some dexterity, as the layshaft assembly, the selector bar and the double gear must be refitted simultaneously without disturbing the correct position of the cam-plate; for this reason these components are entered into the box in a cluster, after pre-assembly on the bench. The double gear lies to the right

GEARBOX AND SECONDARY DRIVE

with the large pinion away from the operator, and on the layshaft the order of assembly by the number of teeth on each of the four gears is 29, 23, 18 and 27, the two middle gears together being moved by the grooved selector fork. The selector bar passes through both forks; the upper portion of the one engaging the double gear points away from the operator, and the same part of the layshaft fork points towards him. The bottom-gear notch will easily be found on the cam-plate, and this component is placed on the selector forks with the bottom-gear notch in line with the selector bar and nearest to the assembler; usually the bottom-gear notch is marked " 1 ". The cam-plate is turned anti-clockwise on the selector pins as far as possible, and the cluster is next put into the gearbox, the double gear to slide inwards on the splines of the final-drive shaft. The indicator lever on the ratchet shaft must be placed in the *bottom-gear* position before the cam-

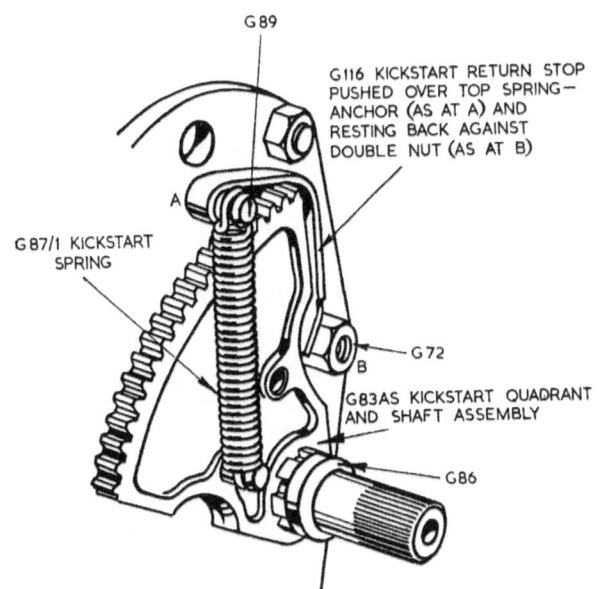

FIG. 41.—FITTING OF KICK-START RETURN AND STOP SPRING.

plate is fully pushed inwards and the correct engagement of the bevels can be observed, and corrected if necessary, before the cam-plate spindle is refitted. All parts should be well lubricated before the cover-plate with clutch shaft is replaced, and care should be taken not to over-tighten the cover-plate set-screws. Finally, the selector pawl and spring are refitted, the plug wired, the cam-plate spindle fully tightened and the kick-starter ratchet components replaced in the reverse order of dismantling. The driving ratchet and spring are the same as on 500-c.c. models.

Ratchet Shaft and Bevel

Correct timing of the ratchet shaft and cam-plate bevels in the bottom-gear position as indicated above is essential, and the ratchet bevel is fitted with a stop indicating the bottom-gear position. On models prior to 1953 the ratchet shaft was located by a sleeve sweated on to the bevel, and normally the shaft can be withdrawn towards the right-hand side of the machine. Trouble will only arise if the sleeve is loose on the bevel, as it will fall down into the gearbox when the shaft is removed. Eventually the female portion of the bevel will be wrenched open by the tongue of the ratchet shaft, and this renders the selector mechanism inoperative. Renewal of the ratchet bevel necessitates splitting the crankcase, but if the sleeve has fallen into the bottom of the gearbox undamaged it can sometimes be refitted without splitting the case, provided the female part of the bevel has not suffered. The procedure is to tin the inside diameter of the sleeve and drive it back into position with a drift inserted through the ball bearing, but care in removing the ratchet shaft is necessary with this temporary repair. On the later type bevel the sleeve is omitted, location being effected by a projection on the shaft and if facilities exist to modify the earlier type shaft in this manner, it can be re-used in conjunction with the later type bevel.

Diagnosing Trouble

Symptoms similar to those produced by failure of a ratchet bevel will be evident if the cam-plate spindle works loose or the boss fractures on the drive-side crankcase due to abuse of the gearbox. If the fracture occurs in a certain gear it may not be possible to disengage this ratio. To rectify this a light-alloy block can be welded into the crankcase, which is then re-machined as required.

If a machine tends to jump into gear of its own accord when leaned over to one side with the engine running in neutral, the selector pins should be examined for signs of wear at the earliest opportunity. More straightforward is the correction of a gear-change which stiffens up when the engine gets hot, caused by slight distortion of the dural right-hand pivot-bearing plate. A nut and locknut are provided on the tube of the battery carrier to correct any slight misalignment of this plate caused by the machine falling over on the right-hand footrest. With the engine hot the adjustment is made just sufficiently to ensure that the actuation-arm peg is again central in the bush of the kick-starter cover.

Due to ample dimensions of the bearings, the Vincent gearbox remains silent in operation after extensive use. A whining noise at low speeds is unlikely to come from the box and, if present, probably emanates from the dynamo drive; see Chapter V.

Chain and Sprockets

Chain sizes and the standard gear ratios for various models are given in the Appendix. On Vincent machines the gear ratio can easily be altered merely by fitting an

ALTERNATIVE REAR-WHEEL SPROCKET SIZES

Rear-wheel Sprocket Part No.	Number of Teeth.	500-c.c. Ratio.	1000-c.c. Ratio.
H5/45 . . .	45	4·35	3·42
H5/46 . . .	46	4·44	3·5
H5/47 . . .	47	4·54	3·58
H5/48 . . .	48	4·64	3·66
H5/49 . . .	49	4·74	3·73
H5/50 . . .	50	4·83	3·82
H5/52 . . .	52	5·02	3·96
H5/54 . . .	54	5·22	4·1
H5/56 . . .	56	5·42	4·26
H5/58 . . .	58	5·61	4·42
H5/60 . . .	60	5·80	4·57

alternative rear-wheel sprocket supplied in sizes ranging from 45 to 60 teeth; even smaller sprockets are available for racing, but these cannot be fitted to the brake drum, and a special adaptor is required.

Correct adjustment of the rear chain gives ¾ in. (19 mm.) up-and-down play at the tightest point. Whilst an efficient chain oiler is provided on the Series C models, it is good practice to remove the chain from time to time in order that it may be scrubbed with paraffin and soaked in warm (not hot) grease. The easiest way to deal with chain replacement is to use an old chain linked to the component in service; this method completely eliminates difficulties in guiding the new or lubricated component over the final-drive sprocket, which is not readily accessible. The rear chain should be renewed when stretch exceeds 2 per cent, which equals ¼ in. per foot (6·35 mm. per 30 cm.). On some Twins the lower run of the chain may foul the crankcase, due to some richness in casting, but the surplus material soon wears away without any detrimental effect whatever.

GEARBOX AND SECONDARY DRIVE

[*Renold Chains Ltd.*

FIG. 42.—CHECKING CHAIN WEAR.

Gear ratios are calculated by the formula:

Ratio =
$$\frac{\text{Number of teeth on clutch sprocket} \times \text{Number of teeth on rear-wheel sprocket}}{\text{Number of teeth on engine sprocket} \times \text{Number of teeth on final-drive sprocket}}$$

The gearbox reductions given in the Appendix are used to calculate the ratio of each intermediate gear when the top-gear ratio is known, and engine r.p.m. are derived from the fact that the Twins turn over at 4600 r.p.m. at 100 m.p.h. on the 3·5 top gear. On a Comet with the standard 48-tooth rear-wheel sprocket, engine revolutions are 610 per 10 m.p.h. (16·1 k.p.h.). The rather high standard ratios give effortless high cruising speeds, reduced wear and tear, as well as fuel economy. An alternative sprocket size is often fitted to the opposite brake drum in order that a ratio better suited to special conditions may be available merely by reversing the rear wheel.

Fig. 43.—Gearbox Details, 500-c.c. Models.

500-C.C. Gearboxes

The 500-c.c. machines are fitted with the Burman BAP gearbox, with the exception of the Grey Flash, which features the Albion component for which a wide choice of internal ratios is available. This gearbox is lubricated with engine oil.

The Burman gearbox can be lubricated with oil, grease or a mixture of both, but experience shows that a fifty-fifty mixture of engine oil and light grease gives the best all-round results. If grease only is used, the recommended quantity to be packed into the box before the end-cover is fitted is 1¾ lb. (0·8 kg.). Gearboxes lubricated in this manner are known to have developed a screeching noise which can easily be cured by the addition of ½ pint (¼ litre) engine oil.

From January 1952 onwards, Comet gearboxes are

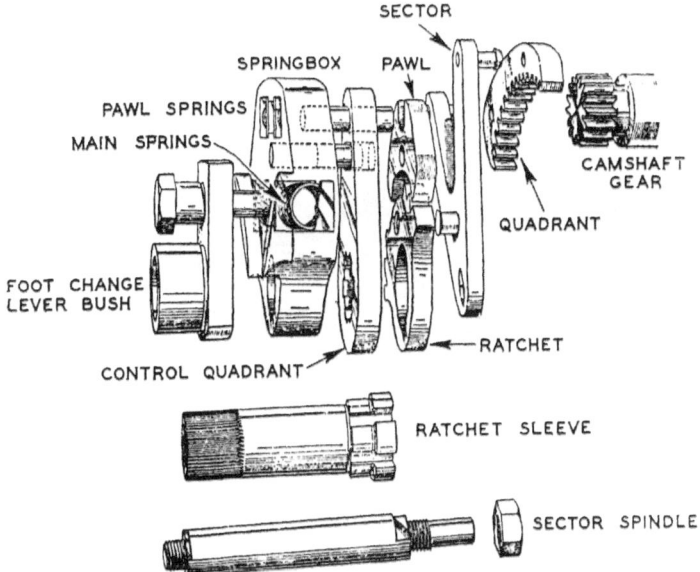

Fig. 44.—Selector Mechanism Details, 500-c.c. Models.

fitted with a drain-plug for the benefit of those owners who prefer oil only. In this case the recommended quantity is 1½ pints (¾ litre); this equals 1¼ in. (32 mm.) on a dipstick inserted through the filling orifice.

With grease, the makers do not consider regular changes of lubricant necessary; it is recommended, however, that the clutch push-rod is greased from time to time and the clutch roller-race packed with grease every 6000 miles (10,000 km.). The gearbox should be topped up with an egg-cup full of oil or grease every 2000 miles (3000 km.), and as core holes are provided in the end-cover, the lubricant can be injected through the orifice closed by the slotted cap. A grease nipple is provided for periodic lubrication of the selector mechanism.

Service Notes

The Burman gearbox less clutch can be removed from the machine without dismantling the pivot plates, but the right-hand pillion footrest plate must be swung clear.

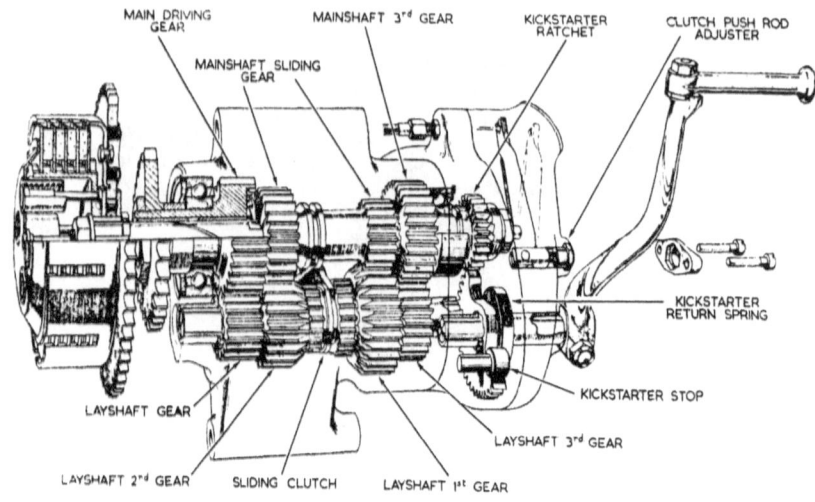

Fig. 45.—Details of the Burman Gearbox.

Mounting the foot-change lever too high causes jumping out of third gear on Comets and Meteors, as the indicator, which is bolted to the end of the selector shaft, fouls the pedal. Mounting the pedal one or two splines lower cures this trouble. The kick-starter spring is fitted on the shaft with the coils running clockwise, and two complete turns on the crank are usually sufficient to return the quadrant firmly to its rubber-bushed stop. A weak spring can be wound up one or two turns more. The selector mechanism on the Burman gearbox is also timed; the engaging tooth and tooth-space on the camshaft pinion and sector are marked " O " to obtain the correct setting, and when assembling, the mark on the camshaft pinion should be in the nine o'clock position.

The selector pawl and spring are located in the bottom of the gearbox shell, retained by a slotted plug, and these parts must be removed if it is intended to strip out the gearbox internals. Removal of the outer kick-starter cover complete with selector mechanism and kick-starter exposes the hexagon ratchet-pinion nut, which is

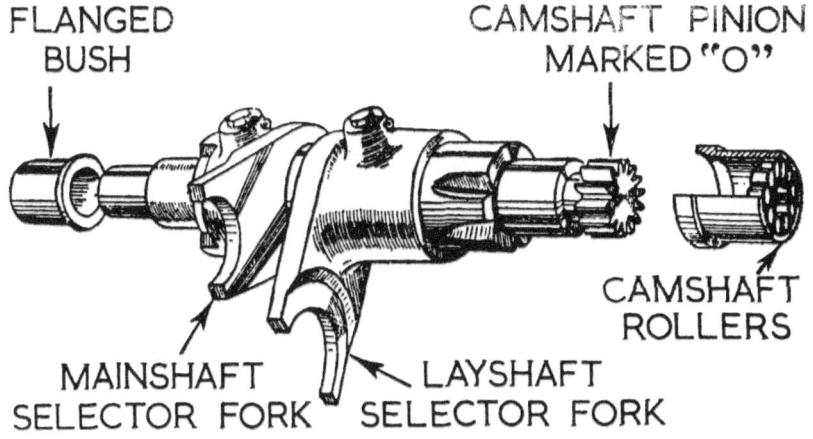

Fig. 46.—Burman Gearbox Camshaft.

next unscrewed together with the four nuts which retain the inner cover. This can then be pulled away, taking care not to loose any of the twelve camshaft bearing rollers. The mainshaft is withdrawn from the clutch side, and the layshaft and camshaft assemblies are taken out from the opposite end. The main driving gear, ball bearing and sprocket are normally left in position; unscrewing the final-drive sprocket nut (note the tab washer) enables withdrawal of the gear to the right.

Inspecting and Re-assembling

The gears are not case-hardened but made from oil-toughened nickel–chrome steel, and need for renewal on account of fractured teeth is rare indeed. The layshaft and mainshaft may show signs of bending after prolonged service, and renewing is advisable if this exceeds 0·005 in. (0·12 mm.). Clearance of the shafts in their bushes and bearings may amount to 0·008 in. (0·2 mm.) before replacement is necessary. The same figure applies to the fit of the mainshaft in the bushes of the main driving gear; these are a press fit in the gear, with a grease space in the middle, and after fitting reaming to a shaft clearance of 0·002 in. (·05 mm.) minimum is necessary.

Minimum end float of the camshaft is 0·002 in. (0·05 mm.), but this tends to increase by wear on the flange of the bush in the gearbox shell. Eventually this may cause jumping out of gear, and as a temporary measure the camshaft can be shimmed up with a hardened washer. Mainshaft end float should not exceed $\frac{1}{32}$ in. (0·79 mm.).

When re-assembling the box the mainshaft sliding gear is fitted with the larger pinion away from the operator, and this gear engages with the smaller of the two selector forks. The layshaft is sub-assembled with the longer splines away from the operator, and the order of the pinions from right to left as fitted in the shell is: third gear, first gear, sliding clutch, fixed second gear and finally the free small gear; the sliding clutch engages with the larger selector fork.

Assuming that the driving gear has been left in position, the sub-assembled parts are entered into the gearbox shell, the mainshaft is re-fitted from the drive side, the mainshaft third-gear pinion installed and the shell packed with a mixture of oil and grease. Finally, the inner cover is re-fitted and the rest of the assembly completed following the instructions given under " Service Notes ".

CHAPTER VII

THE LUBRICATION SYSTEM

OIL is fed to the pump through a large-bore pipe, and the tank union is fitted with a stop valve which prevents the tank from draining, *only when the top end* of the feed pipe is detached.

Circulation of the Lubricant

Internal passages in the crankcase lead the oil to the full-flow filter, which receives the lubricant from the outside of the element and delivers it from the inside to the long banjo bolt which connects the filter chamber with the internal passages of the timing cover. These are positioned so as to conform roughly to the pattern of a letter " H " laid on its side, with the lower bar comprising the aforementioned banjo bolt, the big-end quill and the pressure-relief valve. The vertical passage contains the cylinder feed jet, and the top bar of the H-pattern divides the oil to the camshaft bushes and liner wall of each cylinder.

The lubricant circulated in this manner collects in the sump and is picked up by the scavenge side of the pump; there is no oil bias on the rear cylinder, due to the fact that any excess is diverted from the flywheels by a scraper cast into the sump. The scavenge side of the oil pump has, furthermore, a greater capacity than the pressure side. On its way back to the tank over each cylinder head, the oil lubricates the overhead-valve gear, and here again any excess is returned to the sump through the push-rod tubes and timing chest. Finally, the lubricant can be observed at the return pipe or chain-oiler block inside the filler neck of the tank, and this forms the routine check on the circulation.

Oil Recommendations

The brands listed in the Appendix, Table II, have been chosen in view of their proved suitability and world-wide availability; whilst they cast no reflection upon the quality of alternative oils there is little point in experiments by private owners with lubricants which have not been proved suitable for the Vincent engine.

Viscosity grades are based on average operating conditions. Bearing in mind that it takes approximately 12 miles (19 km.) to warm the contents of the entire system, it is not advisable to use too heavy a grade in postwar machines. If a model is mainly used for runs of short duration, it may even pay to use a slightly lighter grade which will reach important parts of the engine more easily when cold, and—especially on Twins—starting will be facilitated. Conversely, a heavier grade may be advisable if a machine is used for sustained high speeds in hot weather, e.g., continental or sub-tropical touring.

There are no objections to the use of upper-cylinder lubricants; additives mixed with the engine oil, however, may alter the characteristics of the lubricant. Flake graphite must *never* be used.

Colloidal graphite can be used in the form of graphited upper-cylinder lubricant. Applied in this manner, the recommended quantity is usually 1 fluid oz. (2·84 centilitre) to 2 gallons (9 litres) of petrol for running in, and the same amount to 4 gallons (18 litres) thereafter. Those who have a preference for proprietary graphited running-in compound may add this to the engine oil, provided that the instructions of the suppliers are carefully followed, i.e., 1 pint (0·56 litre) to 1 gallon (4·5 litre or 1·2 U.S. gallon) of oil for running in and ½ pint (0·28 litre) to 1

THE LUBRICATION SYSTEM

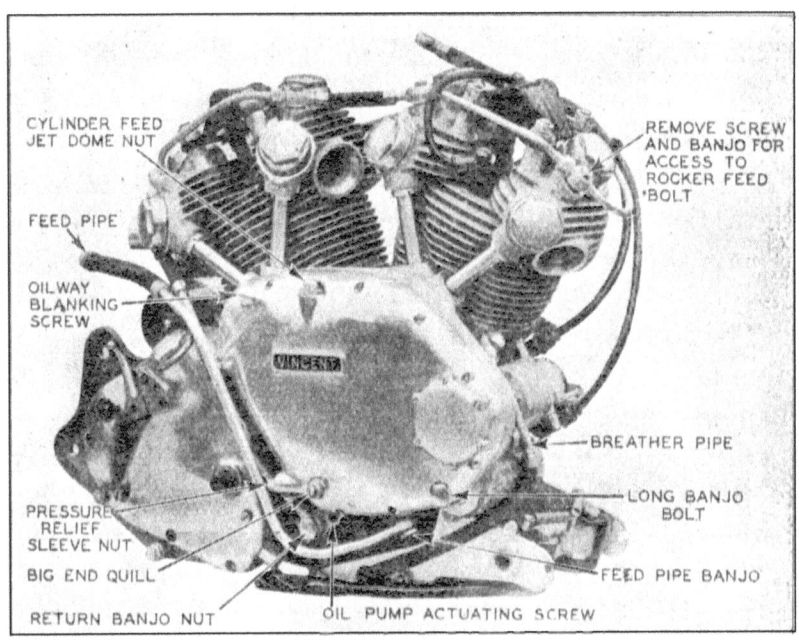

FIG. 47.—ACCESS TO LUBRICATION SYSTEM ON "RAPIDE" ENGINE UNIT.

gallon thereafter. Straight running-in compound is sometimes used for assembly purposes.

Oil consumption at the rate of approximately 200 miles per pint (640 km. per litre) is normal. Most engines use considerably less oil, but, on the other hand, the consumption may be initially higher on a new or reconditioned unit.

Maintenance and Adjustments

Routine attention is confined to frequent visual checks on the circulation and thoroughly cleaning the big-end quill every 2500 miles (4000 km.). Removal of the round-headed screw is not enough, as oil will issue even though the six radial holes in the quill are blocked. The quill can be fractured through over-tightening; clearance in the mainshaft bore is not important, and on a new engine the part may even show signs of slight rubbing on one side : this is not detrimental, provided that the quill is not unduly weakened. A fractured quill must be renewed immediately. The sleeve nut of the pressure-relief valve will break if over-tightened, but an occasional check on the movement of the plunger is advisable; if it sticks in the open position, oil pressure to the big end will be reduced and premature failure may eventually follow.

The lubrication system, being fully automatic, requires no adjustments, but there are three points at which the standard settings can be varied to suit special operating conditions. All later machines are fitted with a 0·020 in. (0·50 mm.) metering wire in the 0·032 in. (0·81 mm.) diameter jet of each rocker feed bolt, and as this wire also reduces the chance of a complete blockage it is not recommended to remove same completely. It is permissible, however, to substitute a slightly thinner wire to increase the flow of oil to a rocker bearing, particularly on the exhaust side.

The cylinder-feed jet size on all post-war models is 170, and on the Twins this jet may be increased up to 200 for racing; this is not necessary on 500-c.c. models, and it should be remembered that a larger jet tends to reduce the flow to the big end. On a 1000-c.c. engine the jet size can be reduced to 140, but this also cuts down the lubrication of the camshaft bushes; for this reason it is better to retain the standard 170 jet in conjunction with an oil-restrictor disc fitted behind the rear rubber washer of each pair inside the timing cover. On 1954 models the hole in each recess of the timing cover has been reduced in diameter and the oil-restrictor disc is not required.

Changing the Oil

Frequent oil changes are beneficial and best done when the oil-tank level is low, but intervals should not exceed

2000 miles (3200 km.). A thorough job includes the removal of the stop-valve union complete from the tank, draining the sump through the plug provided and cleaning or renewing the filter element. Always clean out the filter chamber and renew the element every 10,000 miles. When fitted into the tank the stop-valve gauze is surrounded by a metal shroud which acts as a sludge trap. Removal of this deposit necessitates swilling with degreasing fluid when the tank is dismantled and can be turned upside down.

For a quick oil change it is only necessary to unscrew the lower banjo bolt of the main feed pipe, as the top end of this pipe in position will keep the stop valve open. In this manner the old oil can easily be caught in a tray; a scoop is required if the stop-valve union is removed bodily.

The earlier inspection-cap spanners would not always fit the hexagon of the filter-chamber cap, due to some richness in crankcase casting. If so, the spanner can be ground down on the outer periphery without detriment, but the later pattern tool always fits and the pegs for the push-rod tube nuts are much stronger.

If the oil contains bronze or aluminium dust during running-in or after failure of some component, it is unlikely that this dust will find its way into the bearings, due to the efficiency of the oil filter. Should it be deemed advisable to use flushing oil, the engine must not be run under load and a quantity of approximately 3 pints ($1\frac{1}{2}$ litres) is required.

The alloy banjo bolts are lighter and just as effective as the earlier stainless-steel pattern, and there is no need to over-tighten them to the point of fracture if the washers are in good condition. "Klingerit" washers are an improvement over the earlier copper–asbestos type.

Frequent oil changes are particularly necessary if the

Fig. 48.—Part Sectional View Through "Black Shadow" Showing Oil Tank, External Pipes and Timing-cover Oil-ways.

majority of running consists of short journeys during which the engine rarely reaches a satisfactory working temperature. This increases moisture contamination of the oil, the primary cause of sludge formation.

The Oil Tank

Without accidental damage, the oil tank seldom requires attention, but it is as well to consider the position of the two internal pipes when dealing with the rare occurrence of a tank which drains itself to a certain level. If fracture of the chain-oiler pipe (or the vent pipe on earlier machines) is suspected, the external union can temporarily be replaced by a plug to carry out a check. A leak in the return pipe will lead the oil back into the engine through the rocker feeds. If it is not possible to renew the tank under the Service Exchange Scheme one side of the component can be cut open for access to the broken pipe, this

THE LUBRICATION SYSTEM 99

part repaired and the tank closed by welding. A leaking union boss can easily be rectified by brazing.

Air passing through the space between oil tank and petrol tank cools the oil considerably, and the comparatively low running temperature of the engine is one of the reasons why vegetable-base lubricants are not normally recommended, in spite of their delightful smell !

A carburetter banjo nut fits on the stop valve, and this can be used as a temporary plug if the valve should drip with the top end of the main feed pipe detached.

The Oil Pump

The oil pump is of the duplex rotary plunger type. There is no point in fitting a pressure gauge to the system, as readings will be low when the oil is hot, due to the fact that the roller-bearing big end is not designed to retain pressure. Fittings of this nature merely decrease reliability on account of possible fracture of the extra pipes and hose. Access is gained by removal of the hexagon-headed plug in the lower timing-case wall, and this plug *must* be air-tight, also the slotted locating screw which is punch-locked to prevent loss.

Normally there is no need to disturb these components, but if it becomes necessary to withdraw the plunger a $\frac{1}{4}$-in. B.S.F. bolt is screwed into the end for extraction after the locating screw has been removed.

THE PUMP SLEEVE.—This is a push fit in the crankcase and to extract this part a long bolt threaded $\frac{5}{16}$ in. B.S.F. at one end (e.g., crankcase bolt) is used, the cap at the forward end of the sleeve being tapped for this purpose. For removal of the sleeve it is essential, however, to extract the drive worm, and workshops should note that this involves splitting the crankcase only on those very few models which are fitted with an alternative timing-side outer main bearing of smaller than usual outside

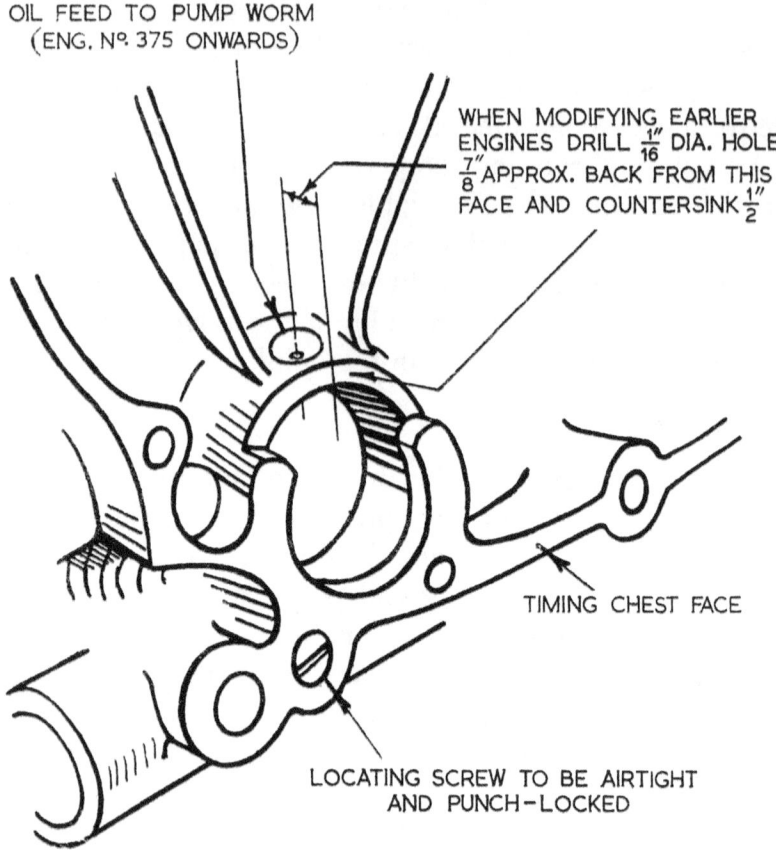

Fig. 49.—Oil-pump Drive Lubrication and Plunger Location.

diameter. On Twins the right-hand pivot bearing plate must be removed.

OIL-PUMP WORM.—In 1949 a steel oil-pump worm became standard in lieu of the phosphor-bronze component used previously; for removal the half-time pinion must first be withdrawn. With the locating screw in position a ¼-in. B.S.F. bolt is used to rotate the plunger clockwise, and slowly turning the engine in the normal direction of rotation will release the worm together with the bearing inner race, which can then be pulled off the

THE LUBRICATION SYSTEM

mainshaft. Two 2 B.A. clutch screws can be used for making up an extractor to finally withdraw the worm, which is tapped for this purpose. Note that one side of the worm is stamped "out". This method of removing the worm will not work if the component has sheared, and in this event the outer main-bearing race must be withdrawn by other means, and this is not always easy; if the race is very tight on the shaft the best method is probably to split the case.

THE OIL-PUMP PLUNGER AND SLEEVE.—These are matched components and only supplied together. When fitted, the plunger must have no tight spots when turned by hand; if necessary workshops should select a different assembly for less contraction when fitted into the crankcase.

Lubrication Troubles

A number of faults, loosely described by the private owner as "lubrication trouble", have no connection whatever with the actual lubrication system, and are merely the result of unsuitable sparking-plugs for certain conditions, a weak magneto, worn valve guides, poor piston-rings, scuffing of pistons or scoring of barrels. The net result is usually plug oiling, smoking from the exhaust, oil leaks, heavy consumption or a combination of these, and it is appropriate, at this juncture, to give some guidance on the tracing of faults of this nature.

SMOKING FROM THE EXHAUST.—This fault, if experienced immediately after the engine has been started up, indicates worn valve guides; on Twins use separate stub pipes to ascertain which cylinder is affected. Excess lubrication in the cylinder head will show up when the return pipe of the pump is led straight back into the tank, by-passing the rocker gear with the aid of a length of rubber hose and running the engine for a few minutes on the stand. If this proves excessive loss of oil into the combustion chamber, metering wires may give an improvement if not already fitted; these wires also tend to reduce consumption.

CONTINUOUS SMOKING.—If an engine smokes continuously without there being any indication that the cylinder head is at fault, the trouble may be in the cylinder feed. A loose jet or holder will fail to meter the correct quantity of oil required for the cylinder feed; but, if no defect is found in this respect, the flow of oil to the cylinder wall may still be too generous. This condition can be observed by running the engine for a few minutes on the stand with a soldered-up jet in the holder.

If this decreases smoking from the exhaust, it indicates that the lubrication of the cylinder wall can be cut down. The best method of doing this is by fitting an oil-restrictor disc to the corresponding feed, as described under "Adjustments". Any reductions in oil supply naturally call for extensive experience with the Vincent engine, and it is bad practice to cut down the supply of oil to cover up a developed mechanical fault; private owners are well advised, therefore, to obtain expert assistance in case of doubt.

AIR LEAKS.—Well within the scope of the private owner is a check on air leaks which reduce the scavenging capacity of the pump and a verification that the return line is unobstructed. A blockage in the far end of this will force oil down the valve guides; any obstruction in the return pipes will overload the oil-pump drive.

Breathing

Some loss of oil through the timed engine breather is normal; the amount of lubricant ejected in this manner is

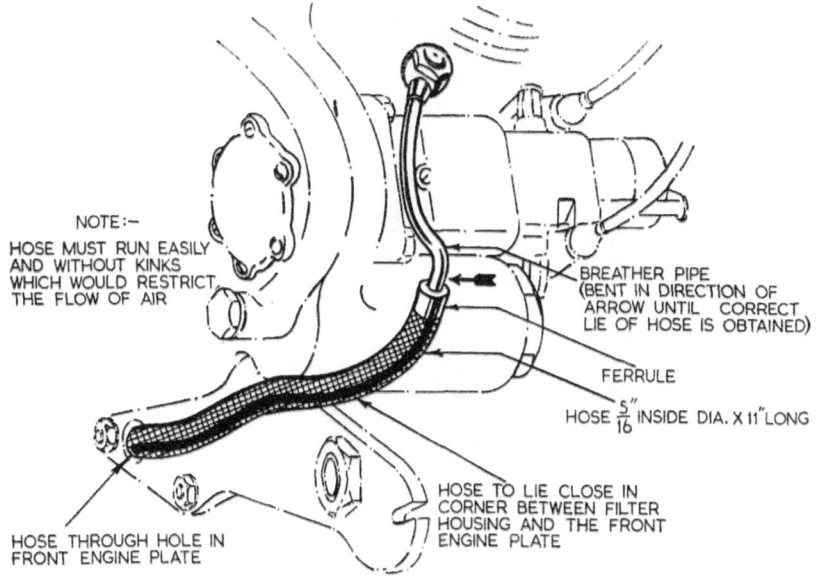

Fig. 50.—Breather-pipe Location, 1000-c.c. Models.

highest at fast tick-over, decreasing at higher engine speeds. This matter can be ignored as long as the oil consumption is not excessive; there are no objections, however, against fitting an extension to the external breather pipe, provided that this does not impede the free escape of the crankcase fumes.

If desired, an atmospheric breather can be added.

The breather is open during 140 degrees of crankshaft rotation, and should close 30 degrees after bottom dead centre of the rear cylinder on Twins. The timing and width of the ports are not unduly critical. This timing should correspond with the meshing of the " B " marks on the front cam-wheel and breather pinion, but will be deranged by the breather spindle moving in the crankcase or the valve sleeve turning in the pinion. On 1000-c.c. models the slot in the spindle should point forwards to the top magneto stud. A loose spindle can sometimes

Fig. 51.—Position of Grease Nipple on Speedometer Gearbox.

[*Photograph by R. S. Allan, A.R.P.S.*]

be plated-up to the required oversize and re-fitted after the case has been heated up locally.

To check the position of the sleeve in the breather pinion, hold a rule across the flats of the $\frac{5}{16}$-in. (7·93-mm.) wide slot: looking at the pinion, the tooth marked " B " should be the first one completely visible below the rule edge. The sleeve is not available as a spare part, and a defective breather valve must be renewed completely. The part has been supplied with alloy, bronze or cast-iron sleeve, and all three types are equally satisfactory. One-piece components of cast-iron are known to have sheared their teeth at very high engine-speeds, and should be replaced by one of the afore-mentioned patterns.

The spindle nut is locked by a tab washer. As the breather turns anti-clockwise, the nut will tighten when the spindle tends to move in the direction of rotation of the pinion.

Cycle Lubrication

Many bushes used on the machine are of the porous-bronze self-lubricating type. But grease nipples are fitted to the brake cam-spindle bosses, speedometer gear-box, hydraulic dampers, front-brake balance beam, head-lug and rear fork pivot bearing. These points should be *sparingly* greased from time to time.

If filling the tool-kit grease-gun presents a problem, try sucking the cork inwards through the hole in the plunger cap, or alternatively buy the grease in a tin provided with a pressure plate for easy filling of grease-guns.

Self-oiling bushes should be removed from parts which are re-enamelled, since the heat used in this process destroys the lubricating properties of these commercial components.

500-C.C. MODELS

In spite of having only one cylinder, the feed jet is 170 as on the 1000-c.c. machine, but—if desired—this size may be reduced to 100 minimum. It has been mentioned previously that a smaller cylinder feed jet also cuts down the supply to the camshaft bushes: on the Singles the better method is to fit an oil-restrictor disc behind the rear rubber washer inside the timing cover, provided that it has been established without doubt that too much oil is getting to the cylinder wall.

The duration of the breather-timing opening is the same as on the Twins, but the slot in the spindle points *downwards* and the valve is driven from the idler gear. The port opens approximately 35–41 degrees after top dead centre and closes approximately 2 degrees before bottom dead centre.

CHAPTER VIII

FUEL SYSTEM, TIMING GEAR AND EXHAUST SYSTEM

ALL post-war petrol tanks are interchangeable, and the "Service Exchange System" operates, but earlier tanks do not have the larger cut-away required for accommodating a T.T.-type carburetter. The tank is stove enamelled and lined with gold leaf. It is surprising how few riders know how to affix a transfer; the following procedure can, however, be recommended :

Fixing Transfer to Petrol Tank.

Brush the dull (silver) side of the transfer with gold size and allow to dry until tacky. The transfer is then affixed to the tank, any air bubbles being carefully smoothed out and the tissue paper washed off with clean water. After drying with a soft cloth, the transfer is finally given one coat of varnish. A few transfers of the cardboard variety have been supplied in the past. This type, which is matt gold on one side, is affixed with methylated spirit; this should not be allowed to dry before fitting as in the case of gold size.

The Tie-bolt and Distance Piece

These components *must* be fitted to the tank bottom lugs, otherwise the component is bound to spring a leak above the rear mounting platform. If this happens, welding is the only way of effecting a satisfactory repair locally. Incidentally, anyone who has witnessed the explosion of a petrol tank during welding is unlikely to be

FUEL SYSTEM, TIMING GEAR AND EXHAUST SYSTEM 107

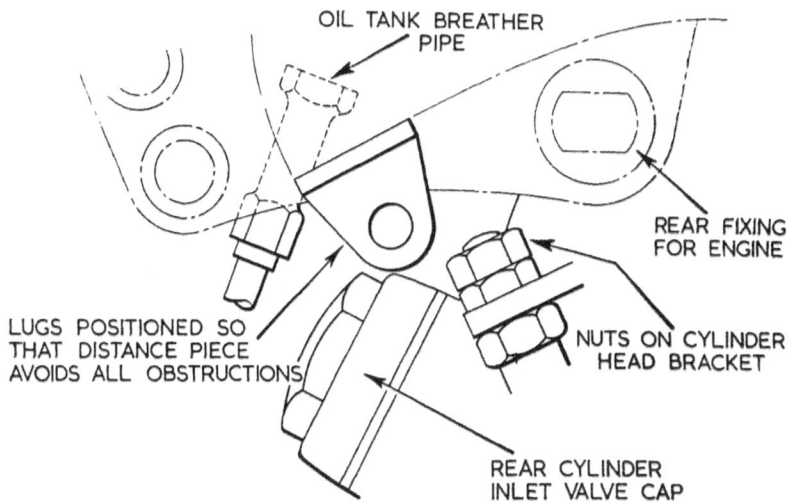

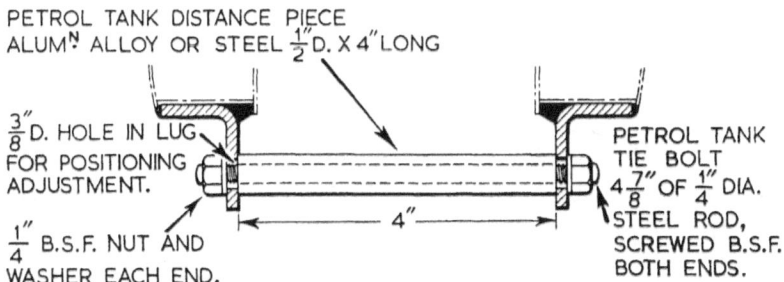

Fig. 52.—Rear Tie Which Must Be in Position to Avoid Petrol-tank Fracture.

careless in respect of the fumes which remain in the empty component for a considerable time!

Knee grips are not a standard fitting on the post-war machine; they tend to give an uncomfortable riding position due to too much spreading of the knees. The pre-war pattern can, however, be fitted if desired.

The " Ewarts " petrol taps are threaded $\frac{1}{4}$ in. B.S.P. both ends, and removal of the round-headed screw enables extraction of the plunger; the cork washer can be expanded by turning the inner head clockwise. Corks which have been dry for some considerable time contract, and should be soaked in castor oil before fitting.

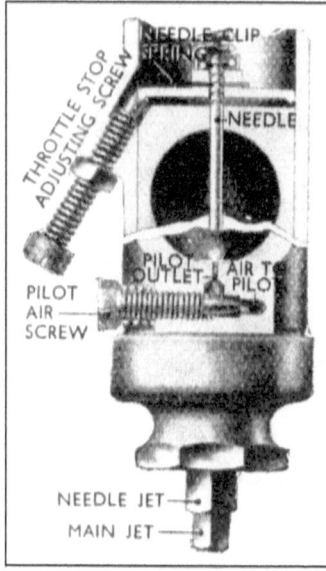

FIG. 53.—AMAL CARBURETTER TUNING PARTS.

Carburetters

In 1948, handed carburetters with extended float chambers—$2\frac{11}{16}$-in. (68·3-mm.) arm—were introduced to facilitate adjustment. The standard Amal carburetter is automatic throughout the throttle range: this, combined with its great reliability in service, probably accounts for the fact that many instruments are found to be poorly tuned in spite of their very wide application on motor cycles. The accompanying illustrations show the parts to tune and the sequence in which the job should be done, preferably on a quiet road with a slight up gradient so that the engine is pulling hard; when the motor is warm the air slide should be fully opened. The standard settings given in the Appendix are very satisfactory for average use, but variations are possible to suit special conditions.

MAIN JET.—This does not affect the mixture strength under three-quarter throttle opening, except when the needle jet is badly worn. The calibration is stamped on every jet. The higher the number, the richer the mixture. With a straight-through or de-baffled exhaust system, the main jet must be increased two to four sizes by experiment until the engine gives maximum power. A slight reduction is recommended for Premier grade fuels unless full throttle openings are frequently used. The main jet is too small should maximum power require throttling back or air-lever correction: the weakness of the mixture will

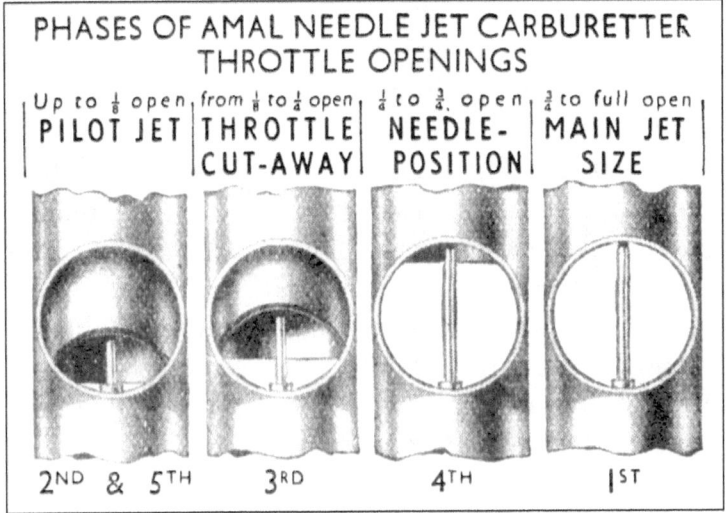

FIG. 54.—SEQUENCE OF TUNING.

then be evident by the greyish appearance of the sparking-plug after a cut-out test.

PILOT JET.—Settings are very important for overall fuel consumption, as so much of the running is done on this jet. The adjustment should therefore be as weak as possible, consistent with good tick-over. On the standard carburetter the pilot air screw is turned clockwise to reduce the air supply, thereby enrichening the mixture, and vice versa. Premier grade fuels usually enable the pilot mixture to be weakened.

THROTTLE VALVE.—The numbers stamped on the top face of the throttle valve indicate the type of carburetter into which it fits, as well as the height of the cut-away in $\frac{1}{16}$-in. (1·58-mm.) steps. Thus a 6/4 and a 29/4 valve have the same amount of cut-away, but the former fits the $1\frac{1}{16}$-in. (26·98-mm.) carburetter, whereas the latter is required for the $1\frac{1}{8}$-in. (28·57-mm.) instrument. The higher the number after the stroke, the weaker the mixture between the pilot and needle-jet range of throttle opening, as the cut-away influences the air flow over the jet and greater economy will be obtained. On the other hand, acceleration will be poor if the mixture is too weak at this stage, and a happy medium must be found to suit specific requirements.

JET NEEDLE.—This controls a wide range of throttle opening as well as acceleration, thereby materially affecting fuel consumption. The five notches are sometimes referred to as weak, half-weak, middle, half-rich and rich or 1, 2, 3, 4 and 5 respectively; lowering the needle by placing the retaining clip in a higher notch weakens the mixture. The needle should be positioned as low as possible consistent with good acceleration, but usually the middle notch gives best all-round results. With Premier fuels the half-weak position, i.e., second groove from the top, can be used in the interest of fuel economy. A rich mixture with the needle in the top (No. 1) groove may indicate that the needle jet has worn, and a needle which is several years old should be renewed as well.

Carburation Troubles

An obstruction in the pilot passage of the jet block causes difficult starting, severe discolouration of exhaust pipes, and sometimes the affected cylinder will fire only with the air lever fully closed. The small drilling is situated in a hemispherical cavity in the lower half of the jet block, and blowing through with *compressed* air is the best way of clearing any particles of dirt accumulated here. For this purpose the jet block must be removed from the mixing chamber, and if tight it should *not* be bashed with a hammer shaft but the mixing chamber warmed up in hot water. Rough handling of the jet block distorts the valve sliding guides and renders the part unfit for further use. In spite of the utmost cleanliness in assembly, pilot obstruction may well occur when a new or reconditioned petrol tank has been fitted.

"SPITTING."—This fault may be a matter of carburation, but can also occur due to the use of too hard a sparking-plug on which the deposit of soot does not burn away easily. "Spitting" when "coming off the pilot" can often be cured by enrichening the pilot setting. If this does not work the pilot must be re-set to its former position and a throttle valve with smaller cut-away fitted. Here again, the pilot may be obstructed, necessitating blowing out with compressed air.

HEAVY FUEL CONSUMPTION.—Instructions for correcting heavy fuel consumption have already been given under "Carburetters", but reference should be made to other causes, such as petrol leakage due to the jet block not being tight in the mixing chamber, worn needle jet and flooding. Retarded ignition settings also give poor consumption figures to a marked degree.

POSITIONING OF FLOAT CHAMBERS.—If a sidecar outfit cuts out on corners the cause is probably that the float chambers are positioned too far to the rear. Re-setting as far forward as possible relative to the mixing chamber usually cures this trouble.

INCORRECT CARBURETTER SYNCHRONISATION.—Very often insufficient attention is paid to synchronisation of the carburetters on 1000-c.c. models; all-round improvement in performance is obtained if both throttle valves come off the stops simultaneously and open up equally. To check, insert a finger of one hand into the air intake of one carburetter so that the movement of the throttle valve can be felt. Operate the twist-grip with the other hand and bend over the machine to observe the lift of the opposite slide.

Cable slack is taken up on the master adjuster between the twist-grip and the junction box; synchronisation of one carburetter relative to the other is provided for by the adjuster on the cable to the *rear* instrument only. This adjuster is purposely positioned behind the right-hand fuel tap to discourage riders from tampering with the synchronisation, which seldom requires correction once accurately set. Note that variations in the lie of the outer cable affect the movement of the throttle valves.

Push-rods and Cam-followers

Stainless-steel push-rods were introduced in November 1949, and this material has the advantage of rapid work-hardening on the ball ends, although comparatively soft when machined. Wear in service is slight, but, during a top overhaul, a push-rod can easily be damaged by careless fitting. The lower ball end must seat properly in the cam-follower cup, otherwise the push-rod will get trapped and bent when the engine is turned. As a temporary measure, a bent push-rod can be straightened; but, if any doubt exists on the correct location, it is as well to remove the timing cover and steady plate for observation.

Three of the cam-followers on Twins are located by a $\frac{3}{8}$-in. (9·52-mm.) thrust washer on the inside and a $\frac{5}{16}$-in. (7·92-mm.) thrust washer on the outside; but the front exhaust follower is fitted with the $\frac{3}{8}$-in. size on both sides. Up to 0·010 in. (0·25 mm.) end float is permissible on the cam-follower spacers; these must always be free enough to be rotated with the fingers.

All cam-followers will show signs of wear in service, but if the groove is not more than $\frac{1}{8}$ in. (3 mm.) wide the component can be refaced on an oilstone. Badly worn followers can be re-claimed by case-hardening and re-grinding; excessive wear may be caused by over-loading due to coil-bound valve springs or the valve-stem collar hitting the lower guide on full lift.

FUEL SYSTEM, TIMING GEAR AND EXHAUST SYSTEM 113

Camshafts

Access to the camshafts and timing gear is gained by removal of the timing cover, which is retained by eleven cheese-headed screws; two of these are $1\frac{1}{8}$ in. (28·6 mm.) long and pass through the hollow dowels which locate the component. Do not forget to unscrew the long banjo bolt before withdrawing the cover, but the big-end quill can remain in position. The steady plate on Twins is retained by five thin self-locking nuts, two $\frac{5}{16}$-in. plain nuts with tab washers and three $\frac{1}{4}$-in. B.S.F. plain nuts with lock washers.

Each camshaft is jig-pressed into the pinion and not keyed. Slipping of the shaft in the cam-wheel may occur, but is most rare. Normally, replacement camshafts are only supplied complete with pinion. The correct clearance on the spindles is 0·0005–0·0015 in. (0·01–0·03 mm.), but up to 0·003 in. (0·07 mm.) is permissible. Re-bushing is a makers' or Vincent repair-specialist's job; the cams are ground with the bushes in position. Thrust washers are fitted only between the pinion and the steady plate in $\frac{1}{2}$-in. (12·70-mm.) and $\frac{5}{16}$-in. (7·93-mm.) sizes, the larger washer innermost. End float may vary between 0·005 and 0·015 in. (0·12 and 0·38 mm.).

Black Shadow camshafts are identical to those fitted to Meteor, Comet and Rapide models. They are, however, specially selected, and the theoretical valve timing is given in the Appendix, Table I. The valve timing of the Black Lightning camshaft enhances performance without necessarily rendering an engine unfit for use on the road, and the *rear* camshaft of this type is common to the Grey Flash.

A small ridge on a cam indicates that the follower should be lined up by adjusting the thickness of the thrust washers. The ridge can be removed with the aid of an oilstone.

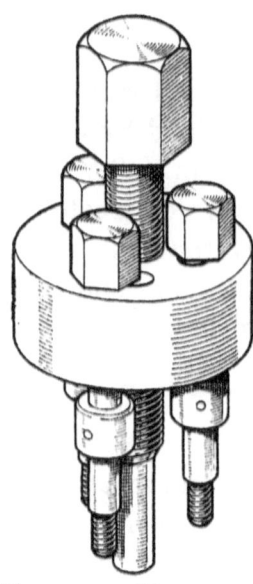

Fig. 55.—Half-time Pinion and Dynamo Pinion Extractor.

Idler Gear

Mounted on an adjustable boss, the idler gear can be re-set to zero backlash against the cam pinions. But, if wear has been considerable, an oversize half-time pinion may be necessary. Backlash at this point is less likely to cause noise than incorrect mesh of the idler with the cam pinion(s). The three nuts retaining the idler gear boss are punch-locked after tightening; the hole in the steady plate for the idler spindle is purposely made oversize. The spindle nut is locked by a tab washer for the same reason as described for the breather valve.

The bronze idler gear has been superseded by the light-alloy component which weighs less, runs quieter and has stood up to racing conditions. For serious racing, however, a steel component is preferable. Some early alloy idlers featured a cast-iron bush, but the majority are unbushed; in this case an extra thrust washer is fitted on the inside of the gear.

The gear has an odd number of teeth (79), and the shaft is a press fit in the boss. This component is stamped " top " to indicate the correct way of fitting, but the direction of the oil hole in the shaft is unimportant.

Half-time Pinion

This pinion has twenty-four teeth and five keyways; as each tooth equals 15 degrees crankshaft rotation, alternative positions can be selected on the mainshaft to obtain a valve timing within $1\frac{1}{2}$ degrees of the theoretical

FUEL SYSTEM, TIMING GEAR AND EXHAUST SYSTEM 115

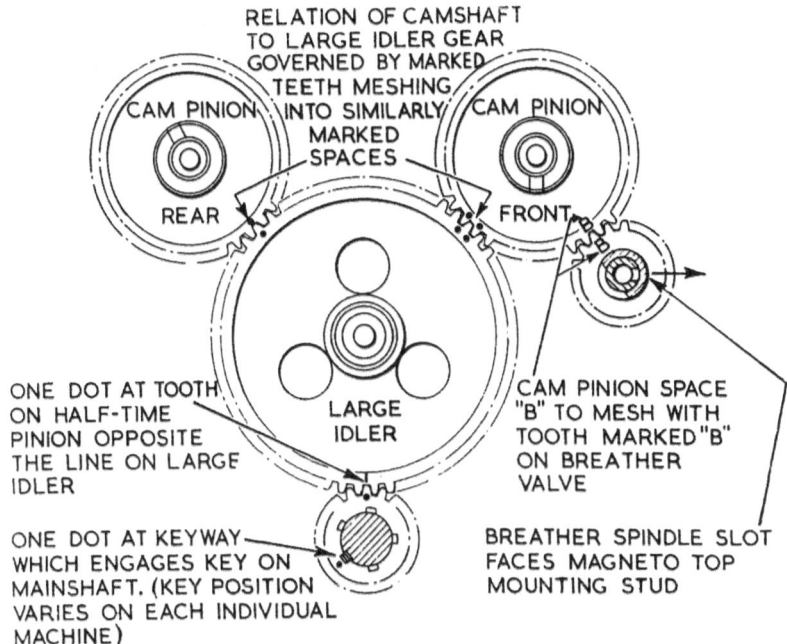

Fig. 56.—Timing-gear Markings, 1000-c.c. Models.

figures. The nut has a right-hand thread, and the pinion is tapped 2 B.A. to take an extractor. Correct backlash is zero to 0·002 in. (0·05 mm.) against the idler gear after this component has been correctly adjusted against the cam pinion(s). Half-time pinions are available in various under-sizes and over-sizes for selection of mesh, and the grade is etched on each component.

Valve Timing

On all engines sent out from the makers the timing gear is fully marked: as this also applies to spares, re-timing usually involves only the lining up of all markings. In this connection, it should be noted that the engaging keyway of the half-time pinion is punch-marked as well. Thus this method can also be used when for any reason this pinion has been disturbed. Careful owners, who like to carry out a check on the markings before dismantling the various gears, may then find that by turning the engine

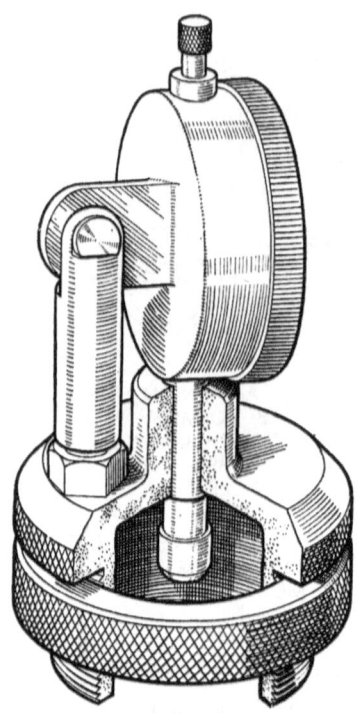

FIG. 57.—HOLDER FOR STANDARD "MERCER" DIAL GAUGE FOR WORKSHOP USE.

they are unable to get everything lined up according to the book! The answer is that due to the odd number of teeth on the idler, the engine has to be rotated many times, and it is probably easier to withdraw just this part in order to line up the pinions by hand.

If a timing disc is available, the opening and closing points of the valves can be accurately determined in degrees of crankshaft rotation. As the figures given in the Appendix are taken at 0·005 in. (0·12 mm.) lift, one or more dial indicators are required to ascertain exactly when this amount of lift is reached. In order to allow for clearances in the valve-operating mechanism, the tappets are adjusted to a nip of 0·001–0·003 in. (0·02–0·07 mm.). Whilst the exact amount is immaterial, the dial indicator is also used to obtain the same tightness on each tappet. Top dead centre must be carefully established, but on Twins this is necessary on one cylinder only, in view of the precise 50-degree angle. The actual valve timing of a used engine is unlikely to correspond exactly with the theoretical figures.

Mark III Cams

Mark III cams were introduced early in 1952 in the interest of mechanical quietness; normally, the figure 3 is stamped on the camshaft end for identification. The valve timing obtained with these cams is identical to the earlier pattern, and they give no loss of performance in any way. Due to the quietening ramps, however, the exact opening and closing points of the valves cannot be ascertained, and for this reason the present method is to measure the lift at top and bottom dead centre with a tolerance of plus or minus three degrees. The figures obtained in this manner will be as follows:

Inlet at T.D.C.: 0·110 in. (2·79 mm.) lift, opening
,, ,, B.D.C.: 0·190 in. (4·82 mm.) lift, closing
Exhaust at B.D.C.: 0·220 in. (5·58 mm.) lift, opening
,, ,, T.D.C.: 0·065 in. (1·65 mm.) lift, closing

Also, on the Mark III cams, the pinions are fully marked, consequently they can be fitted to an earlier engine without re-timing being necessary.

Exhaust Lifter

A spring-loaded linkage operates the lifters. These are retained on their spindles by punch-locked nuts on earlier machines, and by collars on later models. The thrust is taken by a 3 × 5-mm. big-end roller peened into the head of each lifter. On earlier Twins there was no provision for individual adjustment; later machines are fitted with a linkage which is threaded at one end to take an adjuster on the rear component.

Oil retention on the rod is by two rubber washers which can be slipped over the cable abutment. If these washers are in good condition no oil leakage will be experienced, provided that the control cable has $\frac{3}{16}$ in. (4·76 mm.) slack. By way of a temporary measure, the sleeve of the cable abutment can be filled with high-melting-point grease or non-setting jointing compound to rectify quickly an oil leak at this point.

Heavy operation of the exhaust lifter is usually caused by lack of lubrication on the control cable: this can be

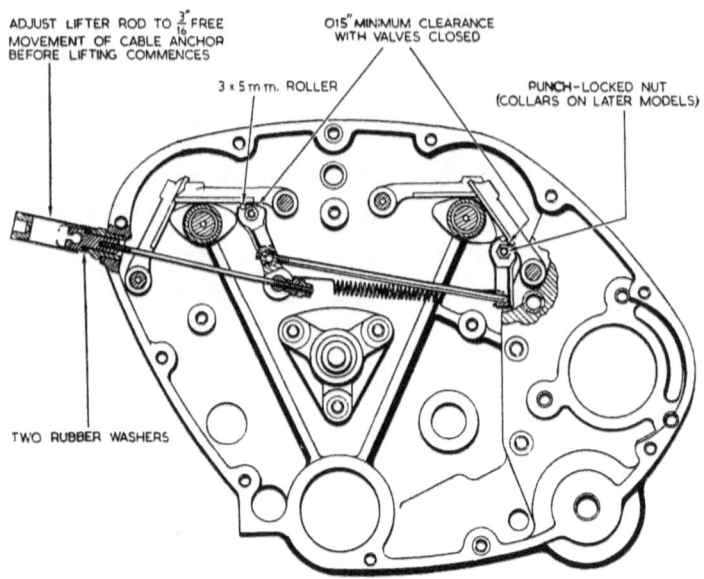

Fig. 58.—Exhaust-lifter Mechanism.

soaked in oil from time to time. If the mechanism does not work properly, a spindle may be loose in the crankcase, and re-tightening this part immediately will prevent damage to the crankcase threads. Loss of the hardened roller out of the lifter—due to operation at too high engine speeds—is not immediately noticeable, as the lifter will still work, and the roller is likely to fall into the bottom of the timing chest, out of harm's way.

When kicking over the Twin engine with the exhaust valves lifted to clear an overrich mixture, always keep the throttle closed.

Exhaust System

Long exhaust pipes are normally supplied complete with nut, since the flange is best made with the aid of a special flanging fixture. The finned nut is threaded $1\frac{7}{8}$ in. × 20 T.P.I. and can be removed by carefully flattening the flange with a hammer on a length of $1\frac{1}{2}$-in. (38·10-mm.)

FUEL SYSTEM, TIMING GEAR AND EXHAUST SYSTEM 119

bar clamped in a vice. A pipe on which the flange has split can be re-flanged, at least once, after cutting off the fractured portion. When fitting exhaust pipes, care is necessary to avoid damage to the fine thread in the exhaust port, inside which a washer is fitted for gas-tightness. Air leaks in the exhaust system may be the cause of banging in the silencer. The standard exhaust-pipe diameter is $1\frac{5}{8}$ in. (41·5 mm.).

Some discolouration of the pipe adjacent to the exhaust port is difficult to avoid on machines fitted with an automatic timing control, but severe blueing is usually the result of an obstruction in the pilot hole of the carburetter jet block; this raises the exhaust-gas temperature considerably, and chromium inevitably changes colour when subjected to excessive heat, irrespective of the thickness of the deposit. It should be noted in this connection that the engine runs fully retarded at tick-over speeds due to the automatic timing control.

A rare phenomenon, which has caused unnecessary worry, is an exhaust pipe which glows dull red in the dark; this has been encountered on Singles as well as on Twins. The main cause is that, during a certain period, exhaust pipes of a lighter material gauge were supplied. Slight mixture weakness, retarded ignition timing or a variation of the valve timing within the theoretical limits may be enough to get an exhaust pipe of this pattern red hot. If attention to these details does not provide a cure, a pipe of heavier material gauge can be fitted, and no detrimental effects to the engine are to be expected.

500-c.c. MODELS

The contents of this chapter are also applicable to the Singles, the main differences in layout being in the timing gear. The idler gear drives the breather pinion as well as

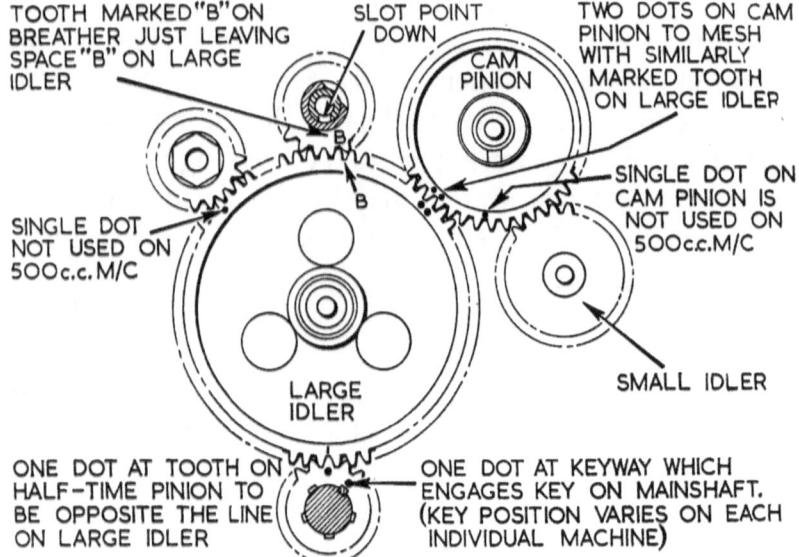

Fig. 59.—Timing-gear Markings, 500-c.c. Models.

the dynamo, and a second (smaller) light-alloy idler drives the magneto from the cam pinion. Most of the parts are fully interchangeable with the Twins, but it is not generally appreciated that the Singles are fitted with the *rear* camshaft of the Twins, not the front assembly.

Various timing-gear thrust-washers are correctly positioned as follows :

Breather :

　One thrust washer ½ in. (12·70 mm.), Part No. E95, inside.
　One thrust washer ⁵⁄₁₆ in. (7·93 mm.), Part No. E98/1, outside.

Large Idler :

　One idler-gearshaft washer, Part No. ET173, outside.
　One thrust washer, Part No. ET173/1, is fitted on the inside, but only with all-alloy gears, i.e., those which do not feature a cast-iron boss.

Camshaft :

　One thrust washer ½ in. (12·70 mm.), Part No. E95.
　One thrust washer ⁵⁄₁₆ in. (7·93 mm.), Part No. ET98/1.
} both outside, larger innermost.

FUEL SYSTEM, TIMING GEAR AND EXHAUST SYSTEM   121

Small Idler :
   One idler-gearshaft washer, Part No. ET173, outside.

Cam-followers :
   One thrust washer $\frac{3}{8}$ in. (9·52 mm.), Part No. ET98, outside.
   One thrust washer $\frac{5}{16}$ in. (7·93 mm.), Part No. ET98/1, outside.

CHAPTER IX

IGNITION AND ELECTRICAL EQUIPMENT

THE original equipment sparking-plugs listed in Table III of the Appendix are, if anything, on the "hard" side, the idea being that it is cheaper and less serious to clean an oiled-up hard plug than to replace a burnt-out soft one. On the other hand, a plug which is too hard for particular conditions of operation is unlikely to reach its correct working temperature, and will foul rapidly, due to deposit forming on the *insulation*. As a general rule the softest grade consistent with conditions of operation is the better choice, and suitable alternatives to the original equipment grades are likewise given. Inspect plugs regularly and renew when earth or centre electrodes appear badly eroded.

At certain stages of the 1000-c.c. models speed range the rear cylinder runs slightly hotter than the front, and this accounts for the fact that the rear plug is often cleaner in appearance than its front-cylinder counterpart. The reason is that any deposit of soot will more easily burn away on the plug with the higher working temperature, and in some cases the fitting of a different grade in front and rear cylinders may be sound practice; some experimentation will enable the best types to be chosen, see also Chapter X.

The standard gaps given in the Appendix may be increased to 0·030 in. (0·76 mm.) maximum to reduce the chances of gap bridging or to increase mileage per gallon at small throttle openings after re-tuning.

Interference Suppressors

Waterproof covers are standard fitting, and home market 1954 models have 5,000-ohm interference suppressors incorporated in the K.L.G. PS-type cover. While not affecting the running of the engine in any way, suppressors tend to show up slight carburetter maladjustments which would otherwise pass unnoticed.

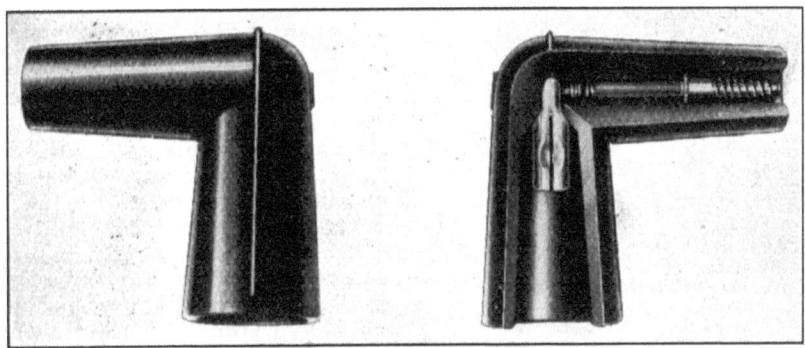

FIG. 60.—K.L.G. SUPPRESSOR COVERS.

In conjunction with the composition of modern fuels and lubricants, poor carburation may lead to "whiskering" of the plug; although removal of the suppressor appears to provide a cure, the actual cause lies elsewhere, and the possibility of a weak spark should not be overlooked. An increase in plug gap often helps, and such increase should be the smallest which just cures the trouble.

Magneto

Automatic timing control is a standard fitting and provides optimum spark intensity when the magneto is fully retarded for starting, as the cam-ring is not moved. Parts for converting the standard magneto to manual control are not supplied. Especially on Twins automatic

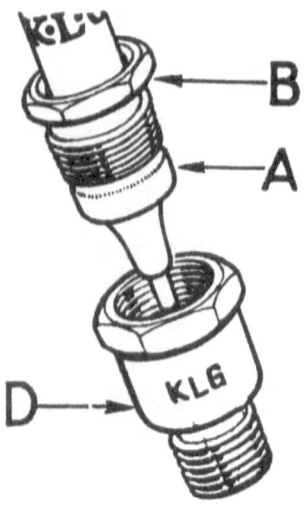

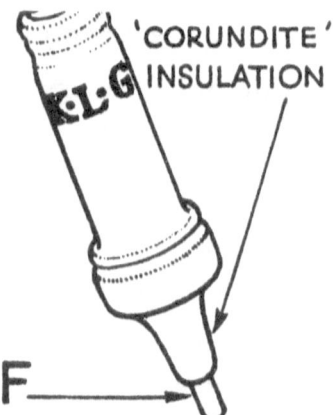

Fig. 61.—Cleaning K.L.G. Plugs.

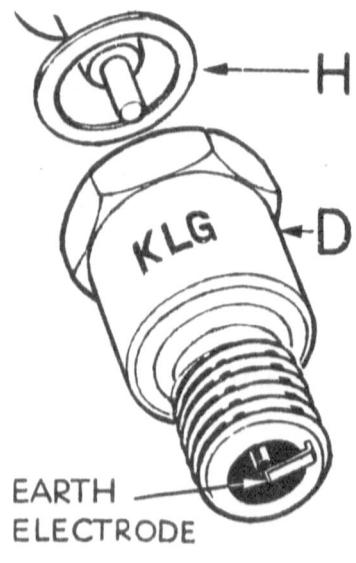

Most K.L.G. plugs are of the detachable type and can be cleaned easily and efficiently by hand. It is best to clean them at regular intervals. To take the plug to pieces, the gland nut (B) should be unscrewed from the body (D) so that the insulated electrode assembly (A) may be withdrawn.

If the " Corundite " insulation is oily, first wash it in petrol or paraffin; then with fairly coarse glass-paper, remove the carbon deposit and wash again. The firing point (F) should be cleaned with a fine emery cloth.

The plug body (D) should be scraped clean internally with a knife or wire brush, paying particular attention to the Earth Electrodes, and finally rinsed in petrol.

The internal washer (H) should be lightly smeared with thin oil. Make sure that it is properly seated in the plug body before reinserting the central electrode assembly. Screw up the gland nut and tighten sufficiently to give a gas-tight joint.

Now adjust the gaps in accordance with the engine makers' instructions. Always remember the golden rule: *never try to move the central electrode. It is embedded in " Corundite " which cannot bend. Move the earth electrodes only.*

IGNITION AND ELECTRICAL EQUIPMENT

control is preferable from a practical point of view unless a machine is mainly used for racing. The magneto rotates clockwise, and it should be noted that no earth brush is fitted behind the contact-breaker. Platinum points are required for the Twin magneto; these are smaller in diameter than the tungsten pattern, which are unsuitable for the 50-degree instrument.

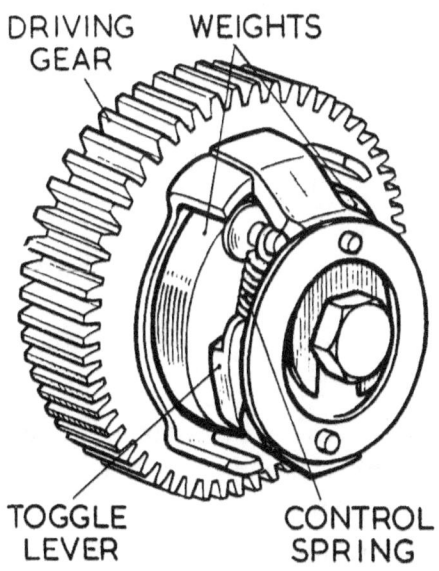

FIG. 62.—AUTOMATIC TIMING CONTROL.

Magneto Maintenance

Every 3000 miles (5000 km.) a few drops of thin machine oil should be applied to the wick in the cam-ring. The contact-breaker must be removed to lubricate the rocker-arm pivot, which should be lightly smeared with clean engine oil. Some of this should also be smeared on the contact-breaker spring.

The contact-breaker should be adjusted every 3000 miles (5000 km.) and cleaned every 6000 miles (10,000 km.). Burnt or blackened points can be cleaned with a fine carborundum stone or very fine emery cloth and cleaned

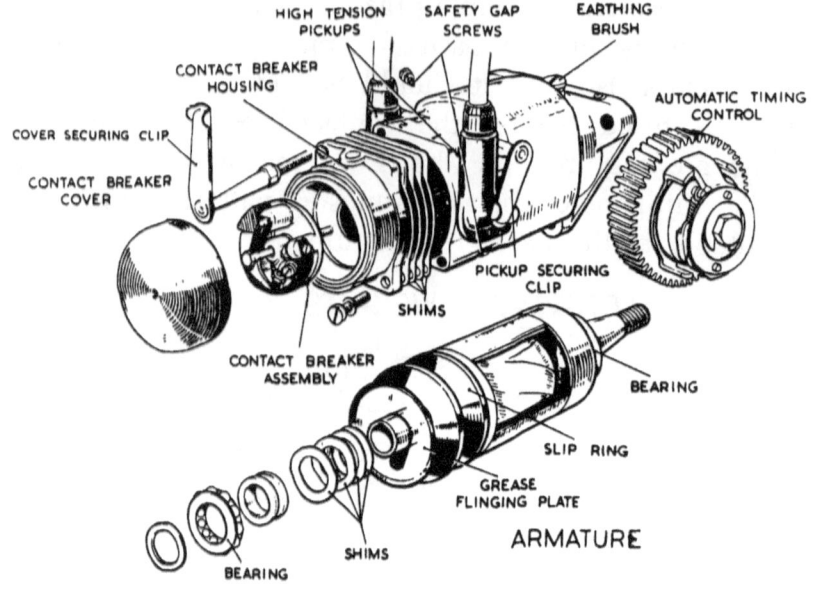

Fig. 63.—Lucas KVF Magneto.

with a rag moistened with petrol. Each high-tension pick-up should be cleaned, and a dirty brush is wiped with a petrol-moistened cloth. The brush must move freely in its holder, and should be renewed when worn to within ⅛ in. (3·17 mm.) of the shoulder. The slip-ring track is cleaned with a soft cloth on a suitably shaped piece of wood while the engine is slowly turned. A piece of paper inserted between the points will assist those who are allergic to electric shocks, but don't forget to remove the paper when the job is done!

The automatic timing control is too tough to dismantle, but new springs may be necessary and a new Tufnol gear can be riveted to the original control. During 1953, the magneto was modified to take a 18-mm. drive-end bearing in conjunction with a spring-loaded oil-seal, and the fitting of this pattern magneto is advisable if oil and condensation from the timing chest tend to enter the instrument.

IGNITION AND ELECTRICAL EQUIPMENT 127

Re-packing the magneto bearings every 20,000 miles (30,000 km.) is good practice, but dismantling or overhauling is best left to experts.

Timing the Magneto

The flange-fitting magneto is retained on studs by means of two plain $\frac{5}{16}$-in. B.S.F. plain nuts and one long sleeve nut, with plain washers; a paper gasket ensures oil-tightness. The automatic control has a self-withdrawing nut, and if rough handling has stripped the extractor threads the nut can be screwed back two or three turns only and given a sharp blow with a hammer after the nuts retaining the magneto have been slackened off sufficiently to allow the Tufnol drive pinion to rest against the timing-case wall. This will free the timing control off the shaft taper, and the magneto can be removed without dismantling the timing cover, simply by unscrewing the inspection plate and leaving the timing control resting inside the timing chest.

Re-timing the magneto with a degree-plate and the timing control wedged open in the fully advanced position gives the most accurate results, but failing a degree-plate, measurements on the firing stroke can be taken, see Table I of the Appendix. On Twins the rear cylinder (No. 1) corresponds with the *bottom* lobe of the cam-ring, and the moment of opening of the contact-breaker points is best ascertained with a blade of cigarette paper gripped between them. Find T.D.C. of the firing stroke and turn the engine backwards through the required number of degrees crankshaft rotation or the equivalent stroke measurement. Turn the contact-breaker until the piece of cigarette paper is just released and tighten the nut without moving the timing control on the armature shaft. When timed at full advance in this manner the spark will occur 4 degrees before T.D.C. with the timing control free and in the fully retarded position; this equals 0·008 in. (0·2 mm.) measured on the stroke, assuming an advance of 39 degrees, which is a good average timing.

A late ignition timing affects petrol consumption adversely, but for higher compression ratios the setting must be retarded in accordance with the following table:

Piston Type.	Compression Ratio.	Ignition Advance.
E7/7	7·3	38–39
E7/8	8	36–37
E7/9	9	36
E7/10	11	35
E7/11	12·5	34

The post-war engines generally require less advance than the pre-war units; racing men may not be concerned with some " pinking " and will time accordingly. With

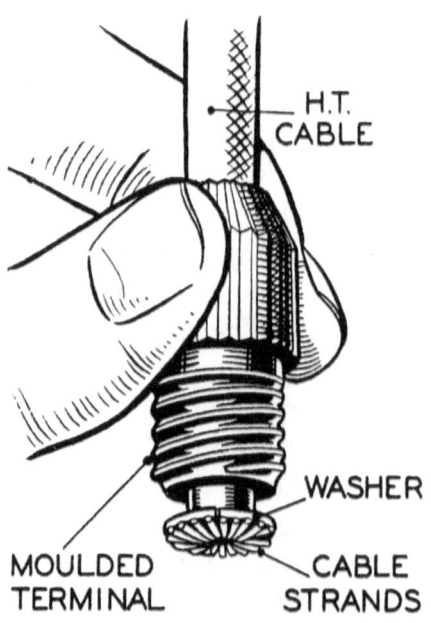

FIG. 64.—REPLACING THE H.T. CABLE.

IGNITION AND ELECTRICAL EQUIPMENT

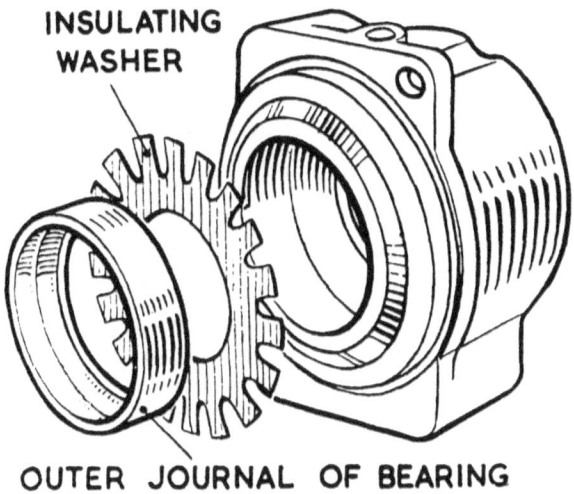

FIG. 65.—USE OF BEARING INSULATING WASHER.

Premier-grade fuels, it may be possible to advance one or two degrees for road work, in the interest of petrol economy.

Ignition Trouble

A strong and regular spark from the cable terminal or end should bridge a gap of about $\frac{1}{8}$ in. (3·17 mm.) from any metal part of the engine when the unit is turned with the plug(s) removed. If the spark is good, the plug is probably at fault. If no spark occurs, the high-tension cable may be perished or burnt by the exhaust pipe and shorting. In spite of a fat spark the engine will run erratically, if at all, when the magneto is incorrectly timed, and workshops should note that the end cover of the instrument *can* be fitted upside down, causing a 50-degree mag to fire on one terminal only.

If the performance of a magneto is not satisfactory, the contact-breaker may require cleaning or adjusting. Badly blackened points and arcing at the contacts indicate condenser failure, in which case a service armature is probably the best and quickest solution; dismantling the armature to fit a new condenser is a specialist's job. The earthing brush is situated in the top of the body adjacent to the identification plate on the mounting flange and retained by a slotted cap. If the magneto has suffered a mechanical breakdown or if an internal fault is suspected specialist attention or service exchange is called for.

Failure of the synthetic-rubber seal in the drive end will cause the ingress of oil and condensation from the timing chest, but with trouble of this nature the timing of the crankcase breather should be checked. Excessive condensation may be the result of specific operating conditions, e.g., when a machine is mainly used for runs of very short duration.

Headlamp

Earlier Series B models were fitted with an 8-in. (20·32-cm.) headlamp, but the later 7-in. (17·78-cm.) component is just as effective and considerably lighter. The main bulb is not adjustable for focus; an incorrect bulb will give a poor beam. Standard fitting is a 24 × 24-watt bulb, and if genuine replacements are not available the type selected should be with one horizontal and one V-filament; the pattern with two horizontal filaments is not always suitable. There are no objections to a 36-watt bulb: a suitable type is the one which gives 36 watts main and 24 watts dipped. The standard bulb should be fitted with the word " Top " facing up. The pilot bulb is of 3-watt rating.

On Brampton pattern forks the top headlamp brackets are mounted to the outside of the girder; on " Girdraulic " forks these brackets are fitted to the inside of the blades. The longer flats on all brackets are bolted to the headlamp. Series C export models for the American market have a slightly different headlamp shell with a split rim retained

IGNITION AND ELECTRICAL EQUIPMENT

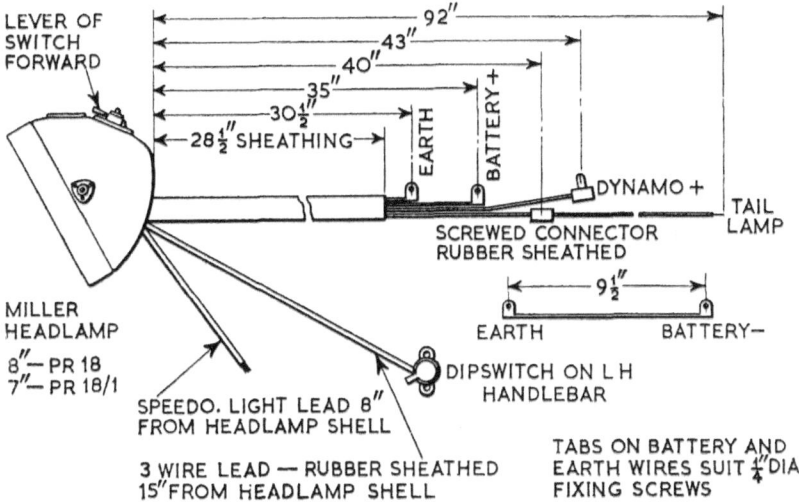

FIG. 66.—WIRING LENGTHS.

by a screw and nut. This shell takes a "General Electric" 4030 sealed-beam unit; the terminals of the detachable connector plug are marked and fit the standard cable ends.

The Miller headlamp is capable of providing good illumination: if the focus of the beam is not satisfactory, the fitting of a different bulb, reflector and/or bulb holder usually improves matters. Naturally, a badly tarnished reflector will give a poor light. A battery in poor condition will not stand up to prolonged night riding unless the voltage regulator is adjusted to balance the consumption of the main filaments. The "Off" position on the headlamp switch is inoperative, and the dynamo charges in this position as well as on "C". Ammeter readings depend on the state of the battery, but—with this component fully charged—the average reading is between 1 and 3 amps charge. At night the charging rate should compensate the current consumption of the main beam at the rider's habitual cruising speed.

Electric Horn

On a motor cycle the output of the electric horn is somewhat restricted by the capacity of the battery: thus the instrument should not be judged by car standards. The Lucas " Altette " horn is adjusted before leaving the Works, and gives long periods of service without attention. The performance may be affected by such defects as a discharged battery, poor condition of wiring, badly earthed

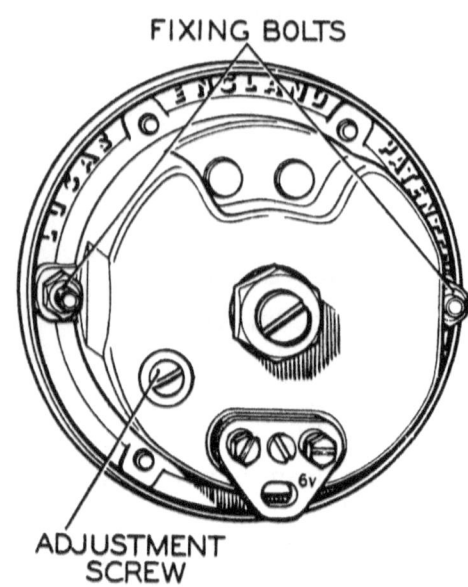

FIG. 67.—LUCAS HIGH-FREQUENCY HORN.

push button, loose fixing bolt or by vibration of some part adjacent to the instrument.

Adjustment does not alter the note, but merely takes up wear of the vibrating parts. In spite of a good note, a horn may be out of adjustment and take excessive current; normal consumption is 3–4 amps noted on an ammeter connected in series with the instrument. When adjusting, the tone-disc nut or other screws in the horn should not be disturbed. Adjustment is made by means of the screw provided, usually by turning in a clockwise direction, two

IGNITION AND ELECTRICAL EQUIPMENT

or three notches at the time before re-testing. If the screw is turned too far, the armature will pull in without separating the points; if no current is taken, the horn may be so adjusted that the contact-breaker is permanently open. When testing do not continue pushing the button if the instrument gives no sound. If used repeatedly when badly out of adjustment, the horn may sustain damage due to the excessive current which it will take. Later type instruments have no screw at the back, and for access to the adjuster the domed nut on the front must be removed.

The long horn lead measures $47\frac{1}{2}$ in. (1·20 m.) from terminal block to push button; the short lead is $15\frac{1}{2}$ in. (39 cm.) long.

Battery

At least once a month the battery should be topped up with distilled water until the plates are just submerged, but the level of the electrolyte should not be allowed to reach the bottom of the filling orifice. The state of charge is indicated by the specific gravity of the electrolyte, and this is checked with a hydrometer. Provided no electrolyte has been spilt, gravity figures will be as follows:

Fully charged	1·285–1·300
Half discharged	1·210
Fully discharged	1·150

Standard equipment is the 6-volt "Exide" motor-cycle battery, type 3EK5AL. If a machine is laid up for several months the battery should receive a trickle charge about once a fortnight to prevent permanent sulphation of the plates.

Connections should be clean and tight, but the use of a spanner on the hexagon terminal nuts is to be avoided, since the terminal will fracture if too much force is applied.

Use some vaseline to prevent corrosion, and never leave a battery in a state of discharge; unless some long daylight runs are made the battery should be charged from an independent source.

Wiring

On the headlamp switch only four of the numbered terminals are in use and in case the wiring has been detached replace the leads by means of their coloured identification sleeves as follows:

Terminal No. 5 . . .	Plain lead to pilot bulb
Terminal No. 6 . . .	Blue lead to discharge side of ammeter (short)
Terminal No. 7 . . .	{ Black lead to tail lamp { Plain lead to speedo bulb
Terminal No. 8 . . .	Red lead to dip-switch
Headlamp shell spring contact	Grey lead to earth on upper frame member or petrol-tank tie-bolt
Charge side of ammeter .	Red lead to positive battery terminal
Discharge ,, ,, .	Blue long lead with plug for dynamo socket

The horn and stop-light circuits are separate and do not register on the ammeter. The tail-lamp and horn-button wire are fitted with a connector to facilitate detaching when removing the upper frame member. A short cable with two drilled terminals connects the negative battery terminal to the earthing screw on the upper frame member or petrol-tank tie-bolt.

Wiring looms supplied with replacement headlamps, or as spares, must be trimmed for length of sheathing and leads. The stop and tail-lamp wires are led through the rear mudguard stay; an easy way of installing these leads is to push them up from below and pick up the end with a bent small paper-clip or wire when they come up at the hole near the mudguard hinge. Note that the horn takes

IGNITION AND ELECTRICAL EQUIPMENT

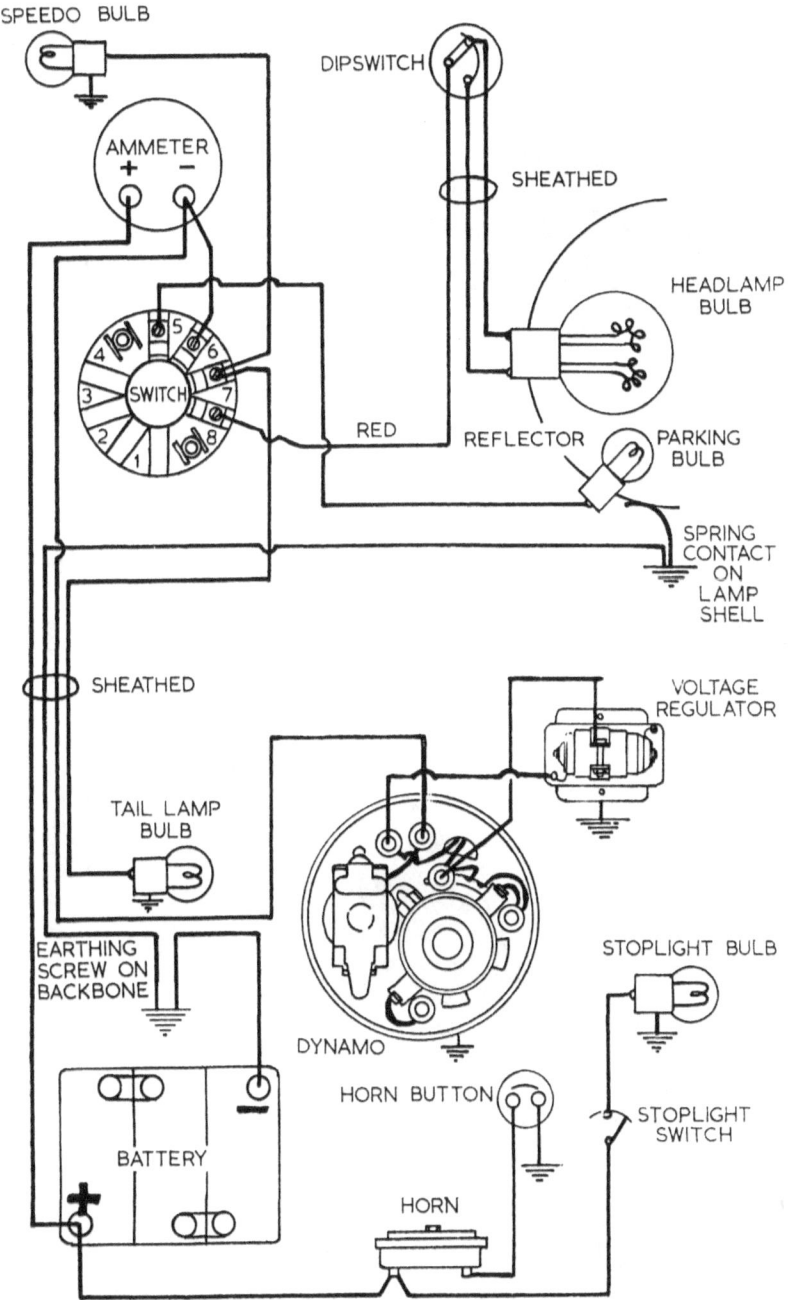

Fig. 68.—Wiring Diagram.

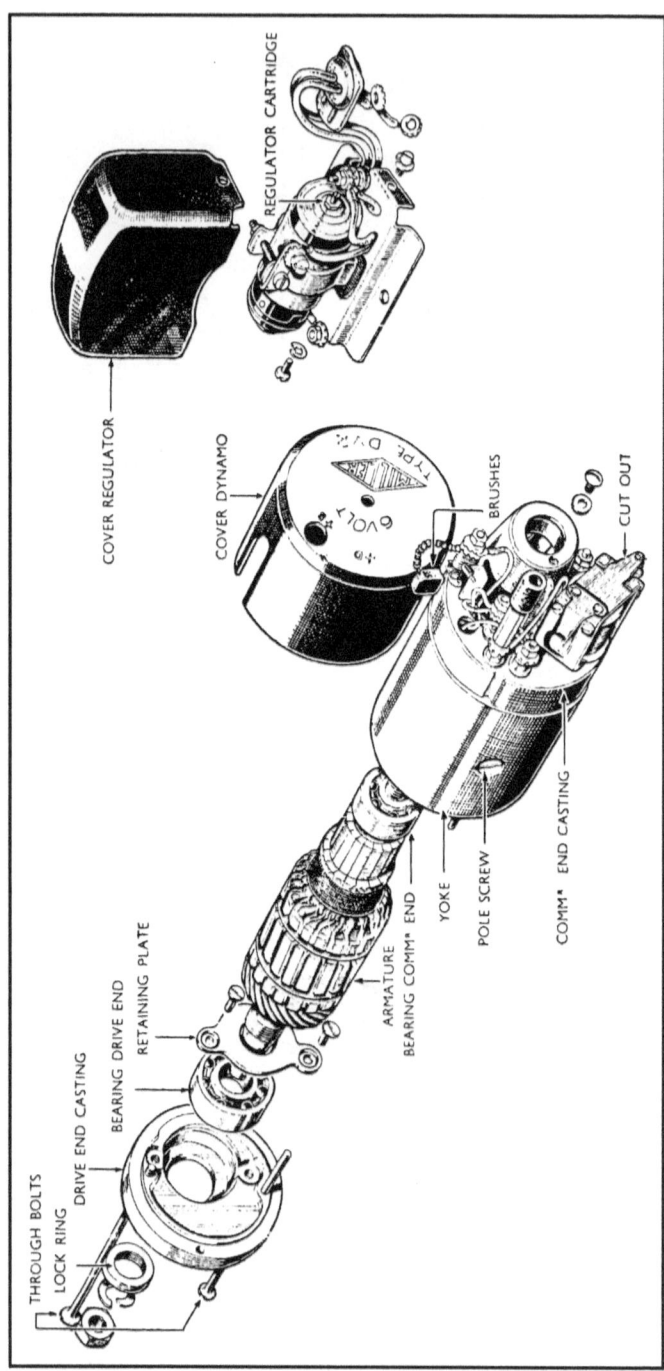

FIG. 69.—MILLER DYNAMO, TYPE D6.

current from the battery direct and that the stop light is fed from the horn terminal block.

Dynamo

On assembly, the dynamo ball bearings are packed with high-melting-point grease, but this does not relieve the owner from subsequent lubrication in service. More often than not this is sadly neglected to the detriment of the bearings, particularly at the drive end. This bearing should be lubricated with oil from time to time, after removal of the grub-screw on top of the bearing housing. The commutator end bearing is oiled through the hole for the screw which retains the black-enamelled end cover. Here again it is good practice to have both bearings re-packed by an expert every 20,000 miles (30,000 km.).

Earlier models were fitted with a $3\frac{1}{2}$-in. (88·9-mm.) dynamo; this type was superseded by the 3-in. (76·2-mm.) instrument, which can be fitted into the $3\frac{1}{2}$-in. cradle by means of an adaptor available for this purpose. Both instruments of Miller manufacture have a rated output of 50 watts and rotate clockwise. The makers' designation is D9S for the $3\frac{1}{2}$-in. type and D6 for the 3-in. pattern. On early crankcases the dynamo cradle was cast integral, but later units feature a detachable component retained by sleeve nuts on two studs in the top wall of the drive-side case.

Oil entering into the dynamo on Twins may indicate that the level in the primary chaincase is too high, and if so, leakage is also likely to occur at the face of the instrument where it abuts against the drive housing on the crankcase. The dynamo itself has a felt washer in the drive end, and the high-melting-point grease used in the bearing also prevents the ingress of oil or condensation. The instrument is very reliable, and an internal electrical breakdown is rare. Dynamo repairs are usually outside the scope of the owner-rider, and should be entrusted to a specialist.

Blanking plates are available for blocking up the drive hole when the dynamo is removed completely for racing.

Voltage Regulator

The regulator base must always be in good earth contact with the clamp; the wires must be kept free from oil and petrol as well as protected from chafing. On Twins the regulator cover should be clear of the battery.

Adjustment to increase the output is performed with the engine stationary. Remove the cover and screw in clockwise the set-screw at the positive flat end of the cartridge (red) *not more than a quarter turn.* Then screw out the set-screw at the negative conical end (black) a quarter to a half turn.

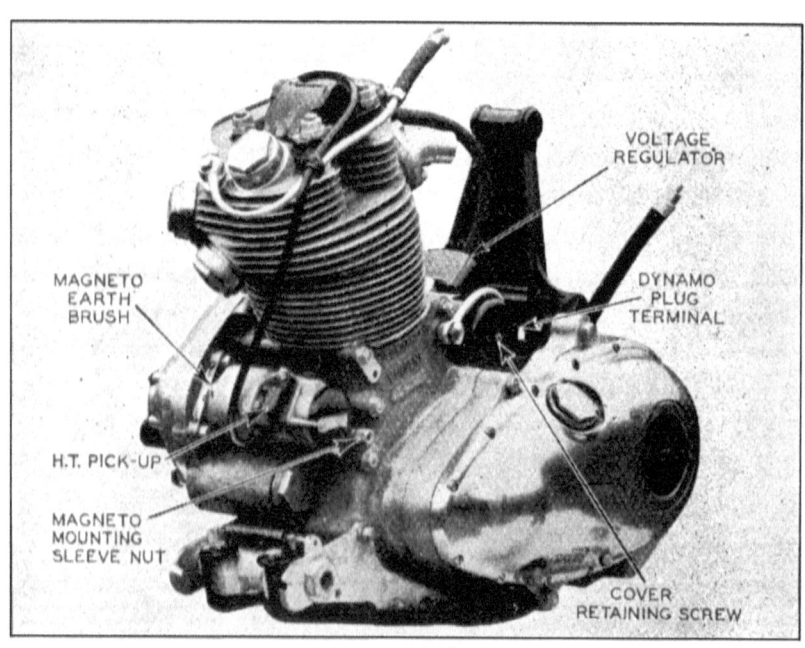

Fig. 70.—500-c.c. "Comet" Engine Showing Ignition and Electrical Equipment.

Over-adjustment renders the cartridge unfit for further use and if the desired results are not obtained the component should be returned to the manufacturers for attention. The dynamo can safely be run with the cartridge removed but the rate of charge will be high. Frequent need for adjustment may be due to vibration and in this case mounting the regulator on rubber may be advisable.

500-C.C. MODELS

The magneto contact-breaker points for the KIF GM2 instrument are made from tungsten and larger in diameter than those used in the Twin magneto; replacement points are cheaper.

Standard fitting of the electric horn is to the rear sidecar lug of the upper frame member. When it becomes necessary to use this lug for sidecar attachment, the horn must be removed to the left-hand pillion-footrest plate and mounted in the same way as on the Twins, i.e., with a distance piece and $\frac{3}{8}$-in. B.S.F. or equivalent bolt and nut.

The dynamo is driven from the idler gear, and when it becomes necessary to remove the instrument the timing cover only must be dismantled. The dynamo pinion is drilled and tapped 2 B.A. to facilitate withdrawal from the taper of the armature shaft with the aid of a simple extractor. The pinion boss must have a smooth, preferably polished, surface for the lip of the spring-loaded synthetic-rubber oil-seal, which is a press fit in the crankcase. This seal is fitted with the spring-loaded lip facing the drive pinion, thus preventing loss of oil from the timing chest. The pinion is retained by a spigot nut with plain washer.

CHAPTER X

RACING

THE standard specification of the road models is a compromise giving a good balance between such factors as performance, longevity, comfort and fuel economy. The aim is to provide the discriminating motor cyclist with a machine on which high average speeds can be obtained on public highways with maximum safety: in fact, certain models of the range are purposely de-tuned. This means that specific characteristics can be enhanced at the cost of sacrificing others, but it should be borne in mind that the road machines are not primarily designed for racing, which, in any case, invalidates the guarantee.

When deviating from the standard specification, the owner should carefully consider the exact purpose he has in mind, and naturally financial considerations enter into the matter to a large degree. A machine entered for speed events must be in first-class mechanical order throughout, and the owner who intends to undertake certain conversions himself should be satisfied that he possesses the necessary equipment and aptitude to do the job properly.

Vincent owners are fortunate, since many special parts for racing are often readily available, and it is possible to carry out a conversion in stages, thereby spreading the cost and labour involved over a longer period. It must be pointed out, however, that success in racing does not depend on the machine alone, and sometimes far too little attention is paid to the ability to *ride*. For high top speed on road or track the engine must be " wound up " in the intermediate gears, and a flat riding position is essential.

Standard Specifications

Standard sports and racing versions of the Vincent range are of great interest to the man who intends to race a road model, and close scrutiny of various details enables him to select such items as are suitable for his purpose. The performance of these versions is often a good indication of the results to be expected.

IA SPECIFICATION.—This derives its name from the engine type symbol, and whilst this specification covers the power unit only, the model is often referred to as a " White Shadow ". A few machines with this power unit have been manufactured, but quite a number of standard Rapides have been converted at a later date. Basically the unit is Rapide but modified to Black Shadow standards as follows :

> Valve rockers fully polished.
> High-compression pistons E7/7 (or E7/8 to order).
> Inlet ports streamlined and blended to carburetter adaptors.
> Combustion-chamber spheres and ports highly polished.
> $1\frac{1}{8}$-in. bore Amal carburetters fitted to bronze adaptors.
> Auxiliary valve springs.
> Lightened clutch-shoe carrier.
> Lightened cam-plate.
> Intermediate-ratio gearbox, giving 7·2 bottom gear.
> Laboratory tested Lucas KVF type magneto.

In cases where the conversion was carried out at an overhaul stage of the engine, polished high-tensile con-rods may have been fitted, in which event the big-end clearance will be to Black Shadow standards. A few assemblies have been fitted with forty-four rollers per row instead of forty-five to increase oil space. The makers have never undertaken the enamelling of used crankcases and covers.

BLACK SHADOW.—All the above mentioned parts also feature in this specification, but auxiliary valve springs were discontinued on later Shadows. Laboratory tested magnetos were no longer available after November 1950. On all Black Shadows, however, the cylinder heads, barrels, crankcase and covers are Pyluminised and finished in black stove enamel to improve heat dissipation and to prevent sea-water corrosion. Special cycle parts include ribbed cast-iron brake drums (ten hub bolts rear) and the exclusive 150-m.p.h. or 250-k.p.h. 5-in. (12·70-cm.) dial speedometer mounted on a central bracket for easy reading at speed.

Black Shadow specification parts are selected and fitted to special limits. The machine requires little preparation for racing, and its specification is well suited to the fast rider who likes to take part in occasional clubman's events.

BLACK LIGHTNING.—This is a stripped racing model based on the Black Shadow and not supplied for road work. Its specification is suitable for sprints, hill climbing, sidecar racing and solo road racing in the unlimited class as well as for establishing national speed records. The combustion-chamber spheres are fully polished, and the inlet ports opened out and streamlined to blend with adaptors for $1\frac{5}{32}$-in. (29·36-mm.), $1\frac{3}{16}$-in. (30·16-mm.) or 32-mm. (1·259-in.) 10 TT carburetters. High-compression pistons are fitted to order, giving compression ratios ranging from 7·3 for 75 octane petrol to 12·5 for alcohol fuels. The "Vibrac" con-rods are highly polished, and 1954 models have a caged-roller big end. Racing contour cams with high lift and long overlap are fitted, and the idler gear is made from case-hardened mild steel. A revolution counter with 8000 r.p.m. dial is standard, and ignition is by a manually controlled Lucas racing magneto. No kick-starter is provided, and a twenty-two-tooth final-drive sprocket is available for speeds in excess of 130 m.p.h. (210 k.p.h.). The racing-pattern rear chain may be $\frac{3}{8}$ in. (9·52 mm.) or

¼ in. (6·35 mm.) wide, with sprockets to suit. The racing gearbox has double backlash on third- and top-gear dogs. The 27-in. (68·5-cm.) diameter wheels with light-alloy rims improve handling and increase ground clearance. Brake plates are made from magnesium alloy, and the front components are fitted with air scoops. Regulation pattern racing mudguards cover 120 degrees of the front wheel and 180 degrees at the rear. Rearwardly mounted footrests have brake and gear levers arranged to suit. The light-weight seat is shaped for solo riding.

Weight Reduction

When preparing a road model for racing, the first step will be to remove all unnecessary equipment; obvious items are all the component parts of the lighting set, registration plates, etc., but the front engine plates with propstands and cowl can be dispensed with as well. If the front mudguard is shortened to 120 degrees the weight of the front stay will be saved, and it is the sum of numerous small savings which gives the required total. If removal of the kick-starter is permitted by the regulations, 4¼ lb. (2 kg.) is gained by dismantling the crank together with sundry parts inside the cover; for some sprints one or more brakes can be removed completely. Smaller savings in weight will be obtained by removing such items as hydraulic damper shrouds and battery carrier; the latter can be substituted by a length of tubing to fit between the pivot-bearing plates.

Substitution of certain parts by components made from lighter material is another good method of saving weight. Examples are the footrest-hanger distance pieces, pillion-footrest plates and brake-plates; some of these components are easy to make up locally, but they are also available as spares, and the time spent on making them up is probably well needed for other jobs. Numerous components can be lightened by drilling, e.g., damper knobs, front engine plates, battery-carrier platform, pillion-footrest plates, pivot-bearing lug, rear-brake torque stays, engine-mounting brackets, sprockets, etc., but care should be taken not to weaken the parts. Examination of a machine prepared by the Works or an experienced racing man is very instructive in this respect.

Engine Tuning

The inlet port of the standard head can be opened out to $1\frac{3}{16}$ in. (30·16 mm.) with safety, but on the rear head care is necessary when grinding, as there is not much metal between the port and the rocker box. A rotary grinder is required only if much material has to be removed, but usually the port and adaptor can be opened out with a strip of coarse emery cloth wound round a $\frac{1}{4}$-in. (6·35-mm.) diameter bar which is slotted at one end. The second finish is obtained with fine emery cloth, and the final mirror finish requires the use of high-speed equipment to rotate a felt mop with polishing soap.

The inlet port can usually be opened out a fair amount between the valve-guide boss and the port wall, but no metal must be removed from the upstream part of this boss; the lower end of the valve guide must not be shortened. On the other hand, it is important to note that the top end of the lower guide must be shortened by $\frac{1}{16}$ in. (1·58 mm.) when Lightning cams are fitted, in view of their higher lift.

The front-inlet rocker box may require grinding adjacent to the valve guide to provide maximum oil drainage, and all rocker bearings should be of the grooved pattern for the same purpose.

The valve rockers should be polished to equal weight, and tappet-adjuster lock-nuts of the later (thicker) pattern are required. Standard valves, springs and guides can be used for racing. Sometimes two front heads are used on Twins to take advantage of the slightly better turbulence of the front component. Auxiliary valve springs are no longer recommended.

COMPRESSION RATIOS.—The choice of ratio depends on the fuel to be used, and by way of a rough guide, for 80 octane a ratio of 8 : 1 is safe, but 9 : 1 is possible, especially on short circuits. Minimum piston clearance at the bottom of the skirt is 0·0055 in. (0·13 mm.), but for long-distance events up to 0·009 in. (0·22 mm.) is required, and although piston dimensions allow for the necessary clearance, an unfinished liner requires honing. The edges of the gudgeon-pin-boss recess should be relieved on both sides with the aid of a smooth file, and the gudgeon pin must be an *easy push fit* when cold. It is good practice to relieve the liner flange adjacent to each valve to increase the gas flow at this point. Rings for E7/9, E7/10 and E7/11 pistons are of wider radial thickness than those used on E7/6, E7/7 and E7/8; it is possible but not advisable to use the narrower rings on the high-compression pistons, but the wider rings must not be fitted to the lower-compression types. See the Appendix, Table VII.

FLYWHEELS.—As the flywheels are machined all over they need not be polished, although they are finished in this manner on Lightnings. Polishing the con-rods is, however, advisable, and the finished weight should be 1 lb. 5½ oz. + ½ oz. (610 grammes + 14 grammes). For serious racing, " Vibrac " rods of the Lightning specification are preferable. The standard big end is perfectly satisfactory for all clubman events, and has been successfully raced all over the world. It should not be over revved, however, and for this reason the machine should be geared to 5800 r.p.m. The caged-roller Lightning big end necessitates modified flywheels, and the supply is restricted to spares for production Black Lightning models only.

GEARS, CAMS AND PINIONS.—Bronze idler gears are unsuitable for racing, and should be replaced by the steel pattern, although the light-alloy gear has been used for racing with much success. The one-piece cast-iron breather may fail under racing conditions, and the assembly consisting of a steel pinion with alloy, bronze or cast-iron sleeve is required. Lightning cams definitely give increased performance, but it is not advisable to press these cams into used pinions. Due to manufacturing tolerances, it is not always possible to obtain the theoretical timing given in Table I of the Appendix, but a variation of 2 degrees is permissible. It is desirable to have the degrees of inlet opening greater than the exhaust closing, e.g., inlet opens 57, exhaust closes 53 is better than inlet opens 54, exhaust closes 58. It is frequently possible to obtain the better setting by using a different keyway in the half-time pinion. The exhaust-lifter mechanism can be removed completely.

LUBRICATION.—A bronze oil-pump worm should be replaced by the later steel pattern. In view of the heavier grades of oil recommended for racing, the cylinder-feed jet on Twins can be increased to 200–220; on Singles this is unnecessary. Metering wires may be removed, especially from the exhaust rocker-feed bolts. It is advisable to increase the diameter of the crankcase breather pipe and extend this to a point behind the rear axle. On Twins an oil-tank vent-pipe union can be used to replace the standard banjo and bolt.

Primary Drive and Gearbox

As fracture of the primary chain causes such extensive damage, it is a wise precaution to renew this component as well as the tensioner blade unless they are in as-new

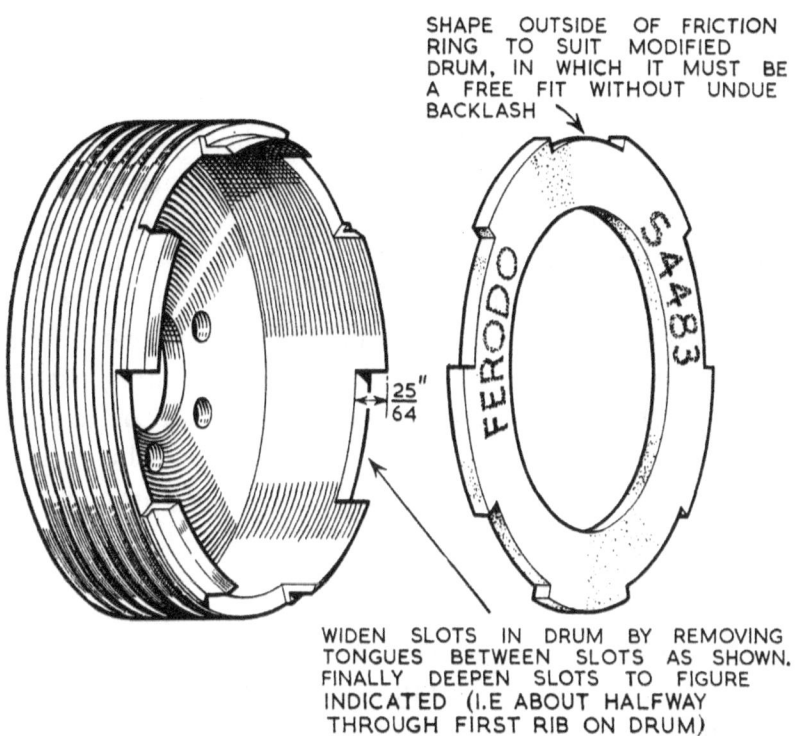

FIG. 71.—FITTING OF FRICTION RING TO EXISTING CLUTCH.

condition. Dynamo blanking plates are fitted with a ¼-in. B.S.F. bolt 1 in. long, with nut and spring washer.

Clutch oil-seals must be in good condition, and for maximum reliability it is as well to fit shoes with Duron P28B moulded linings, as these are impervious to oil. The shoe carrier can be lightened by drilling or a Black Shadow component substituted; the same applies to the plate carrier. The standard floating plate is suitable for clubman events, but for serious racing the Lightning pattern one-piece friction ring is better, and the existing drum can be modified as illustrated. The later type clutch cover with cut-away bottom gives greater ground clearance on left-hand bends, and ventilation is beneficial. An easy way of doing this is cutting a 2-in. (5-cm.)

hole in the centre and drilling a vertical row of ½-in. (12-mm.) holes through the rear portion.

The gearbox must have the latest pattern cam-plate part No. G32/2 or the lightened version G32/3. Fitting the 7·2 bottom gear necessitates a twenty-one-tooth layshaft first gear and a double gear with twenty-seven teeth on the large pinion. Converting the box to double backlash on third and top gear involves changing the constant-mesh pinion, double gear and third-gear pinion, which are all on the mainshaft. The Lightning pattern gears for this conversion may only be used in conjunction with each other and not with any others. The recommendations given in Chapter VI under " Gear-change Adjustment " are also fully applicable.

Carburation and Fuels

The straight-through exhaust system normally used for racing calls for an increase in main-jet size by experiment, and the correct size depends upon conditions obtaining at the time of the event. Rough indications for petrol are 180-200 main jet for $1\frac{1}{16}$-in. carburetters and 200–220 for $1\frac{1}{8}$-in. instruments. The standard carburetters are not suitable for alcohol fuels. The effect of the throttle valve cut-away and needle position on acceleration has already been mentioned in Chapter VIII. When adding Benzol to pump fuel it is not essential to mix equal proportions, and good results have been obtained with 25 per cent Benzol, which just takes the edge off lower octane petrol.

T.T. carburetters can be used with either petrol or alcohol fuels, merely by altering the main jet and needle jet. These carburetters are not provided with throttle stops, the idling speed is set on the control-cable adjusters; they are not normally recommended for road work. Note that on T.T. carburetters the pilot screw is turned

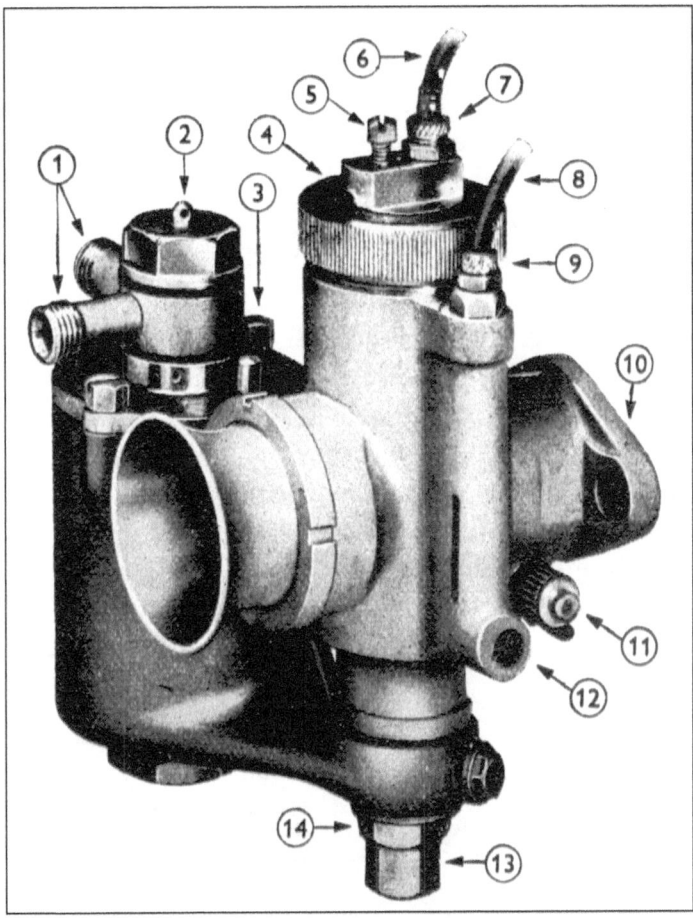

Fig. 72.—"Amal" T.T. Carburetter.

The later models are marked Type 10 T.T.9: they differ from the earlier models prior to 1949 in that they have type 302 top feed float chamber, throttles operated by a large conical spring, and the locking device for the mixing chamber ring is now a leaf spring.

1. Banjo (Twin) 90°, horizontal petrol-pipe connections.
2. Banjo nut with hole for security wire.
3. Float chamber cover screw. See tickler below for flooding.
4. Mixing-chamber Cap and screwed ring.
5. Adjusting Screw * for Lock Plunger, to secure ring No. 4.
6. Throttle Cable.
7. Throttle Cable Adjuster with lock nut.
8. Air Cable for mixture control.
9. Air-cable Adjuster with lock-nut.
10. Flange Attachment to Engine alternative to clip fitting.
11. Pilot-needle, adjustment for slow running.
12. Mixture Control Boss. Air admitted through slot.
13. Jet-holder Plug Screw, remove to get at main jet.
14. Jet Holder, also holds float chamber to mixing chamber body.

* The latest models do not have this screw: the lock ring 4 is now secured by a leaf spring, the end of which presses into the serrations of the ring.

clockwise to weaken the slow-running mixture, and this adjustment covers a wider range than on the standard instruments. The $1\frac{5}{32}$-in. and $1\frac{3}{16}$-in. flange-fitting types are no longer supplied by the Works, nor their adaptors, but excellent results will be obtained with the clip-fitting 32-mm. 10TT9 instruments, for which adaptors are normally available. Tanks which do not have the larger cut-away can be modified by welding, and sometimes an extra rear mounting rubber will assist in obtaining the necessary clearance for the front air intake carburetter. The standard battery carrier will be in the way of the rear float chamber, but if it is essential to retain the carrier it can be modified for mounting over to the left.

Approximate settings are as follows, but given by way of a rough guide only :

Pistons.	Fuel.	Needle Jet.	Throttle Valve.	Main Jet.
E7/7	Petrol over 75 octane	0·109	6	400–460
E7/9	50/50 petrol/Benzol	0·109	7	500
E7/10	33/33/33 blend	0·113	8	1000
E7/11	80/10/10 alcohol	0·120	8	1600–1800

The composition of 33/33/33 is ⅓ methanol, ⅓ Benzol and ⅓ petrol, and in 80/10/10 the alcohol percentage is increased to 80. Alcohol fuels do not give the usual warnings of a weak mixture, such as spitting, etc. Whilst " Dope " runs cool in a correct mixture, over-heating is quite possible due to the oxygen contents of these fuels. Weakness often results in a hole being burnt in the piston crown.

The use of castor-base oils calls for certain precautions and more frequent cleaning of the engine internally, and lubricants of this type are more suitable for the man with vast racing experience.

Ignition and Revolution Counter

When entering a converted standard machine for an important event it is a wise precaution to return the magneto to the manufacturers or a first-class specialist for a check-over, stating the event in which the instrument will be used. Colder (i.e., " harder ") sparking-plugs are necessary for most events (see comparison chart, Fig. 73); for serious racing obtain expert advice on the selection of a suitable racing plug.

The automatic timing control is also suitable for racing, and a manually-controlled instrument is only necessary when it comes to bump-starting a Twin with very high compression. When starting the motor in this manner rock back against the compression of the *rear* cylinder to take advantage of the longer duration of the flywheel inertia.

The Lucas KVF T.T. magneto can, of course, be used for road work as well, but when fitted to a Twin the top pick-up cannot be unscrewed without removing the magneto from the machine. The Tufnol driving gear is mounted on a boss with four 2 B.A. × 1-in. high-tensile bolts which also retain the revolution counter drive dog. This part rotates the drive fork, which is clamped on the tongue of the revolution-counter gear-box screwed to a special drive cover. The gearbox can be of the 1 : 1 reduction type for use with a 2 : 1 reduction head, or alternatively 2 : 1 reduction with a 4 : 1 reduction head; the Works supply the latter set-up, but the two gearboxes are dimensionally identical.

The revolution counter and drive are normally available as spares, and could be fitted to a standard machine but for the fact that the drive parts replace the automatic timing control, which is essential for starting unless the ignition can be retarded by other means. Parts for converting

K.L.G. Racing Plugs—Resistance to Heat and Oil

14-mm. Plugs.	K.L.G. Ceramic (S.749).	K.L.G. Mica.
"Hard" plug (withstanding most heat and least oil)	F.340 FE.340	— —
	F.320 FE.320	875 875.LR
	F.310 FE.310	— —
	F.300 FE.300	731 731.LR
Intermediate	F.290 FE.290	689 689.LR
	F.280 FE.280	646 646.LR
	F.250 FE.250	690 690.LR
"Soft" plug (withstanding most oil and least heat)	F.220 * FE.220 *	— —

* Detachable.

Meaning of K.L.G. Code Letters

```
F  = 14 mm. diameter thread and 12·5 mm. reach
FE =     ,,         ,,         ,,    18      ,,
LR =     ,,         ,,         ,,    18      ,,
```

the standard magneto to manual control are, however, not supplied, and this is the reason why the revolution counter requires the Lucas KVF T.T. magneto which is the only production 50-degree manual magneto available. Designs to take the drive from the stationary portion of the timing control were not successful in practice, and only a few of the Lightning drive parts can be used for this purpose.

RACING

	BERU	FIRESTONE	AUTO-LITE	A.C. U.S.A.	CHAMPION U.S.A.	K.L.G	CHAMPION ENGLAND	A.C. ENGLAND	LODGE	BOSCH	MARELLI	TO CURE FOULING FIT THIS K.L.G PLUG	TO CURE OVERHEATING FIT THIS K.L.G PLUG
HOT	95/14					F20		48	BB 14 BB 14S	W.95T1	CW.95A CW 125		F50
		F 120-F	A.11	49	J.14 J.12	TFS20	J.12		BAN BS 14	W 95T3	CW 95B		TFS30
	E 95/14 95/14/3					FE20	N 7		BL 14	W 95T2			FE30
			A.9	47, 48, 46.5 46, 46 Com 47 Com 48X	J-11	TFS30		47 Com F 9 48 Com		W 125T3	CW 145B CW 125A	TFS20	TFS50
						FE30					CW 145B	FE20	FE50
	145/14 E 145/14		AT 8 AE 6 AN 7	45L	L-10	F50	L-10 L-8	F.10	B.14, C N C 14	W 145T1 W 145T7	CW 145C CW 125C CW 125D	F20	F70
	145/14/5 145/6.16 E 145/14/5	F 80-F	A.7	41, 44 Com 46 X, 44.5 45, 44.5 Com	J-8	TFS50	J-8	VF 9, 45 44 Com	CAN	W 145T3	CW 125B CW 145B CW 145A	TFS30	FS70
14 mm			A E.10	45XL	NA-7 N-8	FE50	N8B. N-8	FL 9	CL 14, CB 14 HLNP, HLNR CLN	W 145T2		FE30	FE70
		F 50-LF	AL 7	44 L 43L Com 45L 45L Com	H-10	FA50	H.10	45L	CS 14				FA70
	175a, 14S E 175/14				L.10S	F70	L.10S		H 14 HNP H 14B, HH.14 2 HN	W 175T1	CW 175A CW 175E	F50	F80
	175/14/5 175/6.16 E 175/14/5	F 40-F	A 5 AN 5 AT 4 A 3	42 S 43 Com	J.7, J.6 J.3, J.6J	FS70	J-10 Com	44	HAN	W 175T4 W 225T3	CW 175B CW 175C CW 175D	TFS50	
	175/14/3 200/14/3		AL 5	43L	NA-8 H 9 H 9 Com	FE70	NA 8		HL 14S HL 14	W 175T2	CW 175F	FE50	FE80
						FA70		43L			CW 225B		
	225/14 225/14LU E 225/14			42 Com		F80			HN	W 225T7 W 225T1 W 225T6	CW 225A CW 225E	F70	F100
	E 200/14/3					FE80			HLN	W 225T2		FE70	FE100
	240/14 260/14 E 240/14				L 11S	F100	L 11S		HHN 3HN	W 240T1 W 240T7 W 260T1	CW 240A CW 260B	F80	
COLD	240/14/3 260/13/3				NA-10	FE100	NA 10		HHLN 3HLN	W 240T8 W 240T2	CW 240B CW 260A	FE80	

FIG. 73.—K.L.G. SPARKING-PLUG COMPARISON CHART.

Exhaust Systems

For full benefit Lightning cams should be fitted in conjunction with high-compression pistons, 32-mm. carburetters and straight-through exhaust pipes, 2 in. (50·80 mm.) diameter and 44 in. (111·7 cm.) long. The latter give an increase in maximum power at the expense of loss of flexibility below 4500 r.p.m. If twin pipes of $1\frac{5}{8}$ in. (41·27 mm.) are used the length should be 54–56 in. (137·1–142·2 cm.), and they are the better choice for short circuits; the 2-in. pipes are more suitable for sprints and fast courses. Twin pipes cannot be used with the standard kick-starter, and their greater width tends to reduce ground clearance on bends. For many events an extension to the standard pipes to replace the silencer is a very good solution; the tail end should be level with the rear axle. The 2-in. pipes are mounted to the standard exhaust port by means of short $1\frac{5}{8}$-in. stubs which take lightened nuts of standard pattern. This gives a certain extractor effect, but megaphones do not answer well to any of the production cams.

Cycle Parts

Light-alloy rims are not suitable for everyday road use, but excellent if a model is mainly kept for racing; high-tensile steel rims have been used in trials and by sidecar racing men, but are not normally available as spares. Racing tyres are essential for all serious racing, but here again it should be borne in mind that a racing cover has not been designed to give maximum long life for everyday road use. The magnesium-alloy air scoops of the racing brake-plates can also be fitted to the standard steel front plates. This job is within the scope of a private owner and well worth doing.

Note that no thin nuts are used on the front hollow axle

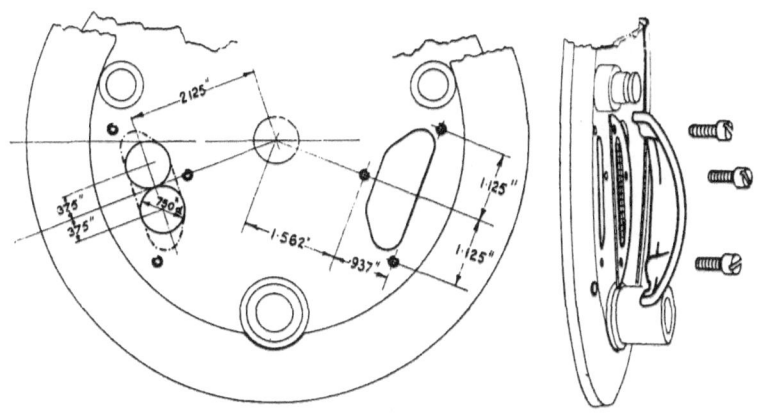

Fig. 74.—Fitting Air Scoops to Standard Front-brake Plates.

with racing brake-plates, as these are endwise located by the fork-ends direct. The brake cam-bushes in these plates are self-oiling.

A shortened Touring pattern handlebar turned upside down makes a good sprint bar, and it is always advisable to shorten the rear chain guard to facilitate wheel removal. A front mudguard which has been shortened too much on a road machine will throw up spray from the wheel straight on to the headlamp. On Series B models the recommended front-fork spring for racing is 180 lb., and this number is usually stamped on the taper nut; the girder should be braced for sidecar racing. The hydraulic damper can easily be fitted to a Series B machine to curb liveliness of the back end. The finger adjusters can be removed from the chain-adjuster assemblies by driving out the pin, and weight is saved by merely using the threaded part with a lock-nut. The racing dualseat lowers the riding position and also saves weight, but there is no attachment for the tool-tray. This seat is not designed for pillion riding. The standard brake and gear-change levers can be reversed for racing or substituted by parts of the Lightning pattern when available. The

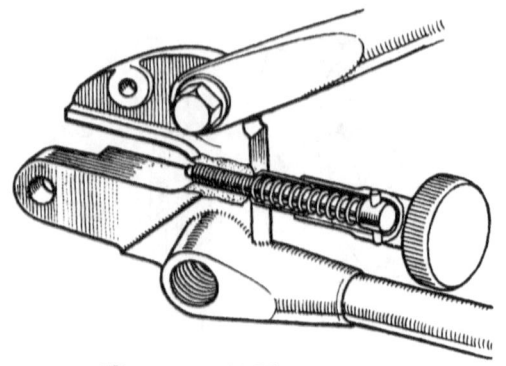

Fig. 75.—Details of Chain Adjuster.

[*By courtesy of "The Motor Cycle", London.*]

drilling and wiring up of sundry bolts and nuts follows normal racing practice; examples are the exhaust-pipe nuts, brake cam-spindle nuts, front-fork spring-box pivots, etc.

Sprockets and Gearing

Some riders labour under the misapprehension that a higher gear ratio will give greater speed, but the reverse is often the case, especially if the run-up for a certain event is less than 1 mile (1·6 km.). The standard models all pull a fairly high top gear, and on the Twins a forty-eight-tooth rear-wheel sprocket is suitable for many circuits. This size is also pleasant for road work, as both acceleration and flexibility are improved. Correct gearing calls for experience as well as experiment, as so many conditions affect this matter. Take, for example, a 1-mile sprint on sand : for a Twin on alcohol fuel forty-five teeth will suit, whereas the same machine on 80 octane petrol requires forty-eight teeth.

As the Vincent engine does not normally suffer from valve bounce at high r.p.m., it is easy to over-rev to the detriment of reliability. Short bursts of 6000 r.p.m. and over are not harmful, but over-indulgence in this respect is bound to lead to trouble sooner or later. The racing

M.P.H. at 6000 R.P.M. (1000-c.c. Engine).

Gear Ratio.	27-in. Wheel.	26-in. Wheel.	Gear Ratio.	27-in. Wheel.	26-in. Wheel.	Gear Ratio.	27-in. Wheel.	26-in. Wheel.
2·9	161·5	157·75	3·63	128·5	126	4·21	111	108
3·04	153	150	3·67	126·5	124	4·32	108·5	105·5
3·19	146·5	143·5	3·73	125·5	122·5	4·45	105	102·5
3·27	143	140	3·79	123·5	120·5	4·54	102·5	101
3·34	140·5	137·5	3·86	121	118	4·62	101·5	99
3·42	137·5	134·5	3·96	119	116	4·70	99·5	97·25
3·47	135	132	4·0	117	114	4·78	97·75	95·5
3·50	133	130	4·06	115	112·75	4·95	95·5	92·25
3·54	131·5	128·5	4·1	114	111			
3·60	130	127	4·16	112	110			

big end of the 1954 Lightning pattern will stand up to longer periods of 6500 r.p.m. and over.

Racing machines can have sprockets and rear chains of ¼ in. or ⅜ in. width; the former are lighter and the better choice for serious racing. Standard chains have been used with success in racing, and indeed in record attempts, but special racing chains are preferable. With either type the connecting link should have soft pin ends for riveting.

500-c.c. Models

The Grey Flash closely follows the Black Lightning specification as far as the engine is concerned. The primary chaincase is ventilated, and standard fitting is the Albion gearbox, for which a wide choice of ratios is available. The racing machine has ratio No. 5, with no provision for a kick-starter, but some machines were supplied in dual-purpose form with kick-starter and No. 16 ratio. Standard fitting is a four-plate clutch, but conversion to five plates and reinforcement of the clutch case is possible. As delivered a forty-six-tooth rear-wheel sprocket was normally fitted.

Sand blasting is the standard finish for crankcase, covers, inspection caps, etc., and cycle parts are either dull chromed or stove enamelled in grey; very few have been finished in black, the engine included. Petrol taps are of the lever type, and the exhaust pipe is a straight-through 2-in. (50·80-mm.) diameter component, except on dual-purpose machines, which feature a 1⅝-in. (41·27-mm.)

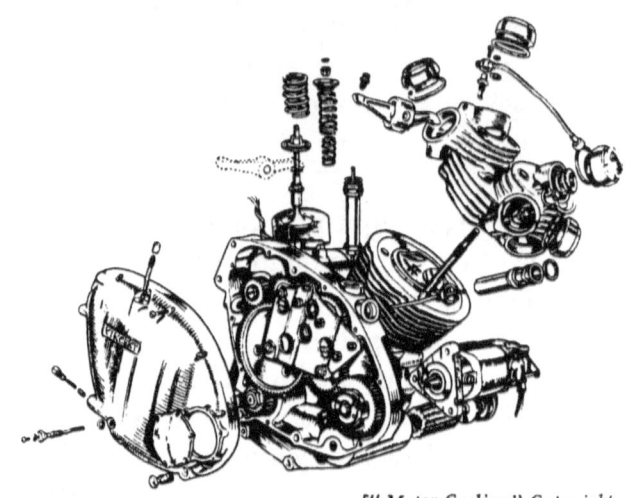

["*Motor Cycling*" *Copyright.*

FIG. 76.—THE "GREY FLASH" ENGINE, DUAL-PURPOSE MODEL.

diameter pipe with standard silencer. Racing wheels complete the specification of the machine, which is very suitable for short-circuit work and so obviously a "Lightningised" version of the Comet that many details are very worth while considering when hotting-up a standard machine.

Gearbox

At one time the Burman BAP gearbox could be converted to close-ratio by replacing all shafts and gears, but at present the necessary parts are not readily obtainable. For serious racing it is possible, however, to fit the Albion gearbox to a Meteor or Comet, and the following fittings are required if available :

RACING 159

1 pivot plate, offside	G50/2
1 gearbox bolt, lower	F48/8
1 ,, ,, upper	F48/9
1 rear frame-tie bolt	F48/10
2 gearbox links instead of one	F102/1 and F102/2
1 pivot-bearing spacer	F103/1
1 battery bracket	F111/1
3 gearbox sleeves	F117/1, /2 and /3

The connecting link of the primary chain must also be of the riveting type, and the use of a cranked double link is not permissible for racing. The B.T.H. T.T. magneto with manual control also fits Comet and Meteor models. Dynamo blanking plates differ from those used on Twins.

Speedway Engine

Reference must be made of the Speedway engine, of which a small batch was manufactured during 1949, some with Y-alloy, others with magnesium-alloy crankcase. The case is very similar to the pre-war " Comet ", but features a different cam-box and four-stud cylinder mounting enabling the use of the post-war " Rapide " head and barrel, the latter with turned-down cooling fins.

The timing gear is of pre-war pattern, with exception of the camshaft, which is a special component, as the relative positions of inlet and exhaust cam are reversed on pre-war and post-war machines. The cam followers are of pre-1940 pattern and not interchangeable with the post-war type; the idler gear is a steel component. There is no engine-shaft shock absorber, and the special drive-side mainshaft takes a sliding sprocket with twenty-three generated teeth for $\frac{1}{2}$-in. pitch single-row chain. The timing-side mainshaft is also a special part, and at the time of delivery alternative engine sprockets from fifteen teeth upwards were available.

Lubrication is by Pilgrim PH152 Duplex oil pump on the total-loss system, for which the cylinder liner is

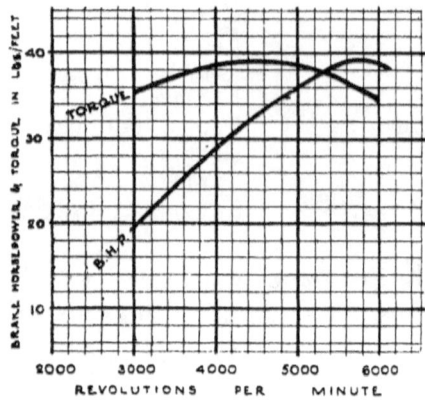

Fig. 77.—Performance Curves of Speedway Engine Equipped with $1\frac{1}{8}$-in. Amal Track-type Carburetter and Using Methanol Fuel.

specially drilled. An external oil pipe with T-piece leads lubricant to the rockers and from there back into the timing chest through push-rod tubes of post-war pattern. These engines are fitted with a $1\frac{1}{8}$-in. (28·57-mm.) twin-float Amal Track carburetter, but for maximum power at high revs a $1\frac{3}{16}$-in. (30·16-mm.) 10 TT carburetter is recommended. The 2-in. diameter exhaust pipe should be 56 in. (1·42 m.) long. The big end has forty-four rollers per row, and auxiliary valve springs are standard. Cam-box retention is by $\frac{1}{4}$-in. B.S.W. Allen screws. Original equipment sparking-plug: Champion NA-14.

CHAPTER XI

SIDECARS, ACCESSORIES AND EXTRA EQUIPMENT

THE Vincent Big Twins are so obviously ideal for sidecar work that the question sometimes arises whether the 500-c.c. models will give equal satisfaction. The answer is that they do, provided due allowance is made for the smaller engine capacity when assessing performance. A sidecar can be fitted to the right or to the left; some British makes are available adapted for mounting alongside a Vincent, and should be ordered as such. Almost any sidecar can be fitted, provided the rear lower connection is brought forward to a point adjacent to the mounting bracket on the machine, and whilst three-point mounting has been used, four-point fixing is preferable. Parts for adapting an existing sidecar should be obtained

FIG. 78.—"BLACKNELL" SIDECAR CHASSIS WITH FITTINGS FOR VINCENT MACHINES.

from the manufacturers of the chassis or sidecar specialists, although a local motor-cycle dealer is often in a position to assist. It is *never* permissible to fit the sidecar to the rear fork of the machine, in spite of the fact that the lugs in the rear fork ends may be tapped ¾ in. × 20 T.P.I.; they were originally intended for torque stays of a special chassis which is not in production.

Recent developments in sidecar design, such as wheel springing or sidecar brake, are also suitable for the Vincent machine. A sidecar outfit is a very attractive

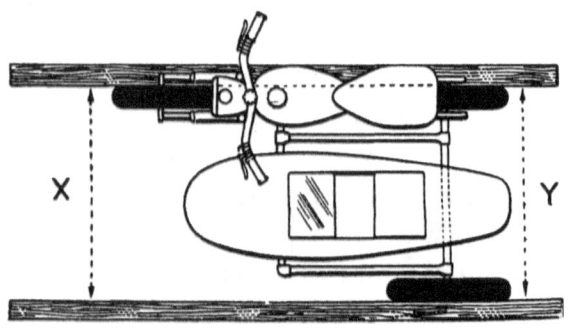

FIG. 79.—TOE-IN EQUALS THE DIFFERENCE BETWEEN DIMENSIONS X AND Y.

proposition from many a point of view, provided the handling qualities are not marred by poor fitting.

Sidecar Alignment

Correct alignment is to some extent a matter of experiment, also influenced by personal preferences of the rider. No hard-and-fast rules apply, but it is generally accepted that the sidecar wheel should be 2 in.–to 3 in. (50·80–76·20 mm.) in front of the rear wheel of the machine, although a lead up to 9 in. (22·86 cm.) is possible. Toe-in of the sidecar wheel relative to the track of the machine should be between ½ in. (12·70 mm.) and 1½ in. (38·10 mm.), and lean-out of the motor cycle measured at the steering-head may vary between ½ in. (12·70 mm.) and 1 in. (25·40 mm.). The inner corner of the sidecar

SIDECARS, ACCESSORIES AND EXTRA EQUIPMENT 163

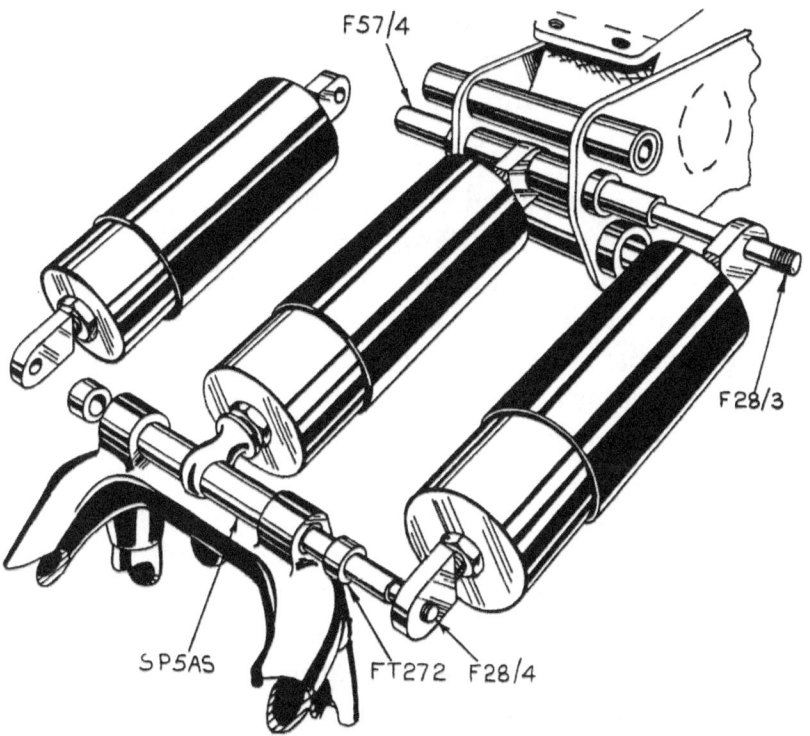

FIG. 80.—THREE-SPRING FITTING.

chassis should be slightly higher than the outside, to ensure that the chassis will be parallel with the ground with the rider seated. For extra heavy loads the hydraulic damper can be substituted by a third spring-box assembly. If front-spoke fracture is experienced, move the sidecar chassis *forward* to increase stability on corners away from the chair, thereby relieving front-wheel stress.

Sidecar Conversion

Conversion of a machine to sidecar trim is straightforward, and for all post-war models the following parts are required:

> Larger *rear-wheel* sprocket, with ten screws, nuts and shake-proof washers.

Heavier rear-frame springs, " O " S.W.G., 0·324 in. (8·30 mm.) wire diameter.

Sidecar-mounting bracket.

Length of rear chain with extra connecting link.

Series B models require in addition, sidecar-type top front-fork links and a 180-lb. front-fork spring, but the latter is standard fitting on all later Series B machines. The " Girdraulic " forks of the Series C range require no additional parts, as variation of trail automatically alters the effective spring strength. The Meteor and the Grey Flash must be equipped with front engine plates and front stand pivot.

Sidecar-pattern handlebars (see Chapter I), whether straight or upswept, are always recommended, in view of their greater leverage. The fifty-six-tooth rear-wheel sprocket is a good all-round size for most outfits, 1000 as well as 500 c.c. The latter require fifty-eight teeth if the sidecar is a heavy two-seater, and on Twins fifty-four or fifty-two teeth can be used for lighter loads by the man who does not object to using his gearbox. The sixty-tooth sprocket, the largest in the range, is suitable for competition work or for towing a light trailer. Sprocket screws are fitted with the nuts and washers on the *inside*

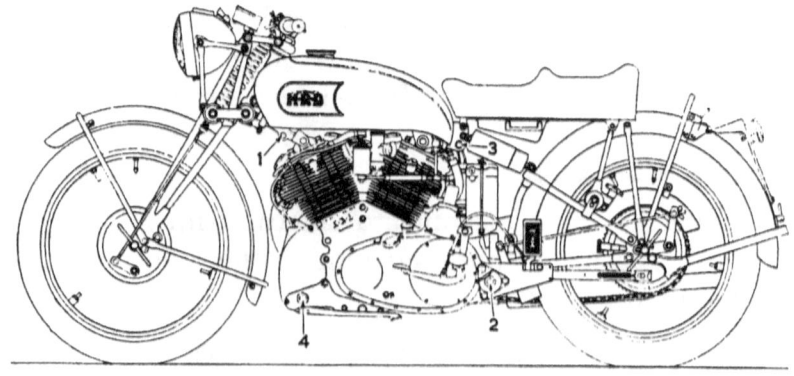

FIG. 81.—SIDECAR PICK-UP POINTS.

SIDECARS, ACCESSORIES AND EXTRA EQUIPMENT

of the brake-drum flange, and should be occasionally checked for tightness.

Touring Models

Touring equipment is optional for Comet and Rapide models, and whilst the mechanical specification remains the same, machines in Touring trim are favoured by riders in certain overseas markets as well as by sidecar enthusiasts. Touring and Sidecar specifications combined give a machine often referred to as " Sidecar Tourer ", and the components making up either trim can easily be incorporated in standard models.

A Touring model as delivered from the Works features " cow-horn " handlebars, and the fitting of these to later standard machines only necessitates a longer throttle-cable assembly, which is available as a spare. The steel mudguards are deeply valanced and black enamelled. A $3 \cdot 50 \times 19$ in. ribbed front tyre is fitted to a WM2 rim, and the rear tyre size is $4 \cdot 00 \times 18$ in. on a WM3 rim. These tyres are run at slightly lower inflation pressures and give greater comfort with better wear.

For solo work, the Touring specification detracts somewhat from the performance, one of the reasons being increased weight. Steel mudguards are $7\frac{3}{4}$ lb. ($3 \cdot 51$ kg.) heavier than a pair of alloy blades, and the Touring wheels increase the weight by a further 7 lb. ($3 \cdot 17$ kg.). From a handling point of view the wider-section tyres are a slight disadvantage when partly worn, but this will be noticeable only on a solo machine.

Tyres and Pressures

The ribbed front tyre enhances the steering qualities of the machine to a remarkable degree, and a studded-tread pattern is only recommended for competitions or sometimes sidecar work. A $4 \cdot 00 \times 19$-in. tyre *can* be fitted

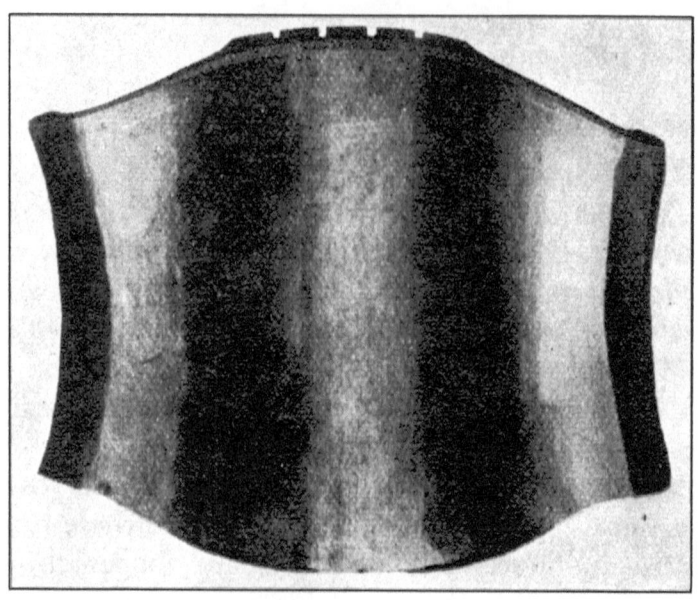

Fig. 82.—Darkening of Inside of Tyre Casing, Indicative of Under-inflation.

to standard models with the later type rear fork, but even on these this size leaves little clearance between cover and mudguard, although fouling is not to be expected. The point is, however, that a 4-in. (10·16-cm.) section tyre requires a WM3 rim for adequate support, and with the standard WM2 rim tyre roll may be experienced. A front tyre will eventually wear somewhat more on one side due to road camber, and it is good practice to reverse the cover when this becomes noticeable.

Most motor cyclists are well aware of the great importance of correct tyre pressures, but the reliability of an old pressure gauge should not be taken for granted; checking the instrument against another of known accuracy may pay dividends. Valve caps are to be regarded as an essential fitting, also from an additional safety point of view. The inflation pressures given in Table IV of the Appendix are to some extent a compromise, and may be varied slightly to suit particular conditions of operation or tyres of other manufacture than the " Avon " original equipment.

The Dualseat

The seat is of " Feridax " manufacture, and component parts other than the cover and tool-tray are not supplied as spares, although the Service Exchange Scheme applies on the home market. Screws at the underside of the component should not be undone, as they are fitted with nuts, and if these come adrift the whole seat must be dismantled !

Adjustment for height is at the rear only by unscrewing the eye ends of the stays. To counteract the rider sliding forwards the front mounting bracket was lengthened by $\frac{5}{8}$ in. (15·87 mm.) on 1954 machines. Early seat-stay assemblies had alloy shanks riveted to the clamps and if trouble with working loose is experienced welding makes a very effective repair. Later machines feature cadmium-plated steel shanks.

The Dualseat cannot be lowered without danger of the rear portion fouling the mudguard, and a rider who is unusually short in the leg can only reduce the seat height by reducing the thickness of the " Dunlopillo " squab.

The Tool-kit

The tool-kit may vary in detail on different machines, but normally the items illustrated are supplied. Workshops should use a $\frac{3}{4}$-in. B.S.W. solid socket wrench for crank-pin and shock-absorber nuts, and a $\frac{5}{8}$-in. B.S.W. ring-spanner for the half-time pinion nut. A $\frac{5}{8}$-in. B.S.W. open-ended flat spanner is handy for the hollow axle and battery-carrier nuts. Box spanners in $\frac{3}{4}$-in. and 1-in. B.S.W. sizes can be used on the steering-column and final-drive sprocket nuts. Useful reamers are $\frac{1}{2}$ in., $\frac{7}{8}$ in. and

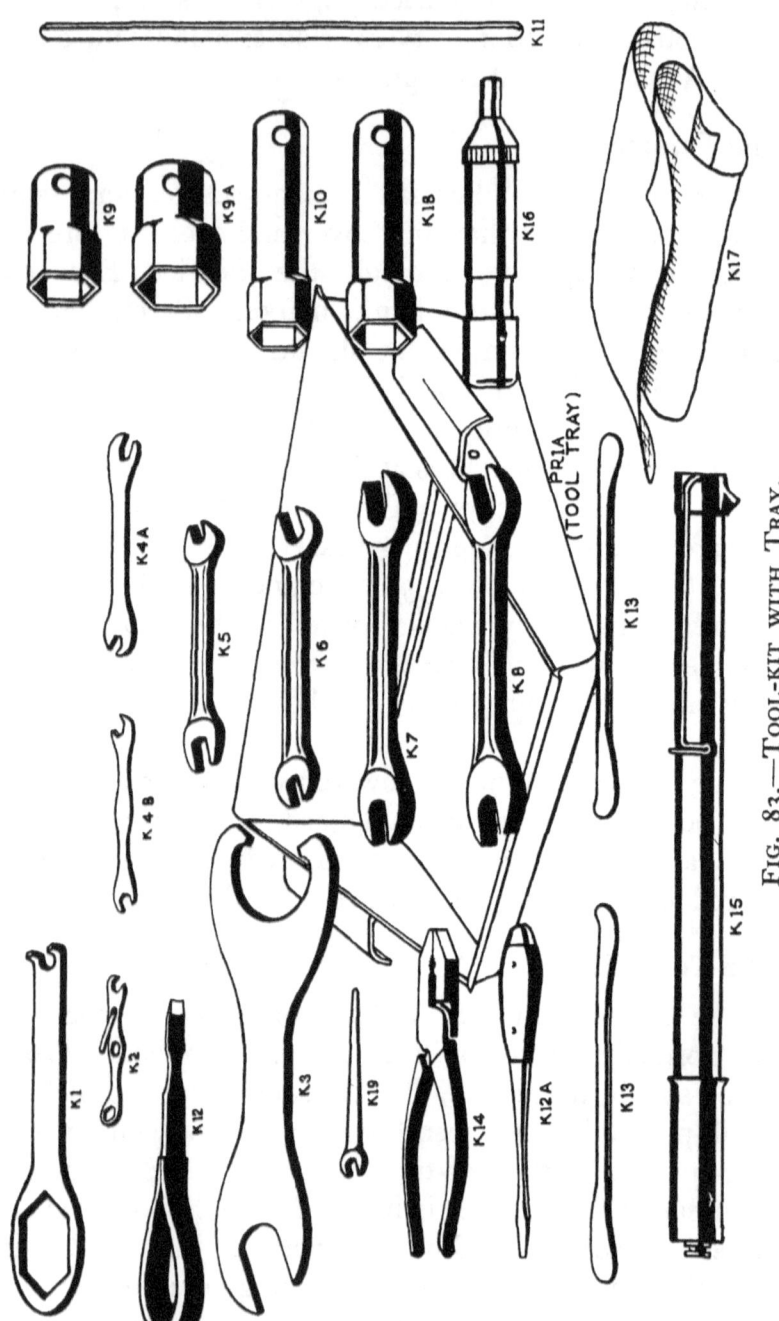

Fig. 83.—Tool-kit with Tray.

1 in. for the clutch shoes, small-end bush, and oil-pump bore in the crankcase respectively.

Panniers and Crashbars

All pannier equipment affects the high-speed handling to some extent, and for this reason the earlier Vincent pannier set was relatively small, the dimensions of the cases being $10\frac{1}{2} \times 11\frac{1}{2} \times 5\frac{1}{2}$ in. ($26 \times 29 \times 14$ cm.). The 1953 Vincent equipment was designed for heavy loads, and at the front end it is attached to a long bolt which replaces the original front mounting bolt of the dualseat. The tool-tray is permanently placed in the runners at the underside of the luggage platform. The horizontal bars of this set are mounted with the rear lug facing *upwards*, and the forward attachment points of the platform also carry the pannier frames, which are further supported by the down tubes. These are fitted to the rearmost hole in each pillion-footrest plate.

Proprietary pannier sets can be fitted or frames made up, but unsprung luggage affects handling, and heavy loads on the rear mudguard should be avoided. The Vincent crashbars have been supplied black enamelled or chromium plated. Proprietary leg-shields can be fitted if desired.

Air Cleaners and Petrol-tank Cover

Amal cleaners of the gauze-element type do not normally require carburetter adjustments. Filters of Vokes manufacture call for a reduction in main jet size to the next lower number, and the three-ply element requires washing out in petrol every 2000 miles. Pink-coloured elements are meant to be wetted with Trifiltrene oil; if this is not available very thin engine oil can be used. Air cleaners reduce the volumetric efficiency of the engine to some extent, but they are recommended if a machine is frequently used in dusty areas, e.g., continental touring. Change the elements every 10,000 miles.

Petrol-tank covers as supplied by the Works protect the tank fully without adding to the width as in the case of knee-grips. Another advantage is that light parcels can be carried and the felt lining damps sound.

Handlebar Screens

Some proprietary screens are available complete with fittings for mounting to a Vincent, and it is now generally accepted that this equipment does not detract from the performance of the machine. As an aid to comfort many riders find a handlebar screen conducive to higher average speeds, and if correctly adjusted for height night riding in wet weather will be facilitated, as goggles are unnecessary. Equipment of this nature amplifies sound, and careful fitting may be necessary in conjunction with a sidecar to avoid side-draughts just behind the rider's screen.

U.S.A. Specification

A number of machines finished in Chinese Red were shipped to the U.S.A., and after 1952 some models featured a higher compression ratio. The sealed-beam headlamp equipment has already been mentioned in Chapter IX.

Service Exchange (Home Market Only)

The " Service Exchange Scheme " covers a wide range of components, and the advantages of rapid service, Works standards of manufacture and inspection, as well as automatic incorporation of the latest improvements, are obvious.

Service Exchange prices apply only if the original part has been received at the Works or Vincent spares stockist and passed as suitable for re-conditioning. The Scheme is automatically in force on all spares orders and repairs unless specifically instructed to the contrary.

Vincent Owners Club

This club, founded in 1948, is not sponsored by the Works, but an entirely independent organisation, whose aim is the furtherance of social and sporting activities in the interests of motor cycling in general and of the Vincent marque in particular. There are numerous local sections in the United Kingdom, as well as in countries and continents overseas. The monthly journal *M.P.H.* is often said to hold a unique position amongst motor-cycle-club publications.

CHAPTER XII

THE SERIES "A" MODELS

WHILST no Series A machines have been manufactured since 1939, this range of models has remained very up-to-date, no doubt due to the advanced design. Many features of the Series A machines have been continued in the B and C Series with only slight detail alterations, and numerous principles described in the previous chapters for the post-war machines are applicable to the Series A machines. Examples are the taper-roller bearings, brakes, rear chains, head-races, Burman gearbox, clutch, carburation, rear suspension, wheels, big end, electric horn, battery, sprockets, etc.

Present owners are fortunate, as many spares are still obtainable, and numerous items such as big-end parts, con-rods, pistons, piston-rings, front-fork components, rims, frame springs, wheel bearings, etc., are interchangeable with the post-war Series. Other Series B and C components, such as mudguards, " Girdraulic " forks, dualseats, etc., can be adapted without much difficulty, and a pre-war model can be modernised with water excluders, finger chain adjusters, $\frac{7}{8}$-in. (22·22-mm.) diameter handlebars, controls, etc.

Maintenance data will be found in the tables of the Appendix, and the following paragraphs give information on matters peculiar to the Series A range.

Frame and Forks

With the engine removed it is advisable to connect one of the gearbox plates with the lower down tube lug of the front frame if the machine is likely to be wheeled;

a strip of mild steel can easily be drilled with two holes for this purpose. Fracture of tubes is most unlikely, but may happen due to incorrect sidecar fitting, and in this event a new tube can be brazed into the frame lugs. Frames which are not too badly crashed can still be returned to the Works for rectification, and when looking for a second-hand replacement remember that the front frame of the preceding J.A.P. and Python engined models interchanges or requires slight modification only.

Originally the head-races were all cups, but the post-war cup-and-cone layout can be used if the outside diameter of the cups is slightly reduced; to avoid exposure of the lower bearing balls these can be enclosed by a simple shroud. Note the screwed location of the steering-damper anchor plate.

Apart from dimensional differences with the Series B forks, the pre-war component is *not bushed* and grease nipples are fitted. Many parts, such as links and spindles, are, however, interchangeable, and Series B self-lubricating porous bronze bushes can be used to overhaul a pre-war set if the lugs are bored out. Insufficient greasing of spindles may cause these to seize in their lugs, and in extreme cases the application of heat and/or penetrating oil will be necessary. A really obstinate spindle can often be removed after cutting one link with a hacksaw.

The pivot bearing is positioned in its own bracket and not in the rear fork, which is the same component on 500- and 1000-c.c. models. Pivot-bearing adjustment is by means of a nut and lock-nut, not shims as on the post-war range.

The spring-boxes can be *sparingly* greased through the nipples provided, and the outer cases are slotted for the inserts of the friction damper bands.

Wheels and Brakes

A wheel which has been completely "written off" in an accident can be replaced by a component with a Series C front hub, and here again numerous parts are interchangeable. Early Series A machines had a light-alloy hub requiring brake drums with a smaller centre hole. The malleable part used later will take the post-war brake drums, and the adjustment of the taper-roller wheel

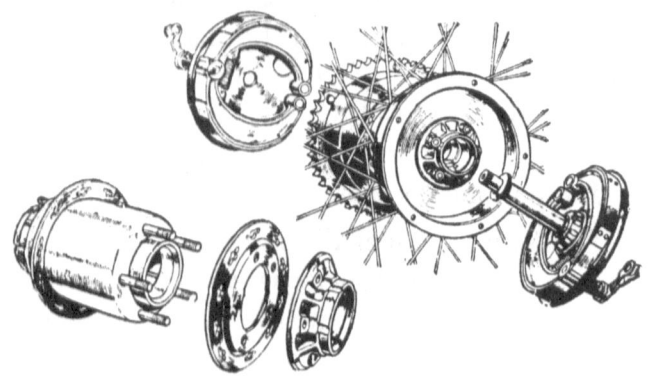

FIG. 84.—SERIES A LIGHT-ALLOY HUB.

bearings on all models follows the principles described in Chapter I. Pre-1940 drums were steel pressings, but composite drums and alloy plates were available for racing.

The speedo gear ring is retained by the five hub bolts, and a feature is the rigid speedometer drive tube, which is no longer available as a spare. When the need for replacement arises a tube can be made up or a flexible drive substituted.

Retention of the brake shoes is by grub-screws, but present-day linings and shoes can be used for replacement. Water excluders are a post-war refinement, but easy to fit; small parts, such as return springs, hub felts, shims, etc., are identical to those used to-day.

Fig. 85.—Speedometer Bracket and Rigid Drive Tube.

Cylinder Head and Barrel

Standard fitting is a cast-iron head, but Comet Special and T.T. replica models feature a bronze component. Originally the head joint was ground, but later a gasket was fitted to facilitate decarbonising by private owners. There are instances on record of a cast-iron head cracking between the sparking-plug hole and the exhaust-valve seat. Experience shows that this need not detract from the performance, although the exhaust valve may eventually burn out. Repair is possible by welding, but this should be entrusted to a firm specialising in repairs of this nature.

VALVES.—The valve seat angle is 45 degrees and the hairpin springs have a wire diameter of 0·160 in. (4·06 mm.); replacement springs are normally available from the Works or Vincent spares stockists. The valve stems have threaded ends which take the spring collars, and these are prevented from unscrewing by locking plates. The 4 B.A. screws have their nuts soldered on to the plates after tightening. Valve grinding is done with a sucking tool or T-handle, and poor seats can often be corrected by backing out with a cutter. Once the seats have sunk too deeply the head requires specialist attention, as new heads are no longer available. The Works can not undertake to build up the seats or fit inserts.

Worn top valve guides can be reclaimed by bushing with cast iron; valve-stem sleeves and lower guides are

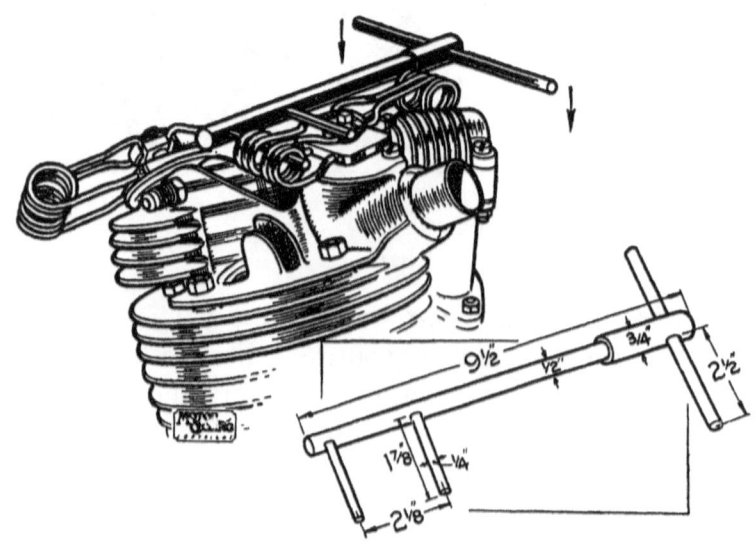

[" *Motor Cycling* " *Copyright.*

FIG. 86.—VALVE-SPRING REMOVING TOOL.

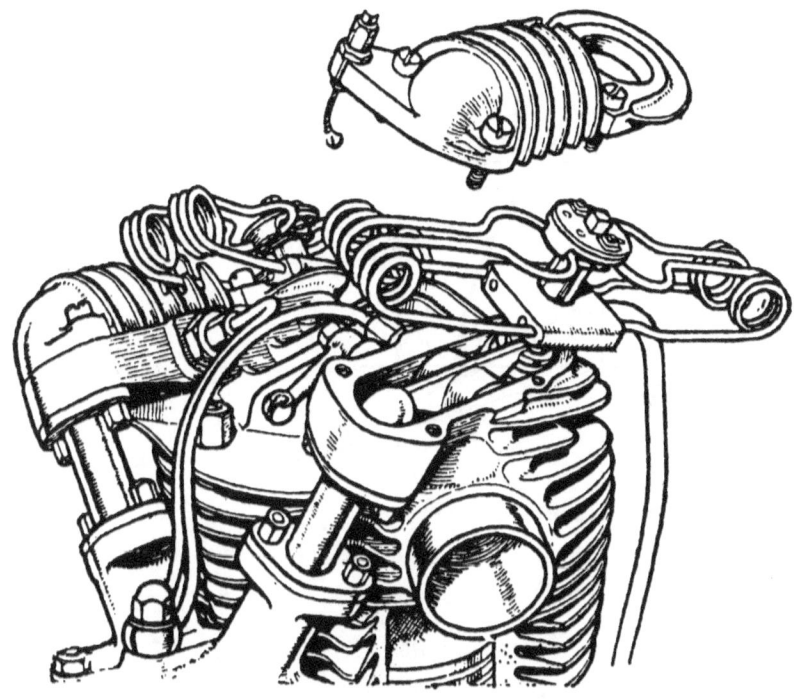

[*By courtesy of " The Motor Cycle ", London.*

Fig. 87.—Cylinder Head with Exhaust Rocker-box Cover Removed.

normally still available as spares. Correct valve-stem clearance is 0·004 in. (0·10 mm.) for inlet and exhaust. The lower guides are a normal drive fit in the head.

The exhaust lifter consists of an arm which operates a cam in an eccentric bush; the latter screws into the boss of the exhaust rocker box and is retained by a screw with lock-nut. On racing heads this boss is often unmachined, in which case it can be drilled and tapped to take the exhaust-lifter parts.

Cylinder Barrel.—On 1935–36 models, the cylinder barrel had a flat base, but in 1937 the part was re-designed with a spigot; the later type barrel can be used on earlier machines. Boring up to 0·060 in. (1·52 mm.) oversize

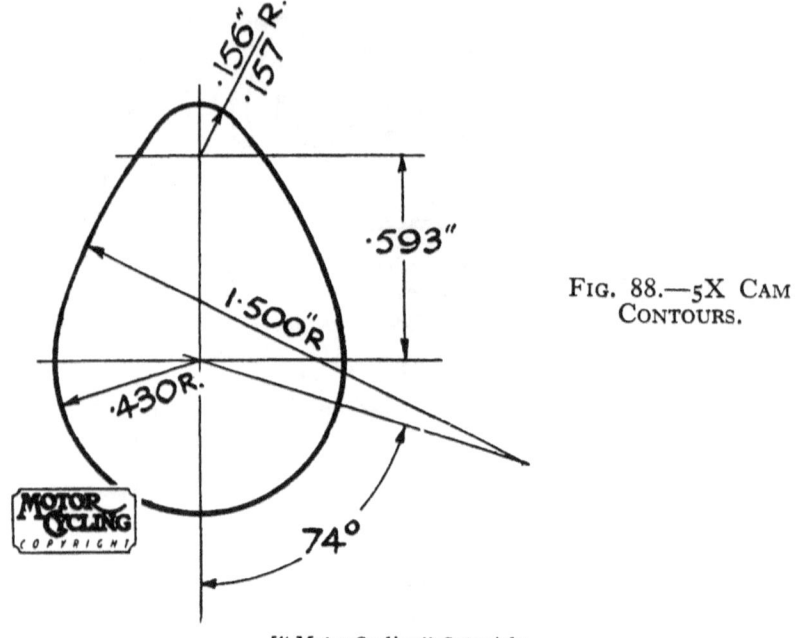

Fig. 88.—5X Cam Contours.

["*Motor Cycling*" *Copyright.*

is permissible, or the component can be linered. Current pistons and rings are readily available as spares, and the same clearances apply. Compression plates have never been supplied by the Works, but cylinder barrels were shortened on some racing engines to adjust compression ratios.

Valve Gear

Tappet clearance is nil with engine cold, and a check on the adjustment every 2000 miles (3000 km.) is recommended. Up to the end of 1938 the push-rods featured cups for the ball ends of the rockers, but 1939 machines have the ball ends on the rods and cupped rockers; with either design adjustment is made on the push-rod after lowering the tube. The rocker pins are drilled for lubrication, and it is advisable to check periodically that these oilways are clear. The pins are fitted with jointing

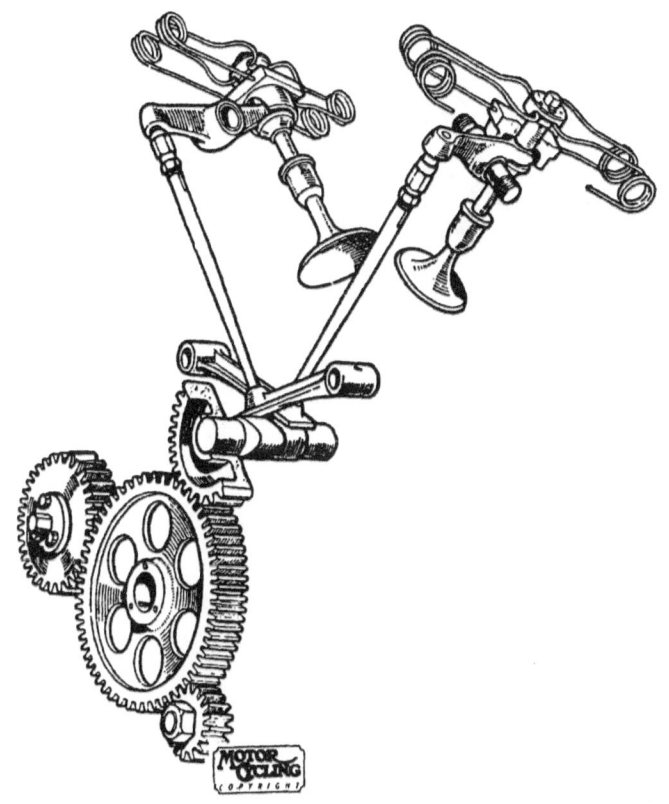

["Motor Cycling" Copyright.

FIG. 89.—CAMS AND EARLY TYPE PUSH-RODS.

compound under the head, and the rockers are sometimes located by washers. Push-rod fracture indicates restricted movement due to excessive wear in the cam-follower cups.

Removal of the cam-box exposes the camshaft with bushes, cam followers with pins and the idler gear, and when lifting the component on its studs the camshaft can be held down to avoid upsetting the timing. No paper washer is fitted at the cam-box base, as its thickness would cause the camshaft bushes to rotate in their housings. These bushes are line-reamed with a $\frac{3}{4}$-in. (19·05-mm.) parallel reamer, and camshaft as well as followers may have up to $\frac{1}{64}$ in. (0·39 mm.) side play. Cam followers are

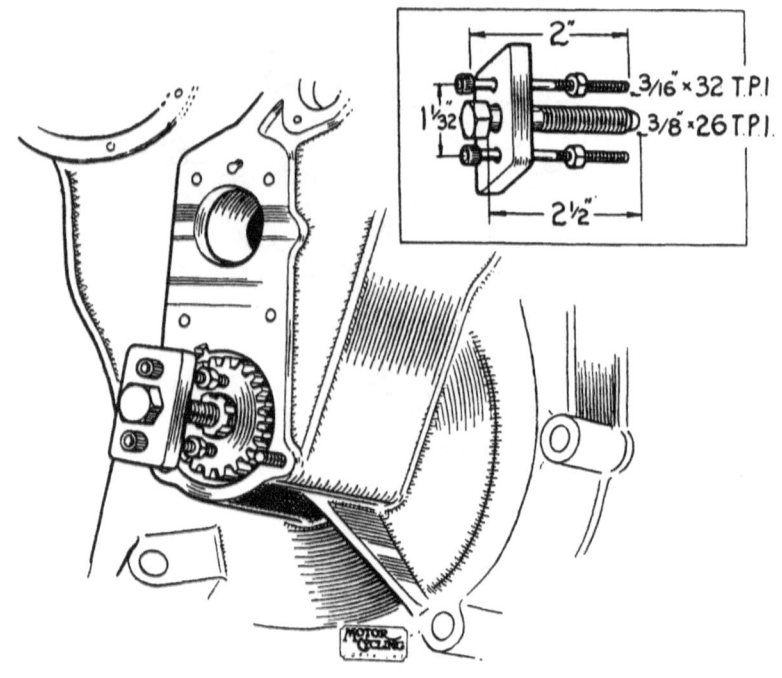

["Motor Cycling" Copyright.
FIG. 90.—HALF-TIME PINION EXTRACTOR.

not interchangeable with the present component, as the centres differ; when badly worn they should be built up, case-hardened and re-ground.

Camshafts were known as 2X, 4X and 5X; they were fitted to Meteors (Rapides), Comets and Comet Specials (T.T. Replicas), respectively. The 5X cam is also very satisfactory for road work, and was at one time the only pattern supplied as a spare. If replacements are not available worn cams can be built up and re-ground.

The idler gear is retained on its spindle by three screws behind the oil pump; after their removal the gear can be lifted out of the top of the timing chest. Unscrewing the timing-hole cover from crankcase and cam-box enables observation of the timing marks. One dot on the idler meshes with two dots on the cam pinion, and the two dots

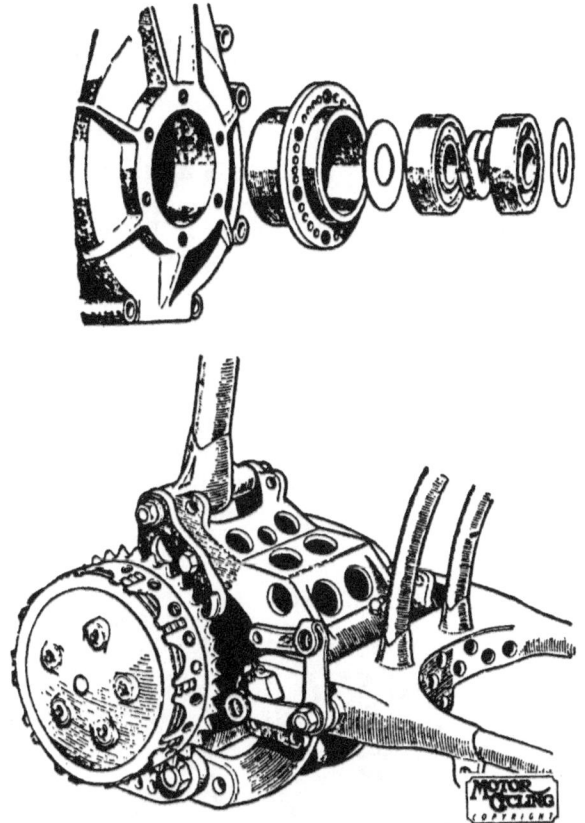

["Motor Cycling" Copyright.

FIG. 91.—(*Top*) DETACHABLE DRIVE-SIDE MAIN BEARINGS (*Below*) RACING CLUTCH AND PIVOT BEARING BRACKET.

of the idler gear mesh with the dot on the half-time pinion, on which the engaging key-way is also marked. On T.T. Replica engines the timing is not normally marked. Idler-shaft bushes are available as spares, or can easily be made up.

The half-time pinion nuts are the same as post-war, and for withdrawal the pinion is tapped $\frac{3}{16}$ in. $\times$ 32 T.P.I.

Crankcase and Flywheel Assembly

The engine number is stamped on the front face of the timing chest. When splitting the crankcase the valve and magneto timing can be left undisturbed, provided the engaging key-way of the half-time pinion is marked. A damaged case can often be repaired by welding, and if threads have stripped bottle-studs can be made up. For the main bearings the following fits apply:

Drive-side roller (lipped outer race) . . . { Press fit in housing
{ Light press fit on shaft
Timing-side roller . . Press fit in case and on shaft
Drive-side ball . . . Push fit in housing and on shaft
Timing-side ball . . Press fit in case, push fit on shaft

The flywheel assembly is located from the *timing* side, and as the layout is rather unusual the following procedure is suggested. Lay the timing-side case flat on the bench and insert ball bearing. Fit distance piece and

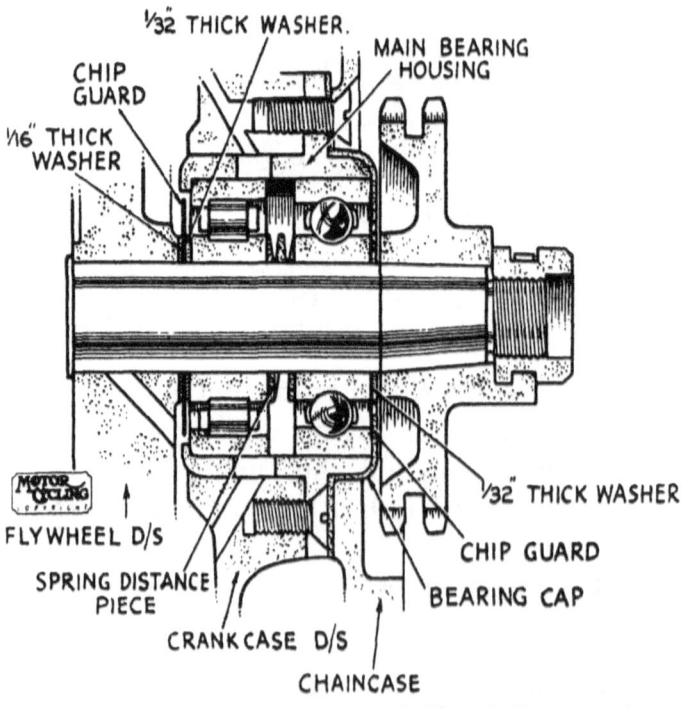

["*Motor Cycling*" Copyright.

FIG. 92.—CROSS-SECTION THROUGH DRIVE-SIDE MAIN BEARINGS.

centre of roller race, which should stand $\frac{1}{64}$ in. (0·39 mm.) proud of the outer sleeve; shim-up inner race as necessary, the shims for this purpose are 0·015 in., 0·010 in. and 0·005 in. (0·38, 0·25 and 0·12 mm.) thick. Finally, instal the flywheel assembly.

On the drive side the layout from flywheel to sprocket is as follows:

$\frac{1}{16}$ in. (1·58 mm.) washer against flywheel.
0·015 in. (0·38 mm.) chip guard.
$\frac{1}{32}$ in. (0·79 mm.) washer.
Roller bearing.
Spring.
Ball bearing.
0·015 in. (0·38 mm.) chip guard.
Bearing cap.
$\frac{1}{32}$ in. (0·79 mm.) washer.
Engine sprocket.

It will be noted that the drive-side ball-race is spring-loaded in the bearing cap against the outer chip guard. This should run just clear of the bearing cap, and for this reason shims between the chip guard and sprocket hold the latter slightly off the taper. If clearance is too great with the sprocket pulled up tight the oil level in the primary chaincase rises rapidly. The thickness of the shims must then be reduced, taking care not to trap the chip guard between bearing and cap.

The fitting of a new big end is a Works' or specialist's job, and post-war Service Exchange con-rods can be used. If the crank-pin bores in the flywheels are worn, re-sleeving to standard is often possible, and new mainshafts can be fitted.

Primary Drive and Clutch

The primary-chaincase oil level is to the edge of the filling orifice. To test the tension of the primary chain the small lever is pulled clear from its recess and turned anti-clockwise. The tension is correct if slight effort is

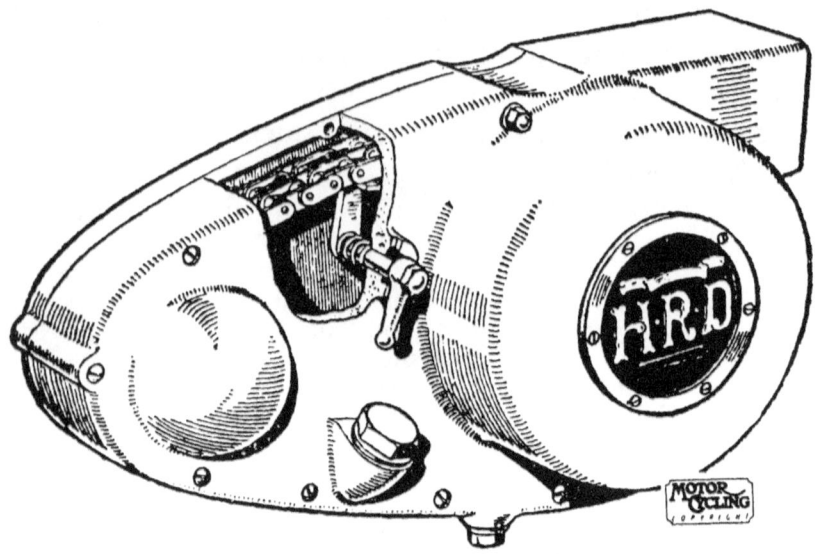

["Motor Cycling" Copyright.
FIG. 93.—CHAIN TENSION CHECKING DEVICE.

needed to push the internal feeler arm over the chain. If considerable effort is required the chain is too tight, and if no resistance is felt at all the chain is too slack. The correct position of the internal arm relative to the external lever is "six o'clock".

The engine-sprocket nut is of the self-withdrawing type, and the Burman clutch has *four* lined plates with four springs. As there is no engine-shaft shock absorber, the clutch sprocket is provided with rubber buffers which require renewal after considerable service. They are standard Burman parts and common to other makes of motor cycle.

Gearbox and Secondary Drive

Pre-war gearboxes were lubricated with light grease, but it is advisable to add a small quantity of engine oil from time to time for the plain bearings. On Series A

Vincent H.R.D. machines the gearbox shell is spot-faced to take a link to a cranked adjuster with lock-nut on the right-hand side of the model. When this lock-nut and the nuts of the gearbox-mounting bolts are slackened off, the square end of the adjuster can be rotated until correct tension of the primary chain is obtained.

In general layout the pre-war box is similar to the current component, and many parts are interchangeable. After prolonged service a gearbox may develop a slight whine in the intermediate ratios, but sometimes this is more due to general wear and tear than excessive wear of one particular part or group of components. As noise of this nature is not necessarily detrimental, it should be duly considered whether a cure by renewal of all internals is justified.

Sidecar gearing is obtained by fitting a larger rear-wheel sprocket, but smaller final-drive sprockets for the Burman gearbox are available. The size can be reduced, taking into account that the rate of wear will be greater, the smaller the sprocket.

Lubrication System

The cylinder-feed outlet of the oil pump is fitted with an adjustable union which should be set to pass 20 drops per minute at 1000 r.p.m. Machines from 1937 onwards are fitted with twin rocker-feed pipes on adjustable unions to the cam-box. The setting of these is: inlet—20 drops per minute; exhaust—30 with the engine warm and running at a fast tick-over (1000 r.p.m.). On earlier models the rocker-pipe banjo stud in the cam-box can be peened to adjust the flow to requirements. On very early models removal of the big-end quill necessitates dismantling the oil pump, but on the BD-type the quill is easily detachable without disturbing the pump. Frequent cleaning is recommended as for the post-war range

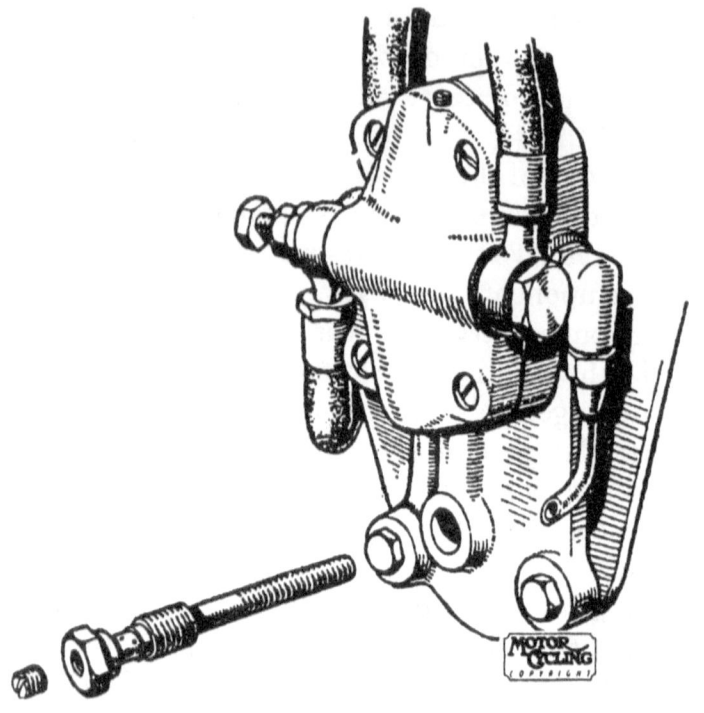

["Motor Cycling" Copyright.
FIG. 94.—DETACHABLE OIL-PUMP QUILL.

and the Series C quill interchanges. This part, however, passes slightly more oil, so that the supply to the rockers must be adjusted accordingly.

The four oil pipes are located as follows :

Pump body, rear . . .	Oil-tank return pipe
Pump body, front . .	Sump scavenge pipe (brass)
Pump cover, rear . . .	Cylinder feed
Pump cover, front . .	Oil-tank feed pipe

A ball and long spring are fitted in the union of the oil-tank feed pipe, and a ball with short spring in the cylinder feed union. The oil pump is of the gear-type and driven by the idler spindle; the light key on the driven side is made from 12 S.W.G. spoke material and intended to shear should the pump become locked by foreign matter.

Series C light-alloy banjo bolts fit. Side clearance of the gears in their recesses is provided by the paper washer, and should not exceed 0·002 in. (0·05 mm.). If more, the pump face can sometimes be carefully rubbed down on a surface plate or sheet of emery cloth. Gears can be reduced in the same manner if their clearance is insufficient. Oil draining from the tank into the sump when the machine is stationary may indicate leakage past the

[" *Motor Cycling* " *Copyright.*
FIG. 95.—POSITION OF EXTERNAL OIL PIPES.

gears and need for an oil-pump overhaul. Check first that the non-return ball is seating properly and the spring undamaged. Lubrication troubles are rare, provided all oil-ways are clear, those in the timing-chest wall and cam-box included. After many years' use most oil pumps can do with a general overhaul, and at the time of writing many component parts are available. On single-cylinder models which are not normally driven hard the oil supply to the rockers can be reduced to 12 drops per minute.

On 1935–36 models a Tecalemit type FG 2363 oil

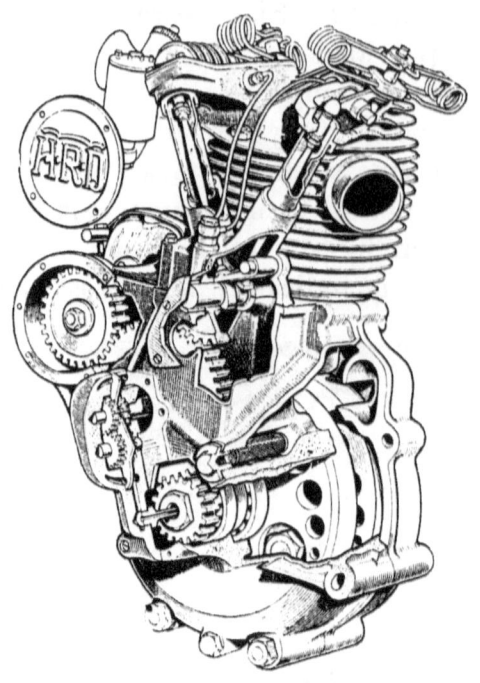

["Motor Cycling" Copyright.
FIG. 96.—1935 500-C.C. VINCENT H.R.D. ENGINE.

filter was positioned high up in the tank, receiving oil from the return of the pump; some very early crankcases featured a filter chamber cast into the timing-side crankcase. From 1937 onwards a gauze element is placed in the feed to the pump, access being gained from underneath the oil tank. Both types of filter should be cleaned every 1500 miles (2400 km.).

The pre-war engine breathes through the exhaust rocker box, from which an external pipe should run downwards to a point between the crankcase and primary chaincase. If the breather pipe has been lost a replacement must be made up, and it is, of course, not permissible to block up the rocker-box union.

Fuel System

Standard fitting on Meteors is a black steel tank; on Comets the tank has polished stainless-steel panels, and the colour is usually maroon. In view of the soldered joints pre-war tanks are cellulosed and not stove enamelled. Some Comet Special and all T.T. Replica machines feature all-stainless tanks in polished finish.

All tanks are easy to remove, and often this facilitates

working on the engine. The component rests on rubber washers, and if a boss for the mounting bolts has stripped, it is sometimes possible to tap this oversize to take a slightly thicker bolt. Alternatively, a new boss can be fitted by a specialist in tank repairs.

["*Motor Cycling*" Copyright.
FIG. 97.—POSITION OF BREATHER PIPE.

The principles of carburation described in Chapter VIII are fully applicable, and for approximate settings, etc., see Table VI of the Appendix. The pre-1940 exhaust pipe diameter is 1¾ in. (44·45 mm.).

Ignition and Electrical Equipment

The sparking-plugs recommended in Table III of the Appendix are all of the short-reach type. Ignition on earlier 500-c.c. models is by a B.T.H. Mag-Generator with the cut-out mounted on top of the tool-box. In 1937 the Miller Dyno-Mag became standard, and most of these are of the three-brush type; some two-brush dynamos were fitted to special order with a voltage regulator

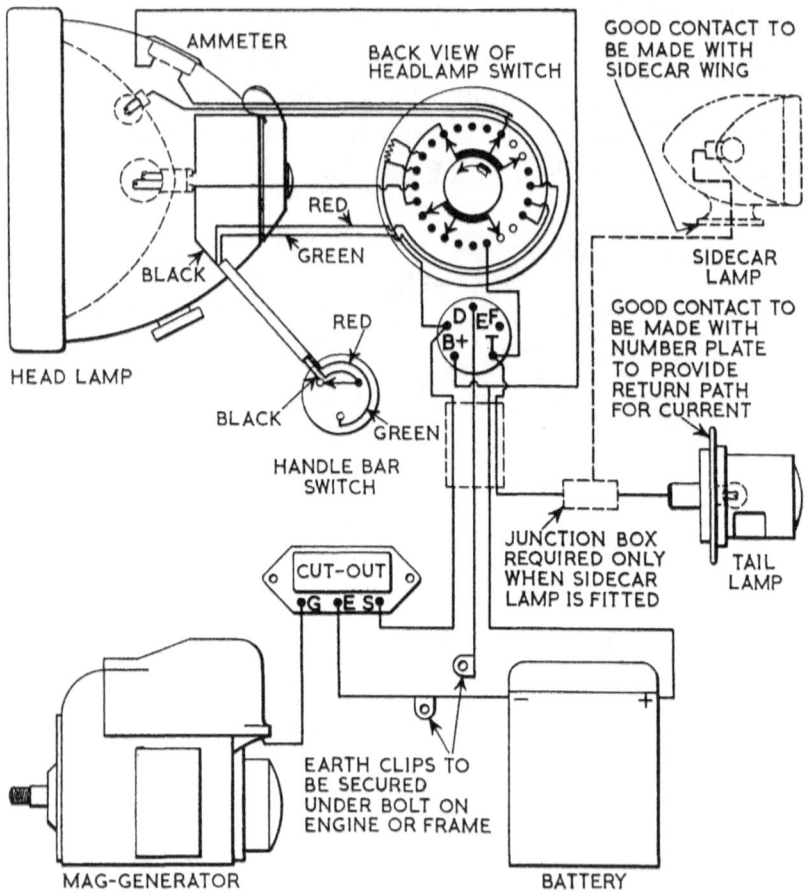

Fig. 98.—Wiring Diagram for Type P.B. Mag-generator Lighting Equipment.

mounted on the tool-box. The B.T.H. instrument calls for a headlamp bulb of 18 watts, but with the Miller Dyno-Mag a 24-watt bulb can be used.

Both instruments are retained by straps, and a thick felt sealing ring ensures an oil-tight drive. The pinion-retaining nut is self-withdrawing, and only the racing magnetos are mounted by bolts inserted from the underside of the platform.

Unfortunately, the afore-mentioned equipment is no

longer in production, which renders the spares position difficult. Bearings, however, can still be obtained. In view of the spindle height of 35 mm. (1·377 in.) alternative mag-dynos are difficult to adapt, but the B.T.H. Mag-Generator of the earlier J.A.P. or Python engined Vincent H.R.D. machines is interchangeable.

The recommended bulb for pilot light and tail-lamp is a single-contact 6-volt 3-watt for all models.

Comet Special

This model was only manufactured during 1935 and 1936, and consists of a de-tuned T.T. replica engine fitted to a machine of standard " Comet " specification. Cycle parts, such as the 1-in. (25·40-mm.) diameter handlebar and 150-lb. frontfork spring, are common to the other single-cylinder machines, but some Comet Specials featured a larger petrol tank.

The cylinder head is a bronze component, and the T.T. type carburetter is usually clip-fitting on a stub. The standard compression ratio is 8 : 1. A " Vibrac " con-rod takes a big end with *four narrow separators*, and the mainshafts are also " Vibrac ". For the valve timing of the 5X camshaft see the Appendix, Table I. The gearbox features close ratios, and a slightly harder sparking-plug is recommended. Narrower flywheels and racing valve springs complete the specification.

Where the original special equipment parts are no longer available as spares, standard pre-war components can be successfully substituted. Series C spares, such as pistons and Black Shadow con-rods, are very satisfactory, and in all other respects the instructions given for the Series A Meteor and Comet apply. The machine was discontinued with the introduction of the Rapide.

T.T. REPLICA

Individual machines of this type vary considerably in detail, but most have a 1½-in. (38·10-mm.) diameter front frame down tube, identical to the Series A Rapide. The composite brake drums have side plates of cast aluminium for greater stiffness and less weight.

The racing valve springs have a wire diameter of 0·170 in. (4·31 mm.), and some cylinder barrels were shortened by $\frac{1}{16}$ in. (1·58 mm.) to raise the compression ratio to 8·95 with the E7/8 piston. No exhaust lifter is fitted. The idler gear is a steel component, sometimes ½ in. (12·70 mm.) wide and drilled for lightness. The revolution counter drive is mounted to a cover which replaces the H.R.D. name plate on the timing side. In all

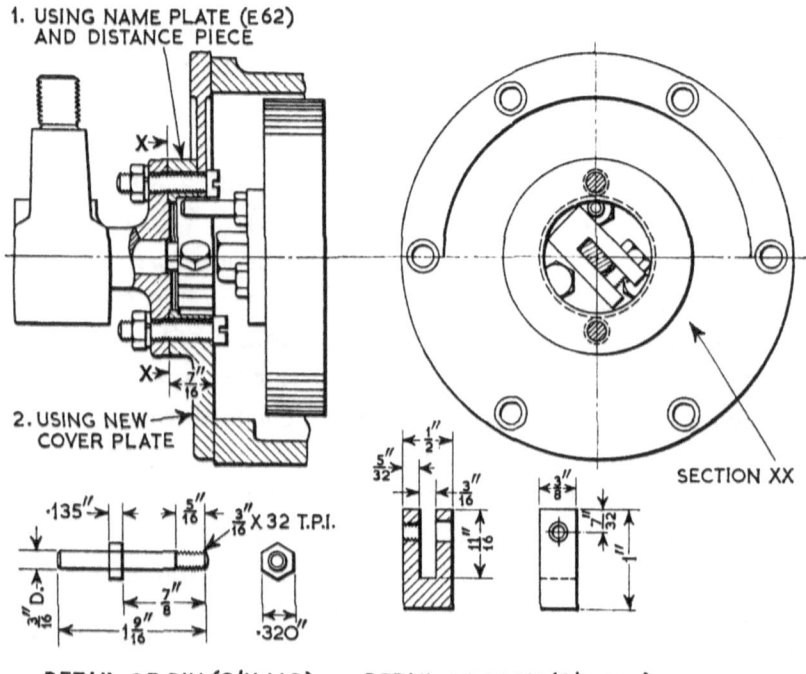

FIG. 99.—REV. COUNTER DRIVE (PRE-1940).

other respects the specification of the Comet Special engine applies.

For maximum power at high revs an exhaust-pipe length of 43 in. (109 cm.) is required, but for low-speed torque on short circuits the recommended length is 56 in. (142 cm.). The gearbox is a special racing component.

When preparing a T.T. Replica certain parts of the Series C Grey Flash can be used, e.g., alcohol piston, " Vibrac " con-rod, " Girdraulic " forks (with adaptor), racing wheels, etc. During the Senior T.T. of 1935, three replicas were won on this model.

Rapide, Series A

Introduced for the 1937 trading season, the Rapide virtually consists of two Meteor cylinder barrels and heads mounted offset on a common crankcase, the aim being effortless high-speed touring with the minimum of wear and tear.

The frame differs from the 500-c.c. models in the longer top tube, and the front down tube is of $1\frac{1}{2}$ in. (38·10 mm.) diameter. There is very little clearance between the rear-cylinder inlet-valve spring and the rear down tube of the frame, and if the spring fouls the top guide can be moved round to clear after some filing of the rocker-box cover. The standard front-fork spring is 150 lb. and 170 lb. is recommended for sidecar work.

Standard compression ratio is 6·8, and whilst some machines feature cast-iron barrels, many have been equipped with light-alloy finning on cast-iron liners. Both types can be bored oversize or re-sleeved to standard by firms specialising in this work. Tappet adjustment is the same as for 500-c.c. models, but the rear exhaust pipe must be removed for access to the front-cylinder inlet push-rod.

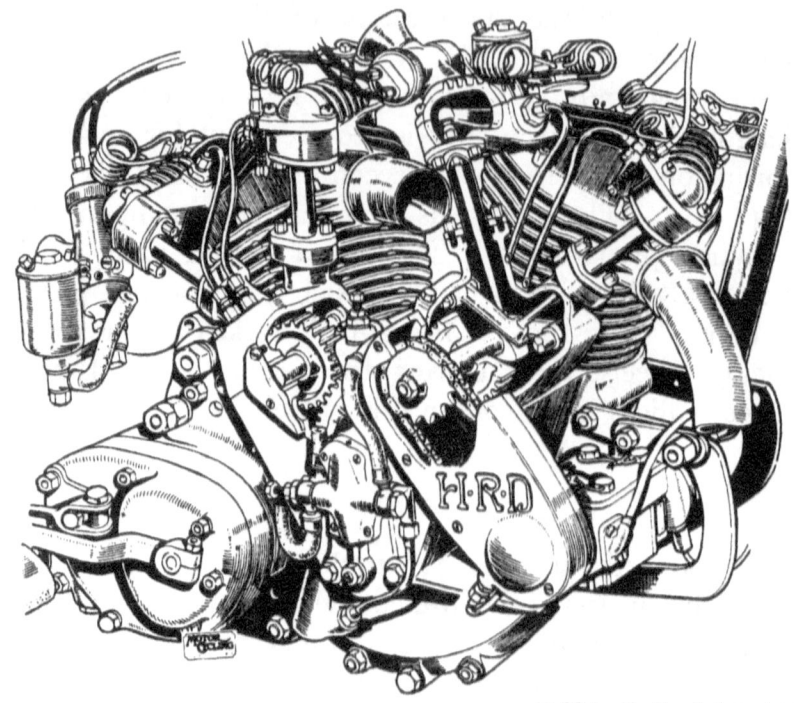

["Motor Cycling" Copyright.

FIG. 100.—"RAPIDE" POWER UNIT.

Some Rapides have 2X cams of the Meteor pattern, others are fitted with 4X cams of the Comet type, and the theoretical timing will be found in the respective columns of Table I, in the Appendix. The front camshaft fits in a flanged sleeve to which the slotted pinion is retained on four studs. This arrangement permits equal timing on both cylinders to be obtained, and normally the nuts can be left undisturbed. The idler gear of the Rapide is retained similarly to the Singles but removed through the slot in the front wall of the timing chest after the cover plate has been dismantled.

On the drive-side mainshaft there is a difference with 500-c.c. models, as an oil-seal is fitted in lieu of the outer chip guard. This seal runs on a thick distance washer, which also holds the sprocket off the taper, and if necessary shims must be added to ensure that the single-coil spring distance piece does not impose thrust upon the ball-race when the sprocket is fully tightened. The flywheels are of the narrow type.

The inner chaincase is interchangeable with the Singles, but the outer case has a larger dome. The clutch has three lined plates, and due to the great power output of the engine slip may occur if the throttle is opened too briskly before the clutch is fully engaged, for instance as in racing-gear changes. The clutch can be reinforced by riveting two inner plates together using countersunk rivets, and the withdrawal plate can be stiffened-up by riveting a suitably shaped piece of $\frac{1}{8}$-in. (3·17-mm.) thick steel plate to the outside. The recommended friction material is Ferodo AS10. When ordering sprockets note that the rear chain is not $\frac{3}{8}$ in. but $\frac{1}{4}$ in. (6·35 mm.) wide; sprockets which are too wide can be turned down.

All twins have a gauze-type oil-filter element in the feed to the pump, and the location of various oil pipes is as follows :

Delivery from tank . .	To front union of oil-pump cover
Return to tank. . .	From rear union of oil-pump body
Sump pipe . . .	To front union of oil-pump body
Cylinder feed, rear cylinder	From rear union of oil-pump cover

The cylinder feed to the front barrel is taken off a union on top of the timing-side crankcase between the two cam-boxes. The rear-cylinder inlet and front-cylinder exhaust rocker boxes drain more easily; consequently their rocker feeds may require a more generous adjustment of the oil supply. Both exhaust rocker boxes have separate external breather pipes.

Correct adjustment for the $\frac{1}{2}$ in. × $\frac{5}{32}$ in. (bicycle size) magneto chain is $\frac{1}{4}$ in. (6·35 mm.) up-and-down play at the tightest point; the chain is endless, with thirty-six rollers. The 36-watt Lucas Magdyno is mounted

Fig. 101.—"Noxal" Sidecar Chassis Showing Pick-up Points.

inverted and protected by a cowl. The cam-ring *must* be 47 degrees, and the foremost high-tension pick-up transmits current to the front cylinder sparking plug.

Sidecars

Fitting a sidecar to a Series A machine necessitates a down-tube clip for $1\frac{1}{4}$-in. (31·75-mm.) tube ($1\frac{1}{2}$-in. on Rapide) with levelling lug and connecting bar. A $\frac{7}{16}$-in.

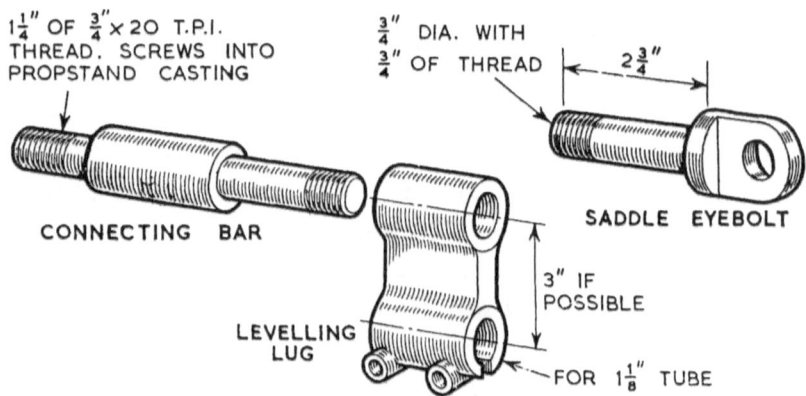

Fig. 102.—Sidecar Rear Fittings, Pre-1940.

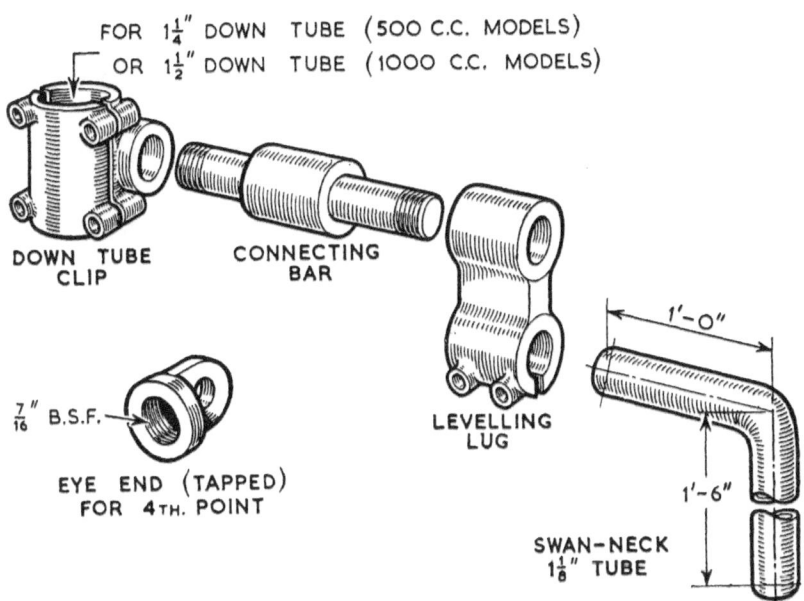

Fig. 103.—Sidecar Front Fittings, Pre-1940.

B.S.F. eye end replaces the nut of the lower engine bolt, and the top rear connection is taken off a saddle eye bolt of ¾ in. (19·05 mm.) diameter. The lower rear connection of the sidecar should be adjacent to the propstand casting on the machine. This casting is tapped ¾ in. × 20 T.P.I especially for sidecar attachment. The sidecar conversion of the machine is identical to the Series B models, but usually a 170-lb. front-fork spring suffices. Pre-war spring claws are slightly different, and may require easing. The recommended rear-wheel sprocket is fifty-six tooth for all models (see also Chapter XI).

APPENDIX

TABLE I.—GENERAL DATA

Series A.

	Meteor.	Comet.	Comet Special.	T.T. Replica.	Rapide.	Speedway Engine.
Engine type symbol	M	C	TTC	TTR	V	F5AB/1 F5MB/1
Frame type symbol	D	D	D	D...TTR	DV	
Bore and stroke:						
Mm.	84 × 90 (All Models)					
In.	3·307 × 3·543 (All Models)					
Capacity:						
C.c.	499	499	499	499	998	499
Cu. in.	30·50	30·50	30·50	30·50	61	30·50
Compression ratio	6·8	7·3	6·8	8	6·8	12
B.h.p. and r.p.m.	25 at 5300	26 at 5600	28 at 5600	34 at 5800	45 at 5500	39 at 5800
Cylinder angle	Vertical	Vertical	Vertical	Vertical	47°	Vertical
Ignition:						
Make	B.T.H. Mag.-Generator or Miller Dyno-Mag.			B.T.H.	Lucas	B.T.H.
Type	PB		MK	T.T. Magneto	MNV1 47°	T.T. Magneto
Contact-breaker gap:						
In.	B.T.H. 0·014	Miller 0·019		0·010	0·012	0·010
Mm.	0·35	0·48		0·25	0·30	0·25
Ignition timing:						
Before T.D.C.	42° = 17/32 in.	42° = 17/32 in.	40° = 1/2 in.	42° = 17/32 in.	42° = 17/32 in.	34° = 3/8 in.
Mm. stroke	13·49	13·49	12·70	13·49	13·49	9·52
Primary chain:						
Type	Duplex ·375	Duplex ·375	Duplex ·375	Duplex ·375	Duplex ·375	1/4 in.
Pitches	94	94	94	94	94	

APPENDIX

Valve timing:						
Inlet opens (B.T.D.C.)	40	44	48	48	40	55
Inlet closes (A.B.D.C.)	52	56	60	60	52	68
Exhaust opens (B.B.D.C.)	65	68	71	71	65	73
Exhaust closes (A.T.D.C.)	33	38	42	42	33	50
Rear chain:						
Size	5/8 in. × 3/8 in.	5/8 in. × 3/8 in.	5/8 in. × 3/8 in.	5/8 in. × 1/4 in.	5/8 in. × 1/4 in.	
Pitches	108	108	108	108	108	
Petrol-tank capacity:						
Imp. gals.	3¼	3¼	3¼	5	3½	
Litres	14·5	14·5	14·5	22·5	16	
Oil-tank capacity:						
Pints	3½	3½	3½	8	4	
Litres	2	2	2	4·5	2·25	
Petrol consumption, approximate:						
M.p.g.	80	70	60	—	45–50	
Km.p. litre	28·3	24·8	21·2	—	15·9–17·7	
Oil consumption, approximate:						
M.p.g.	1800	1800	1600	—	1600	
Km.p. litre	640	640	565	—	565	
Speed range, target:						
M.p.h.	75–80	85–90	87–92	102–110	105–115	
K.p.h.	121–129	137–145	140–148	164–177	169–185	
Weight:						
Lb.	385	385	385	335	430	
Kg.	175	175	175	152	195	
Wheelbase:						
In.	55	55	55	55	56	68–64
Metres	1·40	1·40	1·40	1·40	1·42	31·2–29

TABLE I.—GENERAL DATA (continued)

	Series B.				Series C.			
	Meteor.	Rapide.	Black Shadow.	Comet.	Grey Flash.	Rapide.	Black Shadow.	Black Lightning.
Engine type symbol	F5AB/2	F10AB/1	F10AB/1B	F5AB/2A	F5AB/2B	F10AB/1	F10AB/1B	F10AB/1C
Frame type symbol	R/1	R	R . . . B	RC/1	RC/1A	RC	RC . . . B	RC
Bore and stroke:				84 × 90	(All Models)			
Mm.								
In.				3·307 × 3·543				
Capacity:								
C.c.	499	998	998	499	499	998	998	998
Cu. in.	30·50	61	61	30·50	30·50	61	61	61
Compression ratio	6·45	6·45	7·3	6·8	8	6·45	7·3	To order 9 : 1 C.R.
B.h.p. and r.p.m.	26 at 5300	45 at 5300	55 at 5700	28 at 5800	35 at 6200	45 at 5300	55 at 5700	70 at 5600
Cylinder angle, degrees	25	50	50	25	25	50	50	50
Ignition:								
Make	Lucas	Lucas	Lucas L.T.	Lucas	B.T.H.	Lucas	Lucas	Lucas
Type	KIF GM2	KVF GM1	KVF GM1	KIF GM2	T.T. Magneto	KVF GM1	KVF GM1	KVF T1
Contact-breaker gap:								
In.	0·012	0·012	0·012	0·012	0·010	0·012	0·012	0·010
Mm.	0·30	0·30	0·30	0·30	0·25	0·30	0·30	0·25
Ignition timing:								
Before T.D.C.	38° = 11/32 in.	39° = 15/32 in.	38° = 15/32 in.	38° = 15/32 in.	42° = 17/32 in.	39° = 15/32 in.	38° = 15/32 in.	38° = 15/32 in.
Mm. stroke	11·90	12·30	11·90	11·90	13·49	12·30	11·90	11·50
Primary chain:								
Type	1/2 in. × 5/16 in.	Triplex ·375	Triplex ·375	1/2 in. × 5/16 in.	1/2 in. × 5/16 in.	Triplex ·375	Triplex ·375	Triplex ·375
Pitches	64	94, Endless	94, Endless	64	64	94, Endless	94, Endless	94, Endless

APPENDIX

Valve timing:								
Inlet opens (B.T.D.C.)	40–42	40–42	40–42	40–42	55	40–42	40–42	55
Inlet closes (A.B.D.C.)	60–64	60–64	60–64	60–64	68	60–64	60–64	68
Exhaust opens (B.B.D.C.)	72–70	72–70	72–70	72–70	73	72–70	72–70	73
Exhaust closes (A.T.D.C.)	28–33	28–33	28–33	28–33	50	28–33	28–33	50
Rear chain:								
Size	⅝ in. × ⅜ in.	⅝ in. × ⅜ in.	⅝ in. × ⅜ in.	⅝ in. × ⅜ in.	⅝ in. × ¼ in.	⅝ in. × ⅜ in.	⅝ in. × ⅜ in.	⅝ in. × ¼ in.
Pitches	108	106	106	108	108	106	106	106
Petrol-tank capacity:								
Imp. gals.	3½	3½	3½	3½	3⅜	3½	3½	3⅜
Litres	16	16	16	16	15·25	16	16	15·25
Oil-tank capacity:								
Pints	6	6	6	6	6	6	6	6
Litres	3·25	3·25	3·25	3·25	3·25	3·25	3·25	3·25
Petrol consumption, approximate:								
M.p.g.	80	55–65	55–65	75–80	35	55–65	55–65	—
Km.p. litre	28·3	19·5–23	19·5–23	26·6–28·3	12·4	19·5–23	19·5–23	—
Oil consumption, approximate:								
M.p.g.	2000	1500	1500	2000	—	1500	1500	—
Km.p. litre	700	530	530	700	—	530	530	—
Speed range, target:								
M.p.h.	80	110	125	90	110	110	125	150
K.p.h.	129	177	200	145	177	177	200	242
Weight:								
Lb.	386	455	458	390	330	455	458	380
Kg.	175	206	208	177	150	206	208	172
Wheelbase:								
In.	55¾	56½	56½	55¾	55¾	56½	56½	56½
Metres	1·41	1·44	1·44	1·41	1·41	1·44	1·44	1·44

TABLE II.—

	Models.	Esso.	B.P.
ENGINE :			
Tropical conditions, high-speed touring, racing	Rapide, Series "A", "B" and "C"; Black Shadow, Series "B" and "C"	Essolube 50	Energol SAE 50
Temperate summer		Essolube 40	Energol SAE 40
Temperate winter		Essolube 30	Energol SAE 30
Arctic conditions		Essolube 20	Energol SAE 20
Tropical conditions, high-speed touring, racing	Comet Special Series "A"; Meteor Series "A" and "B"; Comet Series "A" and "C"	Essolube 50	Energol SAE 50
Temperate summer		Essolube 50	Energol SAE 50
Temperate winter		Essolube 30	Energol SAE 30
Arctic conditions		Essolube 20	Energol SAE 20
Racing, tropical or high-speed touring	T.T. Replica Series "A"; Grey Flash and Black Lightning Series "C"	Essolube Racer	Energol SAE 50
Temperate summer, roadwork		Essolube 50	Energol SAE 50
Temperate winter, roadwork		Essolube 40	Energol SAE 40
PRIMARY CHAIN	All Series "A", "B" and "C"	Use oil as for engine.	
GEARBOX :			
Burman	Series "A" Series "B" and "C" 500-c.c.	Esso Grease † Esso Grease †	Energrease AO Energrease AO
Vincent and Albion	Series "B" and "C" 1000-c.c. and Grey Flash 500-c.c.	Use oil as for engine.	
HUBS	All	Esso High-temperature * Grease	Energrease N3
CYCLE PARTS (grease-gun)	All	Esso Grease †	Energrease AO
HYDRAULIC DAMPERS	Series "C"	Essolube 20 Esso Shock Absorber oil	Energol SAE 20 Energol SA Light

* Overseas use Esso Bearing Grease.
† Overseas use Esso Chassis Grease.
‡ Marketed overseas as Mobiloil AF SAE 40.

LUBRICATION CHART

Shell.	Vacuum.	Wakefield.	Remarks.
X-100 50	Mobiloil D SAE 50	Castrol Grand Prix SAE 50	
X-100 40	Mobiloil BB SAE 50 ‡	Castrol XXL SAE 40	⎫ Alternative viscosities
X-100 30	Mobiloil A SAE 30	Castrol XL SAE 30	⎬ permissible for unusual conditions of operation.
X-100 20/20W	Mobiloil Arctic SAE 20	Castrolite SAE 20	⎭
X-100 50	Mobiloil D SAE 50	Castrol Grand Prix SAE 50	
X-100 50	Mobiloil D SAE 50	Castrol XXL SAE 40 ‖	⎫ Alternative viscosities permissible for unusual conditions of operation.
X-100 30	Mobiloil A SAE 30	Castrol XL SAE 30 ¶	⎬
X-100 20/20W	Mobiloil Arctic SAE 20	Castrolite SAE 20	⎭
X-100 50	Mobiloil D SAE 50	Castrol Grand Prix SAE 50	
X-100 50	Mobiloil D SAE 50	Castrol Grand Prix SAE 50	
X-100 40	Mobiloil BB SAE 50 ‡	Castrol XXL SAE 40	
	Use oil as for engine.		
Retinax A	Mobilgrease No. 2	Castrolease Medium	Mixed with engine oil in equal proportions.
Retinax A	Mobilgrease No. 2	Castrolease Medium	No grease to be used in these gearboxes.
	Use oil as for engine.		
Retinax A	Mobil Hub Grease §	Castrolease WB	Use high-melting-point grease only.
Retinax A	Mobilgrease No. 2	Castrolease Medium	No grease to be used on self-oiling bushes.
X-100 20/20W	Mobiloil Arctic SAE 20	Castrolite SAE 20	For temperate climates.
Donax A1	Mobil Shock Absorber oil light	Castrol Shockol	For arctic conditions.

§ Marketed overseas as Mobilgrease No. 5.
‖ Or Grand Prix in U.K.
¶ Or XXL in U.K.

TABLE III.—RECOMMENDED SPARKING-PLUGS

	Reach. (approx.)	Gap, K.L.G.	K.L.G.*		Champion, England.†		Lodge.‡		Remarks.
			Original Equipment and General Use.	Running-in or Oily Engine.	General Use.	Running-in or Oily Engine.	General Use.	Running-in or Oily Engine.	
Series "A", 1935-39:									
Meteor	½ in. (12·70 mm.)	0·018 in. (0·45 mm.)	F70	F50	L-10	L-8	H14	C14	
Comet	½ in. (12·70 mm.)	0·018 in. (0·45 mm.)	F70	F50	L-10, L-10S	L-10	H14	C14	
Rapide	½ in. (12·70 mm.)	0·018 in. (0·45 mm.)	F70	F50	L-10	L-8	H14	C14	For petrol; colder plugs according to time and fuel.
Comet Special	½ in. (12·70 mm.)	0·011–0·013 in. (0·27–0·33 mm.)	F100	F80	L-11S	L-10S	3HN	H14, HN	
T.T. Replica	½ in. (12·70 mm.)	0·011–0·013 in. (0·27–0·33 mm.)	F220		LA-15		R49		
Series "B", 1946-49:									
Meteor	¾ in. (19·05 mm.)	0·018–0·020 in. (0·45–0·50 mm.)	FE70	FE50	NA-8	N-8B	HLN	CB14	
Rapide	¾ in. (19·05 mm.)	0·018–0·020 in. (0·45–0·50 mm.)	FE70	FE50	NA-8	N-8B	HLN	CB14	
Black Shadow	¾ in. (19·05 mm.)	0·018–0·020 in. (0·45–0·50 mm.)	FE70	FE50	NA-8	N-8B	HLN	CB14	
Series "C", 1949 onwards:									
Comet	¾ in. (19·05 mm.)	0·018–0·020 in. (0·45–0·50 mm.)	FE70	FE50	NA-8	N-8B	HLN	CB14	
Rapide	¾ in. (19·05 mm.)	0·018–0·020 in. (0·45–0·50 mm.)	FE70	FE50	NA-8	N-8B	HLN	CB14	
Black Shadow	¾ in. (19·05 mm.)	0·018–0·020 in. (0·45–0·50 mm.)	FE70	FE50	NA-8	N-8B	HLN	CB14	
Grey Flash	¾ in. (19·05 mm.)	0·011–0·013 in. (0·27–0·33 mm.)	FE220		NA-10	NA-8	RL49		For petrol; colder plugs according to tune and fuel.
Black Lightning	¾ in. (19·05 mm.)	0·011–0·013 in. (0·27–0·33 mm.)	FE220		NA-10	NA-8	RL49		

* Equivalent Waterproof K.L.G. plugs are identified by prefix "W".
† Equivalent Champion Suppressor-type plugs are identified by prefix "X" and two red bands on insulator. CB14 will be re-named CL14.
‡ Alternative to Lodge HLN is HLNP with platinum-alloy point.

Note: Gaps may be increased to 0·023 in. (0·58 mm.) when Interference Suppressors are used.

TABLE IV.—TYRE PRESSURES

Model	Tyre Size, in.		Solo Inflation Pressure				Remarks
	Front	Rear	Front		Rear		
			Lb./sq. in.	Kg./sq. cm.	Lb./sq. in.	Kg./sq. cm.	
Series "A" 1935–39:							
Meteor	3·00 × 20	3·25 × 19	20	1·40	21	1·47	
Comet	3·00 × 20	3·25 × 19	20	1·40	21	1·47	
Comet Special	3·00 × 20	3·25 × 19	20	1·40	21	1·47	Racing tyres
T.T. Replica	3·00 × 20	3·25 × 19	20	1·40	22	1·54	
Rapide	3·00 × 20	3·50 × 19	22	1·54	21	1·47	
Series "B" 1946–49:							
Meteor	3·00 × 20	3·50 × 19	20	1·40	20	1·40	Touring models as Series "C", Touring
Rapide	3·00 × 20	3·50 × 19	22	1·54	21	1·47	
Black Shadow	3·00 × 20	3·50 × 19	22	1·54	21	1·47	
Series "C" 1949 onwards:							
Comet, Standard	3·00 × 20	3·50 × 19	24	1·68	20	1·40	
Comet, Touring Model	3·50 × 19	4·00 × 18	17	1·19	17	1·19	
Rapide, Standard	3·00 × 20	3·50 × 19	26	1·82	21	1·47	
Rapide, Touring Model	3·50 × 19	4·00 × 18	18	1·26	17	1·19	
Black Shadow	3·00 × 20	3·50 × 19	26	1·82	21	1·47	
Grey Flash	3·00 × 21	3·50 × 20	20	1·40	18	1·26	Racing tyres
Black Lightning	3·00 × 21	3·50 × 20	21	1·47	22	1·54	
Sidecar wheel	3·25 × 19	3·50 × 19	16	1·12			

The above are approximate indications for average conditions, as tyre pressures are dependent upon weight normally carried, cruising speed, road conditions, etc. Average increase for habitual pillion riding 7 lb./sq. in. with standard machines and 3 lb./sq. in. with touring models (rear tyre only). For racing tyres approximate starting pressures are given.

TABLE V.—SPROCKET SIZES AND RATIOS

	Sprocket Sizes.				Box Ratio.				Gear Ratio.			
	Engine.	Clutch.	Gear-box.	Rear Wheel.	Top.	3rd.	2nd.	1st.	Top.	3rd.	2nd.	1st.
Series "A", 1935–39:												
Comet and Meteor, solo	30	56	19	46	1	1·26	1·69	2·67	4·6	5·8	7·4	12·4
Comet and Meteor, sidecar	30	56	19	56	1	1·26	1·69	2·67	5·5	6·9	9·3	14·7
Comet Special and T.T. Replica	30	56	19	46	1	1·16	1·45	1·82	4·3	5	6·2	7·8
Rapide	32	56	22	45	1	1·26	1·69	2·67	3·58	4·51	6·49	9·55
Series "B", 1946–49:												
Meteor	23	40	18	48	1	1·26	1·69	2·67	4·64	5·94	8·17	12·4
Rapide	35	56	21	46	1	1·19	1·61	2·60	3·5	4·16	5·5	9·1
Black Shadow	35	56	21	46	1	1·19	1·61	2·07	3·5	4·2	5·5	7·25
Series "C", 1949 onwards:												
Comet Standard	23	40	18	48	1	1·26	1·69	2·67	4·64	5·94	8·17	12·4
Comet Trials	23	40	18	48	1	1·47	1·98	3·14	4·64	6·82	9·2	14·6
Rapide, Black Shadow, after Engine No. 7076. Black Shadow, up to Engine No. 7076.	35	56	21	46	1	1·19	1·61	2·60	3·5	4·16	5·64	9·1
Grey Flash, No. 5 Ratio	35	56	21	46	1	1·19	1·61	2·07	3·5	4·16	5·64	7·25
Black Lightning	23	42	18	48	1	1·18	1·4	2·13	4·87	5·75	6·82	10·36
	35	56	22	45	1	1·19	1·61	2·07	3·27	3·89	5·26	6·77

Safe Speeds Intermediate Gears

	M.p.h.			Gear Ratio.		
	Top	3rd	2nd	Top	3rd	2nd
Comet, sidecar (H5/58)	60	47	31	5·61	7·7	9·5
Comet, solo (H5/52)	71	51	35	5·02	6·3	8·5
Black Shadow, high bottom gear and H5/56	90	70	53	4·26	5·06	6·85

TABLE VI.—AMAL CARBURETTER STANDARD SETTINGS

Machine.	Type.	Internal Bore.	Main Jet.	Throttle Valve.	Needle Position.	Needle Jet.	Remarks.
Series "A", 1935–39:							
Meteor	76/022	1 1/16 in.	160–170	6/4	3	Std.	Clip fitting, 15° float chamber.
Comet	89/011	1 1/8 in.	170–180	29/4	3	Std.	Clip fitting, 15° float chamber.
Rapide { Front	6/301	1 1/16 in.	180	6/3	3	Std.	
{ Rear	76/022	1 1/16 in.	170	6/4	3	Std.	Clip fitting, 15° float chamber.
Comet Special	10I I	1 5/16 in.	330–350	6	4	0·109	With open exhaust pipe fit 460–500.
T.T. Replica (petrol)	10TT	1 5/16 in.	360	7	4	0·109	Vary settings for each event as required.
Series "B", 1946–49:							
Meteor	276DQ/1DV	1 1/16 in.	170	6/4	3	Std.	
Comet	276CJ/1DO	1 1/16 in.	170	6/4	3	Std.	
Rapide { Front	276CH/2DS	1 1/16 in.	170	6/4	3	Std.	
{ Rear	289M/1DO	1 1/16 in.	180	29/4	3	Std.	
Black Shadow { Front	289N/2DS	1 1/8 in.	180	29/4	3	Std.	
{ Rear							
Series "C", 1949 onwards:							
Comet	229F/1DV	1 1/16 in.	200	29/3	3	Std.	
Rapide { Front	276DQ/1DV	1 1/16 in.	170	6/4	3	Std.	
{ Rear	276CH/2DS	1 1/16 in.	170	6/4	3	Std.	
Black Shadow { Front	229E/1DV	1 1/8 in.	180	29/4	3	Std.	29/3 throttle valve fitted from 1953 onwards.
{ Rear	289N/2DS	1 1/8 in.	180	29/4	3	Std.	
Grey Flash (alcohol)	10II9	32 mm.	1700	7	4	0·120	Same approximate settings apply for 1 3/16-in. and 1 5/16-in. 10TT carburetters. Vary for each event as required.
Black Lightning (petrol)	10TT9	32 mm.	360	7	4	0·109	

TABLE VII.—PISTON RINGS

For Piston.	Width.		Radial Thickness.		Recommended Closed Gap.		Recommended Side Clearance.		Number Per Piston.
	In.	Mm.	In.	Mm.	In.	Mm.	In.	Mm.	
E7/6, E7/7 and E7/8	1/8	1·58	0·118	3	0·016–0·020	0·40–0·50	0·001–0·002	0·02–0·05	Compression 2
	1/8	3·17	0·118	3	0·010–0·020	0·25–0·50	0·003–0·005	0·07–0·12	Scraper 1
E7/9, E7/10 and E7/11	1/16	1·58	0·135	3·42	0·025–0·030	0·63–0·76	0·001–0·002	0·02–0·05	Compression 2
	1/8	3·17	0·125	3·17	0·025–0·030	0·63–0·76	0·003–0·005	0·07–0·12	Scraper 1

Table VIII.—Power Unit Ball and Roller Bearings

	Vincent Part No.	Dimensions.	B.S.S. Reference Symbol.	R. and M.	S.K.F.	Hoffmann.	Fisher.
Series "A":							
Mainshafts: Drive-side Ball	E91	1 × 2½ × ¾	BRM1	MJ1	RMS8	MS10	
Drive-side Roller	E93	1 × 2½ × ¾			CFM8		
Timing-side Roller, inner	E92	1 × 2½ × ¾	RRM1	MRJ1	CRM8	RMS10	
Timing-side Ball, outer	E94	¾ × 2 × 11/16	BRM¾	MJ¾	RMS6	MS8	
Burman gearbox: Drive end	PR50-219X	1½ × 72 × 17					61207
Kick-starter end	PR50-37BA	20 × 52 × 15	BRM020	MJ20	6304	320	6304
B.T.H. Mag.-Generator: Magneto, both ends	PR22T	15 × 35 × 8			EN15	A15	
Miller Dyno-Mag.: Magneto, both ends	PR22T	15 × 35 × 8			EN15	A15	
Dynamo drive end	PR24/1V/1	15 × 35 × 11	BRL015	LJ15	6202	115	
Commutator end	PR24/1V	10 × 30 × 9	BRL010	LJ10	6200	110	
Series "B" and "C":							
Mainshafts: Drive-side Ball	E91	1 × 2½ × ¾	BRM1	MJ1	RMS8	MS10	
Drive-side Roller	ET92	1 × 2½ × ¾	RRM1	MRJ1	CRM8	RMS10	
Timing-side Inner	ET92	1 × 2½ × ¾	RRM1	MRJ1	CRM8	RMS10	
Timing-side Outer	ET94	¾ × 1⅞ × 9/16	RRL¾	LRJ¾	CRL6	RLS8	
Vincent gearbox: Layshaft, drive side	G15	⅞ × 2 × 9/16	BRL⅞	LJ⅞	RLS7	LS9	
Layshaft, timing side	G15	⅞ × 2 × 9/16	BRL⅞	LJ⅞	RLS7	LS9	
Mainshaft, drive side	E91	1 × 2½ × ¾	BRM1	MJ1	RMS8	MS10	
Mainshaft, timing side	G14	1¼ × 2¾ × 11/16	BRL1¼	LJ1¼	RLS10	LS12	
Ratchet shaft	G41	½ × 1⅛ × ¼	BRE½		EE4	S5	
Burman gearbox: Drive end	PR50-219X	1½ × 72 × 17					61207
Kick-starter end	PR50-37BA	20 × 52 × 15	BRM020	MJ20	6304	320	6304
Lucas Magneto; Early type, both ends	PR22T	15 × 35 × 8			EN15	A15	
Later type, drive end only	PR22T1	18 × 40 × 9				A18	
Miller Dynamo: 3½-in. 1947, drive end	PR24/1V/1	15 × 35 × 11	BRL015	LJ15	6202	115	
Commutator end	PR24V	½ × 1 5/16 × ⅜	BRL½	LJ½	RLS4	LS5	
3-in. 1948 onwards, drive end	PR24/1V/1	15 × 35 × 11	BRL015	LJ15	6202	115	
Commutator end	PR24/1V	10 × 30 × 9	BRL010	LJ10	6200	110	

Note.—ET92 is used with ⅝ in. wide outer race.

Table IX.—Rear Frame Springs

RATES: Comet   .   .   0·276-in. wire   121 lb./in. (obsolete)
        Rapide .   .   0·300-in. wire   189 lb./in.
        Sidecar .   .   0·324-in. wire   264 lb./in.

Possible Combinations
One or Two Springs

1 Comet	121 lb./in.
1 Rapide	189 lb./in.
2 Comets	242 lb./in.
1 Sidecar	264 lb./in.
1 Comet and 1 Rapide	310 lb./in.
2 Rapides	378 lb./in.
1 Comet and 1 Sidecar	385 lb./in. (near enough to 2 Rapides)
1 Rapide and 1 Sidecar	453 lb./in.
2 Sidecar	528 lb./in.

Three Springs

3 Comets	363 lb./in.
2 Comets and 1 Rapide	431 lb./in.
2 Rapides and 1 Comet	499 lb./in.
2 Comets and 1 Sidecar	506 lb./in.
3 Rapides	557 lb./in.
2 Rapides and 1 Sidecar	642 lb./in.
2 Sidecar and 1 Comet	649 lb./in.
2 Sidecar and 1 Rapide	717 lb./in.
3 Sidecar	792 lb./in.

Table X.—Service Exchange
(*Parts normally covered, Home Market only.*)

Part No.	Description	Scheme
C7AS	Clutch shoe	Returned to specification exactly as received.
C7/1AS	Clutch shoe	
C24AS	Clutch floating plate, 1000-c.c.	
D1AS	Hydraulic damper	
E4/3S	Big-end assembly, 500-c.c.	
ET4/2S	Big-end assembly, 1000-c.c.	
ET21AS	Cylinder barrel, relinered	
FFAS	"Girdraulic" fork, complete 1000-c.c.	
FF2AS	"Girdraulic" fork, 500-c.c.	
FT1/4AS	Upper frame member assembly	
FT6/2AS	Rear fork	
FT208AS	Brampton pattern fork girder, bare	
H8AS	Brake shoe	
PR1	Dualseat	
PR22B	Magneto armature, 1000-c.c.	Lucas B90 Service Exchange Scheme.
PR22/2B	Magneto armature, 500-c.c.	
PR22S	Magneto, KVF, 1000-c.c.	
PR22/2S	Magneto, KIF, 500-c.c.	
PR24A	Voltage regulator	
PR30AS	Brampton pattern girder forks, complete	
PR32	Speedometer gearbox	Smith's F.R.U. Service Scheme.
PR33	120 m.p.h. speedometer head	
PR33/1	180 k.p.h. speedometer head	
PR33/4	180 m.p.h. speedometer head	
PR33/5	280 k.p.h. speedometer head	
PR33/2	150 m.p.h. speedometer head	
PR33/3	250 k.p.h. speedometer head	
PR50-3X(S)	Clutch plate "Comet" and "Meteor"	
T1/6AS	Petrol tank	

Table XI.—Detail Modifications

POWER UNIT	ENGINE NO.
Grooved rocker bearing ET 26/1, front-cylinder inlet only	193
Second gear pinion G 8/1, 23 teeth instead of 24	309
Selector pawl spring G 36/1	350
Timing-side crankcase oil-catchment hole to pump worm	375
Two single holes in crank-pin instead of two groups of 3 holes	380
Clutch-retaining nut with ground face for bonded carrier seal	594
Dowty bonded rubber/steel washer behind retaining nut	656
Miller 3-in. dynamo with adaptor instead of $3\frac{1}{2}$-in. instrument	746
Cam-plate with larger radius on notches, hand ground	746
Clutch shoe pivot G 5/1, circlip type	853
" Wellworthy " piston rings	1128
Metering wires in rocker-feed bolts	1128
Composite breather valve assembly, cast-iron sleeve with steel pinion	1141
Tappet adjuster lock-nut ET 45/1, thicker section	1211
Solid head bolts ET 55/2	1310
Locking tabs ET 220 to idler and breather spindle nuts	1314
Breather-valve assembly ET 141/3AS, bronze or alloy sleeve with steel pinion	1400
Cam-plate G 32/2, modified slot contours and notches	1590
Grooved rocker bearing ET 26/1, all rockers	2340
Steel oil pump worm	2991
First " Vincent "-embossed crankcase	3090
Stainless-steel valve push-rods	3132
Small-idler gear E 50/4, one-piece pattern	3477
Low clearance pistons	3716
Alloy idler gears, Comet	3815
Alloy idler gears, all models except racing	4548
Auxiliary valve springs, last Black Shadow so equipped	5336
One-piece clutch adjuster C 42/1, without ball	5398
Rapide bottom gear also standard for Black Shadow	7076
Mark III quiet cams	8343
Modified ratchet-bevel assembly G 39/1	8509
Forged gear-change actuating arm G 66/2	8697
Bush G 111 no longer fitted to clutch shaft	8821
Duron moulded clutch linings	9106
Oil-restrictor discs ET 234 in timing cover	9238
Pawl-carrier centraliser G 61/1	9669
Stellited clutch lever G 91/1	9701
Timing cover with small oil holes obviating ET 234 discs on 1000-c.c. machines	10000
Divided clutch push-rods G 96/1 with ball	10021

CYCLE PARTS	FRAME NO.
Lucas stop-light switch	2340
Petrol-tank tie-bolt and distance piece	2416
180-lbs. front fork spring	(approx.) 3000
Cast-iron brake drums	,, 3050
Upper frame member slotted for hydraulic damper	,, 3500
Spring boxes plated instead of enamelled (inner)	3616
Rear chain oiler in tank filler neck	(approx.) 3800
Rear fork FT 6/1, 18-in. centres	3900
Modified head-lug and cylinder-head bracket FT 3/2	8614
Duron moulded brake linings	10250
Drain plug to Burman gearbox shell	10497
SAE 20 engine oil in hydraulic dampers	11288
Steering damper with two friction plates	11937

INDEX

Adjuster, chain, 38, 155, 185
Advance, ignition, 128
Air cleaners, 169
Air leaks :
  exhaust system, 119
  oil pump, 99
Air scoops, 143, 154
Albion gearbox, 74, 88, 157, 158
Alignment :
  sidecar, 162
  wheel, 24
Amal carburetters, 108, 149
Ammeter, 131
Anchor plate, steering damper, 21, 173
Angle, valve seat, 44, 176
Arm :
  actuating, 85
  brake cam, 40
  brake torque, 38
Armature, magneto, 130
Automatic timing control, 123, 151

Balance factor, 60, 63
Balance, wheel, 24
Battery, 133
  carrier, 143
Bearings :
  big-end, 62, 160
  dynamo, 137
  head-lug, 14
  hub, 26
  magneto, 126, 191
  main, 60, 182
  power-unit, data, 208
Bevel, gear ratchet, 84
Big-end, connecting-rod, 62, 141, 145, 160, 183, 191
  quill, 95, 185
Black Lightning, 58, 142, 157
Black Shadow, 60, 79, 113, 141
Blanking plates, dynamo, 138, 147, 159
Bolts :
  banjo, 97, 185
  holding-down, 44, 48
  rocker feed, 46
  security, wheel, 25
Brakes :
  front, 27, 174
  linings, 28, 40
  rear, 39, 174
Brampton front forks, 16
Breather-pipe modification, 103
Breathing, 66, 75, 102, 105, 120, 146
Brush, pick-up, 126
B.T.H. Mag-Generator, 189
Bulb, headlamp, 130, 190
Burman gearbox, 88, 158, 185, 191, 193
Bushes :
  camshaft, 179
  front fork, 16–18

Bushes (contd.) :
  idler gear, 114
  pad, 14
  self-oiling, 16–18, 105, 155

Cam-box, 160, 179
Cam contours, 178
Cam-plate, 79, 148
  spindle boss, 85
Cam-ring, Series A, 196
Camshaft :
  Burman, 92
  Mark III, 116
  Series A, 179, 194
  timing gear, 113, 121, 144
Carburetters, 108, 142, 148, 189, 191
  standard settings, 207
Chain :
  adjuster, 38, 155, 185
  connecting link, 157, 159
  magneto, Series A Rapide, 195
  oiler, 75, 93
  rear, 86, 157, 172, 195
  tension, checking, 183
  wear, checking, 87
Chamfering rear-brake linings, 40
Chip guard, Series A, 194
Chromium, 119
Circlips, main bearing, 61
Clutch, 68, 74, 183, 195
  control cable, 73
  cover, 147
  slip, 71
Comet Model, 88, 113, 159, 165, 180, 188
Comet Special Model, 175, 180, 191, 188
Compression plates, 49, 178
Compression ratio, 128, 145, 178, 191, 193
Condensation, 65
Condenser, 129
Connecting-rod, 62, 141, 142, 145, 183, 191
Connector, cable, 134
Consumption :
  oil, 95
  petrol, 111, 128
Contact-breaker, 122, 127, 139
Control cables, 30, 73, 117
Conversion, sidecar, 163
Crankcase, 54, 137, 142, 181
  splitting, 55
Crank-pin, 58
Cylinder barrel, 48, 177, 193
Cylinder head, 44, 144, 175, 191
  removal, 44
Cylinder oil feed, 96, 105, 195

Damage :
  accidental, 17, 36, 173, 174
  crankcase, 54, 146

INDEX

Damper:
  friction, 16, 24, 33, 37
  hydraulic, 22
  steering, 21, 17
Decarbonising, 43
Dial indicator, 116
Dipstick, 75
Discoloration of exhaust pipes, 119
Drain-plug, 65, 73, 75, 89, 97
Drum, clutch, 68
Dualseat, 33, 155, 167, 172
Dynamo, 137, 139
  blanking plates, 138, 147, 159
Dyno-Mag, 189

Electrolyte, 133
Engine:
  data, 181–201
  mounting bolts, 15
  number, 181
  plates, 143, 164
  Speedway, 159
Exchange Service, 28, 36, 130, 167, 170, 183, 210
Excluder, water, 41
Exhaust lifter, 117, 177, 192
Exhaust pipes, 118, 154, 158, 189, 193

Flange, exhaust pipe, 118
Floating plate, 147
Flywheels, 58, 145
Followers, cam, 112, 121, 179
Forks, front:
  Brampton pattern, 16, 130
  Girdraulic, 18, 130, 172
  spring boxes, 18, 21
Forks, rear, 35, 162, 173
Frame:
  Series A, 172, 193
  springs, 34
  upper, member, 12
Friction dampers, 16, 24, 33, 37
Front stand, 31
Fuels, 148, 150
  premier grade, 49

Gap, sparking-plug, 122, 204
Gaskets, 37, 175
Gauge, tyre pressure, 166
Gear:
  idler, 114, 146, 179
  ratios, 86, 157, 206
  ring, speedo, 30, 174
Gearbox:
  Albion, 74, 88, 157, 158
  Burman, 88, 158, 185, 191, 193
  Vincent, 77, 141
Girdraulic front forks, 18, 130, 172
Graphite, 94
Grease-gun, 105
Grey Flash Model, 32, 63, 74, 88, 113, 157, 164
Grinding:
  front inlet rocker box, 144
  valve, 44
Grooved pin:
  mainshaft, 60
  right-hand fork, 17
Gudgeon pin, 50, 145

Handlebar, 29, 155, 164
  screen, 170
Head bracket, 15
Headlamp, 130
Head-lug, 12, 14
Head-races, 14, 172
High-melting-point grease, 14, 137
Holding-down bolts, cylinder, 44, 48
Horn, 132, 139
H.T. cable, replacing, 128
Hubs, 26, 174
Hydraulic damper, 22
Hydrometer, 133

Idler gear, 114, 121, 146, 180, 194
Ignition, 122
  timing, 127, 182, 198, 200
Indicator:
  dial, 116
  gear, 90
Inlet port, 144
Interference suppressors, 123

Jet, cylinder feed oil, 96, 105
Jets, carburetter:
  block, 110
  main, 108
  pilot, 109, 148
  standard settings, 207
Jointing compound, 48, 57, 80, 178

Key:
  half-time pinion, 114
  oil-pump worm, 100
Kick-starter, 142
  cover, 78, 90
  left-hand, 79
Knee grips, 107

Leads:
  horn, 133
  wiring loom, 134
Lean-out, 162
Lift, valve, 116
Liner, cylinder, 48
Linings:
  brake, 28, 40
  clutch, 71, 147
Lock-rings, valve guide, 46
Lubricant, upper cylinder, 94
Lubrication:
  chart, 202–3
  cycle, 105
  engine, 185
  troubles, 101, 187

Magdyno, Lucas, 195
Mag-generator, B.T.H., 189
Magneto, 123, 151, 159, 190
  cowl, 31, 32
  timing, 127, 182, 198, 200
Main bearings, 60, 182
Mainshaft:
  engine, 58
  gearbox, 91
  oil seal, 61–3
Meteor Model, 32, 90, 113, 158, 164, 180, 188
Metering wires, 96

INDEX

Miller:
  Dyno-Mag, 189
  Dynamo, 136
Mudguards, 143, 165

Needles, jet, 108–10, 148, 207
Nipples, spoke, 25

" O "-rings, 23, 71, 81
Oil:
  change, 96
  consumption, 95
  filter, 93, 97, 188, 195
  lubrication chart, 202–3
  pipes, Series A, 187, 195
  pump, 93, 99, 159, 186
  pump worm, 100, 146
  recommendations, 94
  restrictor discs, 96, 102, 105
Oil-hole:
  cylinder barrel, 49
  small-end bush, 51
Oil-seals:
  clutch, 147
  dynamo drive, 139
  gearbox, 80
  magneto, 126
  mainshaft, 61, 62
  Series A Rapide, 194
Oversize pistons, 49

Pad:
  bolts, 19
  bushes, 14
Panniers, 41, 169
Pinion:
  breather, 105
  camshaft, 113, 194
  dynamo, 139
  half-time, 114, 181
  magneto, 127
Piston-rings, 51, 178
  data, 207
Pistons:
  engine, 49, 128, 145, 178
  hydraulic damper, 23
Pivot bearing, 35, 173
  plate, 85
Plunger:
  oil pump, 101
  petrol tap, 107
  pressure-relief valve, 96
Primary chain, 66, 146, 183
Primary chaincase, 63, 137, 183, 195
Propstands, 31, 143
Push-rod:
  clutch, 89
  valve, 112, 178

Racing, 140
  gearbox, 146
Rapide Model, 59, 79, 113, 165
  Series A, 180, 193
Rear suspension, 33
Rebushing front forks, 17, 173
Reduction:
  gearbox, 87, 206
  rev counter, 151
  speedometer gearbox, 30

Reduction (*contd.*):
  weight, 143
Regulator, voltage, 138
Relief valve, oil, 96
Rev counter, 151, 192
Rims, wheel, 24, 154
Rings:
  piston, 51, 178, 207
  valve seat, 47
Rockers, valve, 45, 144, 178, 188, 195
Roller, exhaust lifter, 118
Running-in, 52

Sealed beam unit, 131, 170
Security bolt, wheel, 25
Selector, gearbox:
  mechanism, 90
  pins, 85
Shims for:
  flywheel assemblies, 60, 182
  gearbox, 79
  Girdraulic fork, 19
  hubs, 27
  rear axle, 33, 35
Shock absorbers, 58, 67, 73, 184
Sidecars, 161, 196
  alignment, 162
  conversion, 163
  gearing, 185
  links, 16
  spring damper for, 22
Smoking from exhaust, 101
Spacer, main bearing, 60
Spanners, 167
  oil inspection cap, 97
Sparking-plugs, 122, 151–53, 160, 189
  cover, 123
  gaps, 122, 204
  recommended, 204
Specifications:
  1A, 141
  touring, 165
  U.S.A., 51, 130, 170
Speedometer, 30, 142
Speedway engine, 159
Spigot nuts, 13, 15, 139
Spindles:
  brake cam, 27
  breather, 104, 105
  cam-plate, 82
  crankcase, 54
  fork, 16–19, 173
  idler gear, 114, 180
" Spitting ", 111
Spokes, 25
Spring-boxes:
  front fork, 18, 21
  rear frame, 34, 164, 173
Springs:
  front fork, 31, 155, 164, 191, 193, 197
  kick-starter, 90
  oil pump, Series A, 185
  rear frame, 34, 41, 164, 209
  selector pawl, 84, 90
  shock absorber, 58, 68
  valve, 47, 141, 145, 176, 191, 192
Sprockets:
  engine, Series A, 184
  clutch, 74, 184

INDEX

Sprockets (*contd.*):
  final drive, 86, 142, 164, 185, 195
  rear-wheel sizes, 86, 165
  sizes and ratios of, 206
Stays:
  seat, 33, 37
  torque, 162
Steering damper, 17, 21
Stop valve, 97
Suppressors, interference, 123

Tank:
  oil, 12, 98, 187
  petrol, 106, 150, 188
  petrol, cover, 169
Tappet adjustment, 42, 178, 193
Tensioner, primary chain, 66
Tiebolt, petrol tank, 106
Timing:
  control, 125, 151
  disc, 116, 127
  magneto, 127, 182
  marks, 115, 120, 180
  valve, 115, 146, 181, 191, 194, 199, 201
Throttle:
  cable, 165
  valve, 109
Toe-in, 162
Tools, 167
Touring Models, 165
Trail, sidecar, 164
Transfers, 106
T.T. Replica, 175, 180, 181, 191, 192
  carburetters, 148, 191
Tuning:
  carburetters, 108, 148
  engine, 144

Tyres, 154, 165, 166
  pressures, 205

Upper frame member, 12
Upper-cylinder lubricant, 94

Valve:
  bounce, 156
  grinding, 44
  guides, 46, 144, 176
  push-rods, 112, 178
  rockers, 45, 144, 178, 188
  seat angle, 44, 176
  seat rings, 47
  seats, 176
  spring-removing tool, 176
  springs, 47, 141, 145, 176, 191, 192
  timing, 115, 146, 181, 191, 194, 199, 201
Vibrac connecting-rods, 63, 142, 145, 191
Vincent Owners' Club, 171
Voltage regulator, 138

Washers:
  rubber, exhaust lifter rod, 117
  thrust, cam follower, 113
  thrust, timing gear, 120
Water excluder, 41, 174
Wear, cylinder bore, 48
Wheels, 24, 38, 143
  rims, 24, 154
White Shadow Model, 141
Wiring:
  bolts and nuts, 156
  diagrams, 135, 190
  electric, 134
  lengths, 131
Worm, oil pump, 100

VINCENT
Breaks the World Sidecar Speed Record at 155 m.p.h.

Riding a **privately-owned,** totally-enclosed Vincent Black Lightning, on 18th December, 1954, Robert Burns of Christchurch, New Zealand, formerly of Scotland, recaptured this coveted record for Britain and the Empire.

Bob Burns' machine is a **standard model** — not supercharged — bought from Stevenage, England. The same superlative quality of workmanship will be found in every Vincent machine whether Black Prince, Black Knight or Victor.

THE WORLD'S FASTEST AND SAFEST STANDARD MOTOR CYCLE

VELOCEPRESS MANUALS - MOTORCYCLE

1930'S BRITISH MOTORCYCLE CARBS & ELEC COMPONENTS (BOOK OF)
1930'S BRITISH MOTORCYCLE ENGINES (OVERHAUL & MAINTENANCE)
1930'S BRITISH MOTORCYCLE GEARBOXES & CLUTCHES (BOOK OF)
AJS 1932-1948 SINGLES & TWINS 250cc THRU 1000cc (BOOK OF)
AJS 1945-1960 SINGLES 350cc & 500cc MODELS 16 & 18 (BOOK OF)
AJS 1955-1965 SINGLES 350cc & 500cc (BOOK OF)
ARIEL UP TO 1932 (BOOK OF)
ARIEL 1932-1939 PREWAR MODELS (BOOK OF)
ARIEL 1933-1951 (WORKSHOP MANUAL)
ARIEL 1939-1960 4 STROKE SINGLES (BOOK OF)
ARIEL 1958-1964 LEADER & ARROW (BOOK OF)
BMW R26 R27 (1956-1967) FACTORY WORKSHOP MANUAL
BMW R50 R50S R60 R69S (1955-1969) FACTORY WORKSHOP MANUAL
BRIDGESTONE 90 SERIES FACTORY WSM & PARTS CATALOGUE
BRIDGESTONE 175 SERIES FACTORY WSM & PARTS CATALOGUE
BSA BANTAM ALL MODELS FROM 1948 ONWARDS (BOOK OF)
BSA SINGLES & V-TWINS UP TO 1927 (BOOK OF)
BSA SINGLES & V-TWINS UP TO 1930 (BOOK OF)
BSA SINGLES & V-TWINS UP TO 1935 (BOOK OF)
BSA SINGLES & V-TWINS 1936-1939 (BOOK OF)
BSA OHV & SV SINGLES 250-600cc 1945-1959 (BOOK OF)
BSA OHV & SV SINGLES 250cc (ONLY) 1954-1970 (BOOK OF)
BSA OHV SINGLES 350 & 500cc 1955-1967 (BOOK OF)
BSA TWINS 1948-1962 (BOOK OF)
BSA TWINS 1962-1969 (SECOND BOOK OF)
CYCLEMOTOR (BOOK OF)
DOUGLAS 1929-1939 PREWAR ALL MODELS (BOOK OF)
DOUGLAS 1948-1957 POSTWAR ALL MODELS FACTORY SHOP MANUAL
DUCATI 160cc, 250cc & 350cc OHC MODELS FACTORY SHOP MANUAL
HONDA 50 ALL MODELS UP TO 1970 INC MONKEY & TRAIL (BOOK OF)
HONDA 90 ALL MODELS UP TO 1966 (BOOK OF)
HONDA 125-150cc TWINS C/CS/CB/CA FACTORY WORKSHOP MANUAL
HONDA 250-305 TWINS C/CS/CB FACTORY WORKSHOP MANUAL
HONDA C100 SUPER CUB FACTORY WORKSHOP MANUAL
HONDA C110 SPORT CUB 1962-1969 FACTORY WORKSHOP MANUAL
HONDA TWINS & SINGLES 50cc THRU 305cc 1960-1966 (BOOK OF)
HONDA TWINS ALL MODELS 125cc THRU 450cc UP TO 1968 (BOOK OF)
J.A.P. ENGINES 1927-1952 & MOTORCYCLES 1934-1952 (BOOK OF)
LAMBRETTA 1947-1957 ALL 125 & 150cc MODELS (BOOK OF)
LAMBRETTA 1957-1970 LI & TV MODELS (SECOND BOOK OF)
MATCHLESS 1931-1939 ALL MODELS 250cc THRU 990cc (BOOK OF)
MATCHLESS 1945-1956 350 & 500cc SINGLES (BOOK OF)
MATCHLESS 1955-1966 350 & 500cc SINGLES (BOOK OF)
NEW IMPERIAL ALL SV & OHV FROM 1935 ONWARDS (BOOK OF)
NORTON 1932-1939 PREWAR MODELS (BOOK OF)
NORTON 1932-1947 (BOOK OF)
NORTON 1938-1956 (BOOK OF)
NORTON 1955-1963 MODELS 19, 50 & ES2 (BOOK OF)
NORTON 1955-1965 DOMINATOR TWINS (BOOK OF)
NORTON 1957-1970 TWINS FACTORY WORKSHOP MANUAL
NSU PRIMA 1956-1964 ALL MODELS (BOOK OF)
NSU QUICKLY 1953-1963 ALL MODELS (BOOK OF)
PANTHER 1932-1958 LIGHTWEIGHT MODELS 250 & 350cc (BOOK OF)
PANTHER 1938-1966 HEAVYWEIGHT MODELS 600 & 650cc (BOOK OF)
RALEIGH MOPEDS 1960-1969 (BOOK OF)
RALEIGH MOTORCYCLES 1919-1933 (BOOK OF)
ROYAL ENFIELD 1934-1946 SINGLES & V TWINS (BOOK OF)
ROYAL ENFIELD 1937-1953 SINGLES & V TWINS (BOOK OF)
ROYAL ENFIELD 1946-1962 SINGLES (BOOK OF)
ROYAL ENFIELD 1958-1966 250cc & 350cc SINGLES (SECOND BOOK OF)
ROYAL ENFIELD 736cc INTERCEPTOR FACTORY WORKSHOP MANUAL
RUDGE 1933-1939 (BOOK OF)
SUNBEAM 1928-1939 (BOOK OF)
SUNBEAM 1946-1957 S7 & S8 (BOOK OF)
SUZUKI 50cc & 80cc UP TO 1966 (BOOK OF)
SUZUKI T10 1963-1967 FACTORY WORKSHOP MANUAL
SUZUKI T20 & T200 1965-1969 FACTORY WORKSHOP MANUAL
TRIUMPH 1935-1939 PREWAR MODELS (BOOK OF)
TRIUMPH 1935-1949 (BOOK OF)
TRIUMPH 1937-1951 (WORKSHOP MANUAL)
TRIUMPH 1945-1955 FACTORY WORKSHOP MANUAL
TRIUMPH 1945-1958 TWINS (BOOK OF)
TRIUMPH 1956-1969 TWINS (BOOK OF)
VELOCETTE 1925-1970 ALL SINGLES & TWINS (BOOK OF)
VESPA 1951-1961 (BOOK OF)
VESPA 1955-1963 125 & 150cc & GS MODELS (SECOND BOOK OF)
VESPA 1955-1968 GS & SS (BOOK OF)
VESPA 1963-1972 90, 125 & 150cc (THIRD BOOK OF)
VILLIERS ENGINE UP TO 1959 INC. 3 WHEELERS (BOOK OF)
VILLIERS ENGINE UP TO 1969 (BOOK OF)
VINCENT 1935-1955 (WORKSHOP MANUAL)

FOR A DETAILED DESCRIPTION OF ANY OF THE TITLES LISTED ABOVE PLEASE VISIT OUR WEBSITE www.VelocePress.com

VELOCEPRESS TECHNICAL BOOKS – MOTORCYCLE

CATALOG OF BRITISH MOTORCYCLES (1951 MODELS)
INDIAN PONYBIKE, BOY RACER & PAPOOSE ILL PARTS LIST & SALES LIT
MOTORCYCLE ENGINEERING (P.E. Irving)
SPEED AND HOW TO OBTAIN IT (Motor Cycle Magazine UK)
TUNING FOR SPEED (P.E. Irving)

VELOCEPRESS MANUALS - THREE WHEELER'S

BSA THREE WHEELER (BOOK OF)
VINTAGE MORGAN THREE WHEELER (BOOK OF)

VELOCEPRESS MANUALS - AUTOMOBILE

ALFA ROMEO GIULIA WORKSHOP MANUAL 1300 TO 2000cc 1962-1975
ALFA ROMEO GIULIA TECH MANUAL CARBURETED CARS FROM 1962
ALFA ROMEO GIULIA TECH MANUAL FUEL INJECTED CARS FROM 1969
AUSTIN-HEALEY 6-CYLINDER WORKSHOP MANUAL
AUSTIN-HEALEY SPRITE & MG MIDGET WORKSHOP MANUAL 1958-1971
BMW 600 LIMOUSINE FACTORY WORKSHOP MANUAL
BMW 600 LIMOUSINE OWNERS HAND BOOK & SERVICE MANUAL
BMW 2000 & 2002 1966-1976 WORKSHOP MANUAL
BMW ISETTA FACTORY WORKSHOP MANUAL
CORVAIR 1960-1969 WORKSHOP MANUAL
CORVETTE V8 1955-1962 WORKSHOP MANUAL
FIAT 500 FACTORY WORKSHOP MANUAL 1957-1973
FIAT 600, 600D & MULTIPLA FACTORY WORKSHOP MANUAL 1955-1969
JAGUAR E-TYPE 3.8 & 4.2 SERIES 1 & 2 WORKSHOP MANUAL
JAGUAR MK 7, 8, 9 & XK120, 140, 150 WORKSHOP MANUAL 1948-1961
METROPOLITAN FACTORY WORKSHOP MANUAL
MGA & MGB OWNERS HANDBOOK & WORKSHOP MANUAL
MG MIDGET TC, TD, TF & TF1500 WORKSHOP MANUAL
PORSCHE 356 1948-1965 WORKSHOP MANUAL
PORSCHE 911 2.0, 2.2, 2.4 LITRE 1964-1973
PORSCHE 912 WORKSHOP MANUAL
TRIUMPH TR2, TR3, TR4 1953-1965 WORKSHOP MANUAL
VOLKSWAGEN TRANSPORTER, TRUCKS & WAGONS 1950-1979 WSM
VOLVO 1944-1968 ALL MODELS WORKSHOP MANUAL

VELOCEPRESS TECHNICAL BOOKS - AUTOMOBILE

FERRARI 250/GT SERVICE AND MAINTENANCE
FERRARI GUIDE TO PERFORMANCE
FERRARI OWNER'S HANDBOOK
FERRARI TUNING TIPS & MAINTENANCE TECHNIQUES
HOW TO BUILD A FIBERGLASS CAR
HOW TO BUILD A RACING CAR
HOW TO RESTORE THE MODEL 'A' FORD
MASERATI OWNER'S HANDBOOK
OBERT'S FIAT GUIDE
PERFORMANCE TUNING THE SUNBEAM TIGER
SOUPING THE VOLKSWAGEN
SOLEX CARBURETORS (EMPHASIS ON UK & EU AUTOMOBILES)
SU CARBURETORS (EMPHASIS ON UK AUTOMOBILES)
WEBER CARBURETORS (EMPHASIS ON ALFA & FIAT)

VELOCEPRESS BOOKS & GUIDES - AUTOMOBILE

ABARTH BUYERS GUIDE
COMPLETE CATALOG OF JAPANESE MOTOR VEHICLES
FERRARI 308 SERIES BUYER'S AND OWNER'S GUIDE
FERRARI BERLINETTA LUSSO
FERRARI BROCHURES AND SALES LITERATURE 1946-1967
FERRARI BROCHURES AND SALES LITERATURE 1968-1989
FERRARI OPP, MAINTENANCE & SERVICE H/BOOKS 1948-1963
FERRARI SERIAL NUMBERS PART I - ODD NUMBERS TO 21399
FERRARI SERIAL NUMBERS PART II - EVEN NUMBERS TO 1050
FERRARI SPYDER CALIFORNIA
HENRY'S FABULOUS MODEL "A" FORD
MASERATI BROCHURES AND SALES LITERATURE

VELOCEPRESS BOOKS – RACING

CARRERA PANAMERICANA - MEXICAN ROAD RACE (BOOK OF)
DIALED IN - THE JAN OPPERMAN STORY
IF HEMINGWAY HAD WRITTEN A RACING NOVEL
VEDA ORR'S NEW REVISED HOT ROD PICTORIAL

AUTOBOOKS WORKSHOP MANUALS & BROOKLANDS ROAD TEST PORTFOLIOS

FOR A COMPLETE LISTING OF THE AUTOBOOKS & BROOKLANDS TITLES
THAT WE CURRENTLY HAVE AVAILABLE, PLEASE VISIT OUR WEBSITE.

Please visit our website

www.VelocePress.com

for a complete up-to-date list of titles, descriptions, and secure online ordering using PayPal.

www.ingramcontent.com/pod-product-compliance
Lightning Source LLC
Chambersburg PA
CBHW020124240426
43673CB00038B/582